MW00779731

JAMES

.

BELIEF

*A Theological Commentary
on the Bible*

GENERAL EDITORS

*Amy Plantinga Pauw
William C. Placher†*

JAMES

MARTHA L. MOORE-KEISH

WESTMINSTER
JOHN KNOX PRESS
LOUISVILLE • KENTUCKY

First edition
Published by Westminster John Knox Press
Louisville, Kentucky

19 20 21 22 23 24 25 26 27 28—10 9 8 7 6 5 4 3 2 1

Book design by Drew Stevens
Cover design by Lisa Buckley
Cover illustration: © David Chapman/Design Pics/Corbis

Library of Congress Cataloging-in-Publication Data
Names: Moore-Keish, Martha L., author.
Title: James / Martha L. Moore-Keish.
Description: First edition. | Louisville, Kentucky : Westminster John Knox
 Press, [2019] | Series: Belief: a theological commentary on the Bible |
 Includes bibliographical references and indexes. |
Identifiers: LCCN 2019002007 (print) | LCCN 2019007699 (ebook) | ISBN
 9781611649598 (ebk.) | ISBN 9780664232641 (prntd. case : alk. paper)
Subjects: LCSH: Bible. James--Commentaries.
Classification: LCC BS2785.53 (ebook) | LCC BS2785.53 .M665 2019 (print) |
 DDC 227/.91077--dc23
LC record available at https://lccn.loc.gov/2019002007

Contents

Publisher's Note

William C. Placher worked with Amy Plantinga Pauw as a general editor for this series until his untimely death in November 2008. Bill brought great energy and vision to the series and was instrumental in defining and articulating its distinctive approach and in securing theologians to write for it. Bill's own commentary for the series was the last thing he wrote, and Westminster John Knox Press dedicates the entire series to his memory with affection and gratitude.

William C. Placher, LaFollette Distinguished Professor in Humanities at Wabash College, spent thirty-four years as one of Wabash College's most popular teachers. A summa cum laude graduate of Wabash in 1970, he earned his master's degree in philosophy in 1974 and his PhD in 1975, both from Yale University. In 2002 the American Academy of Religion honored him with the Excellence in Teaching Award. Placher was also the author of thirteen books, including *A History of Christian Theology*, *The Triune God*, *The Domestication of Transcendence*, *Jesus the Savior*, *Narratives of a Vulnerable God*, and *Unapologetic Theology*. He also edited the volume *Essentials of Christian Theology*, which was named as one of 2004's most outstanding books by both *The Christian Century* and *Christianity Today* magazines.

Series Introduction

Belief: A Theological Commentary on the Bible is a series from Westminster John Knox Press featuring biblical commentaries written by theologians. The writers of this series share Karl Barth's concern that, insofar as their usefulness to pastors goes, most modern commentaries are "no commentary at all, but merely the first step toward a commentary." Historical-critical approaches to Scripture rule out some readings and commend others, but such methods only begin to help theological reflection and the preaching of the Word. By themselves, they do not convey the powerful sense of God's merciful presence that calls Christians to repentance and praise; they do not bring the church fully forward in the life of discipleship. It is to such tasks that theologians are called.

For several generations, however, professional theologians in North America and Europe have not been writing commentaries on the Christian Scriptures. The specialization of professional disciplines and the expectations of theological academies about the kind of writing that theologians should do, as well as many of the directions in which contemporary theology itself has gone, have contributed to this dearth of theological commentaries. This is a relatively new phenomenon; until the last century or two, the church's great theologians also routinely saw themselves as biblical interpreters. The gap between the fields is a loss for both the church and the discipline of theology itself. By inviting forty contemporary theologians to wrestle deeply with particular texts of Scripture, the editors of this series hope not only to provide new theological resources for the church but also to encourage all theologians to pay more attention to Scripture and the life of the church in their writings.

We are grateful to the Louisville Institute, which provided funding for a consultation in June 2007. We invited theologians, pastors, and biblical scholars to join us in a conversation about what this series could contribute to the life of the church. The time was provocative, and the results were rich. Much of the series' shape owes to the insights of these skilled and faithful interpreters, who sought to describe a way to write a commentary that served the theological needs of the church and its pastors with relevance, historical accuracy, and theological depth. The passion of these participants guided us in creating this series and lives on in the volumes.

As theologians, the authors will be interested much less in the matters of form, authorship, historical setting, social context, and philology—the very issues that are often of primary concern to critical biblical scholars. Instead, this series' authors will seek to explain the theological importance of the texts for the church today, using biblical scholarship as needed for such explication but without any attempt to cover all of the topics of the usual modern biblical commentary. This thirty-six-volume series will provide passage-by-passage commentary on all the books of the Protestant biblical canon, with more extensive attention given to passages of particular theological significance.

The authors' chief dialogue will be with the church's creeds, practices, and hymns; with the history of faithful interpretation and use of the Scriptures; with the categories and concepts of theology; and with contemporary culture in both "high" and popular forms. Each volume will begin with a discussion of *why* the church needs this book and why we need it *now*, in order to ground all of the commentary in contemporary relevance. Throughout each volume, text boxes will highlight the voices of ancient and modern interpreters from the global communities of faith, and occasional essays will allow deeper reflection on the key theological concepts of these biblical books.

The authors of this commentary series are theologians of the church who embrace a variety of confessional and theological perspectives. The group of authors assembled for this series represents more diversity of race, ethnicity, and gender than most other commentary series. They approach the larger Christian tradition with a critical respect, seeking to reclaim its riches and at the same time to acknowledge its shortcomings. The authors also aim to make available to readers a wide range of contemporary theological voices from many parts of the world. While it does recover an older genre of writing, this series is not an attempt to retrieve some idealized past. These commentaries have learned from tradition, but they are most importantly commentaries for today. The authors share the conviction that their work will be more contemporary, more faithful, and more radical, to the extent that it is more biblical, honestly wrestling with the texts of the Scriptures.

William C. Placher
Amy Plantinga Pauw

Acknowledgments

This book represents a moment in a conversation among many people, over a long period of time. I am grateful to all the people and institutions that have been part of the conversation that yielded this book.

To Columbia Theological Seminary and its board of trustees, for my sabbatical leave in 2017 to complete the writing, and for the consistent encouragement of President Leanne Van Dyk in my research.

To my colleagues on the faculty, especially my faithful writing group sisters who spurred me on: Beth Johnson, Kim Long, Kathleen O'Connor, and Christine Yoder; and more recently, Kelly Campbell, Anna Carter Florence, Kim Clayton, Kathy Dawson, Christine Hong, Mindy McGarrah Sharp, and Rebecca Spurrier. You all have given me courage and joy in finding my voice. I am also grateful to Brennan Breed, Bill Brown, and Mark Douglas, who offered input on key issues regarding wisdom literature, reception history, and ethical implications of James.

To the congregations and presbyteries who invited me to teach or preach on the book of James as I was writing: First Presbyterian Church, Atlanta; St. Luke's Presbyterian Church, Atlanta; the Presbytery of Greater Atlanta; and especially the women of Central Presbyterian Church, Atlanta, and the Presbytery of Utah, both of whom invited me to lead weekend retreats on James. Your questions and comments have helped me to see how James continues to speak to the church today.

To Michael Morgan, for a fascinating afternoon exploring translations of James from the sixteenth century to the present, in his incomparable private collection of English Bibles. Never forget the "floure of the giraffe" (Jas. 1:10).

To Barrett Payne and Gail Baylor, student assistants during the academic years 2016–17 and 2017–18, for helping with my research, and to Nick Carson for his careful editorial eye in the last stages of preparing the manuscript.

To Amy Plantinga Pauw and Don McKim for inviting me into this project and for your patient and encouraging editorial guidance along the way.

And as always, to my family, especially Chris, Miriam, and Fiona, for welcoming James to our table for the past few years. Thank you for your hospitality to him, and for your patience and good humor with me. This book is dedicated to you, with my enduring love.

Introduction
Why James? Why Now?

"Let everyone be quick to listen, slow to speak," says James early in this book (1:19), for "if any think they are religious, and do not bridle their tongues but deceive their hearts, their religion is worthless" (1:26). In the middle of the book, the author says, "the tongue is placed among our members as a world of iniquity; it stains the whole body, sets on fire the cycle of nature, and is itself set on fire by hell. . . . No one can tame the tongue—a restless evil, full of deadly poison" (3:6, 8). Repeatedly this writer warns against the dangers of words misused: grumbling, boasting, disputing, cursing. It is ironic indeed to write a volume of so many words about James, when he raises such serious concerns about the "unbridled tongue."

Why spend so many words on James? Why engage in such unbridled verbosity regarding such a terse text? Three simple reasons: because of the uniqueness of the book in the New Testament canon, because of its history of bad press (especially among Luther-influenced Protestants), and because of its timely wisdom for our world today.

Uniqueness of James: What Is This Book?

If you are approaching James for the first time, or for the first time in a long while, you may initially find it puzzling to read. There is no narrative or plot, and the characters that appear briefly (Abraham, Rahab, Job, Elijah) are moral exemplars whose real significance requires knowledge outside the text. If we try to read it as a letter, it seems oddly disjointed and impersonal, hardly like a letter written to "brothers and sisters." It seems to jump from one topic to another without a consistent theme. We cannot immediately tell what has prompted the writer to address his community, though we recognize that they are enduring trials and temptations from outside as well as struggling with internal divisions. It begins without fanfare, and it ends without so much as a "farewell."

Many readers of James, especially in recent centuries, have wrestled with these features of the book, wondering how we should interpret it and whether it is really a "letter" at all. Martin Dibelius, in his influential commentary, classifies the book as loosely connected "paraenesis" (exhortation to moral living), not a letter addressed to a specific community or situation. He claims that "the entire document lacks continuity in thought" and has no "theology."[1] This judgment regarding James has had lasting impact on interpreters through the twentieth century, leading many to dismiss the book as no more than an ad hoc collection of wisdom sayings without clear purpose or theme. More recent interpreters, however, have employed rhetorical analysis and discovered James's deft use of strategies from the Greco-Roman literary world. Several have pointed out that, like other similar texts of the time, James uses his rhetorical skill to persuade the audience to adopt certain values (here, values such as patience, endurance, and equity). Margaret Aymer, for instance, interprets James as an epistle to communities in diaspora, written in the tradition of other Jewish letters composed to bolster identity among dispersed Jewish communities in the Hellenistic world. By comparing James to other writings of the time, these interpreters have uncovered more coherence and purpose in James than previously recognized. Though the debate continues as to whether James constitutes a letter, most contemporary scholars have greater respect for its literary unity and skill than did earlier generations. Other interpreters, attending to the sociocultural history of similar texts like Q and Thomas, have begun to glimpse the religious, cultural, and socioeconomic conditions out of which James may have

---

1. Martin Dibelius, *James*, 5th ed., translated from the 1964 German ed. (Philadelphia: Fortress, 1976), 2, 21.

emerged.[2] Though it is still impossible to reconstruct exactly James's original context, these new scholarly approaches have opened up fresh appreciation for James as a significant source for learning about Christian origins.

But what sort of writing is this? Amid the surge of publications on James in the past twenty-five years, scholars have variously emphasized it as a wisdom text, as eschatological/apocalyptic writing, and as prophetic literature.[3] Many have followed Dibelius in highlighting James as wisdom literature, similar to Ben Sira, sometimes referring to this as the only wisdom text in the New Testament. Todd Penner affirms the wisdom character of James, but he argues that its eschatological framing is key to understanding the letter, illuminating the relationship of wisdom and eschatology in early Christianity as a whole. John P. Keenan concurs that James is a wisdom text, but one that also anticipates an apocalyptic reversal beyond history.[4] Unlike Penner, Keenan prefers the term "apocalyptic" to "eschatological," because he sees James emphasizing a "reversal of historical time," not "the end period of history."[5] Through his moral teachings, James is seeking to motivate engagement in compassionate justice here and now, not removal from the world. Elsa Tamez and Pedrito Maynard-Reid likewise highlight this book's call for justice, but they emphasize the continuity of James with the prophetic tradition, noting how James, like Amos, focuses on God's condemnation of the rich and preference for the poor.[6]

In this commentary, I will not mount a specific argument regarding James's genre, though I have learned much from the biblical commentators who have engaged in these discussions, especially

2. See Todd C. Penner, "The Epistle of James in Current Research," *Currents in Research: Biblical Studies* 7 (1999): 267–300 for discussion.

3. See, e.g., Luke Timothy Johnson, *The Letter of James,* Anchor Yale Bible (New Haven: Yale University Press, 1995); Todd C. Penner, *The Epistle of James and Eschatology: Re-reading an Ancient Christian Letter* (Sheffield: Sheffield Academic Press, 1996); John P. Keenan, *The Wisdom of James: Parallels with Mahayana Buddhism* (New York: The Newman Press, 2005).

4. "It is not the culmination of history but the abeyance of history. . . . God is in charge from beginning to end, and no human effort can pretend to engender wisdom or trigger the final revelatory reversal. There is no human strategy for coping with the world" (Keenan, *The Wisdom of James,* 21).

5. Ibid., 22.

6. Elsa Tamez, *The Scandalous Message of James: Faith without Works Is Dead,* rev. ed. (New York: Crossroad, 2002) and Pedrito Maynard-Reid, *Poverty and Wealth in James* (Maryknoll, NY: Orbis, 1987).

in recent decades. Instead, what strikes me most in reading James today is how the author weaves together insights from the law (especially Leviticus 19), prophets (such as Amos and Isaiah), and wisdom (especially Ben Sira) into one powerful whole, offering his audience then and now a genre-defying piece of biblical interpretation. Is it perhaps a mistake to try and classify him? He does draw on Hellenistic rhetorical strategies, of course, but perhaps above all he seeks simply to interpret for his own time the richness of the whole Hebrew Bible, not just one piece. And he does so to inspire his audience to lives of righteousness. For James, the word (*logos*) of God, law (*nomos*), and wisdom (*sophia*) are nearly interchangeable terms, and God implants/imparts this word in order that we, the readers, might not just hear it but also do it.

Uniqueness of James: A Minority Report in the New Testament

The book of James offers a minority report in the New Testament, an alternative view to the ones we more often hear from the Synoptic Gospels, Paul, and John. Unlike the Gospels, James has no explicit references to narratives of Jesus, including his death and resurrection; indeed, he says little directly about Jesus at all. Unlike Paul, he says nothing about a distinction between Jews and Gentiles, which is vital to Paul's understanding of Christ's reconciling work. Further, unlike Paul, James does not describe the church as the body of Christ, which would explicitly connect the Christian community to the ongoing work of Jesus in the world. Unlike John, who portrays serious tension between the Jews who recognized Jesus as Messiah and those who did not, James recognizes no such divide. Unlike almost all the New Testament texts, the moral teachings of James are not connected to any experience of conversion or becoming a Christian. Apparently, he did not see a significant divide between pre-Christian and Christian life.

Instead, James preaches to his community on the same texts that Jesus did: the ancient Israelite Scriptures—Torah, prophets, and wisdom. His audience must have been well versed in these texts, as

well as in the communal practices these texts inform. James's hearers
may have been part of the community later called "Ebionite," whose
name means "the poor" and who were Jewish Christians later condemned as heretics.[7] As interpreter John Keenan says, "There was a
period when Christians were all Jews at peace within their tradition,
and that, I think, is the time and the world of the Letter of James."[8]
There is no hint of distance in this writing between the Jewish community and earliest followers of Jesus. This is one distinctive gift that
James offers us today.

Though James says very little about Jesus, his teachings echo
Jesus' teaching at many points. In particular, James challenges the
economic and social divide in his community, repeatedly encouraging "the lowly" and chastising "the rich," like Jesus in the Gospel
of Luke. In doing this, the author speaks directly to the economic
situation of Palestine in the first century, in which there was growing wealth for a few but great poverty for most, provoking social and
religious unrest.[9] Most of the early followers of Jesus were of this
poor and uneducated group.

Thus, while James knows no conflict between Torah followers
and Jesus followers, he describes pronounced conflict between the
privileged and the oppressed. The book may have been written at a
time when people of higher social status were being welcomed into
the nascent Jewish-Christian community, as we glimpse unequal
treatment of rich and poor in "the assembly" in chapter 2. Elsa
Tamez suggests that in response, James was insisting that "the vocation of the church, its mission, is the poor, who are rich in faith and
the heirs of God's reign."[10] From the text, we can see that the writer
seeks to nurture a community of solidarity, characterized by sharing,
compassion, and mercy. James explicitly condemns boasting (3:14),
arrogance (4:6, 10), and the rich who use their power over those
who have less (1:11; 2:6–7; 5:1–6). He focuses attention on establishing a community that seeks to heal the sick and raises up those
who have little. In his teaching, then, though he rarely mentions

7. See Keenan, *The Wisdom of James,* 10.
8. Ibid., 14.
9. Maynard-Reid, *Poverty and Wealth in James,* 17–18.
10. Tamez, *The Scandalous Message of James,* 26.

Jesus at all, James "possibly represents the heart and soul of the ministry of Jesus as a reformist prophet within Judaism."[11]

Who Is "James"?

This is an appropriate point to pause and ask what we can know
about the author of this book called "James." As I will discuss further in the commentary on 1:1, the author identifies himself simply
as "James, a servant of God and of the Lord Jesus Christ," without
further specification, suggesting that those originally hearing the letter did not require any more identification than this. But we wonder:
Who was this "James"?

   The New Testament offers three main characters called James:
two of the twelve disciples, and James "the brother of the Lord." Of
the two disciples named James, the first is the more well-known:
the brother of John and son of Zebedee (Matt. 4:21; 10:2), who,
with Peter and John, is one of the inner circle of disciples present at
the transfiguration (Matt. 17; Mark 9). This James was martyred by
Herod Agrippa, as mentioned in Acts 12:1–2, in about the year 44.
The second disciple is "James son of Alphaeus" (Matt. 10:3; Mark
3:18; Luke 6:15). He is not mentioned again after Jesus' resurrection. The third James is the brother of Jesus (Matt. 13:55), represented as the head of the Jerusalem church in Acts (12:17; 15:13;
21:18), likely from about 44 to 62. Almost all interpreters of this
letter from the earliest centuries to the present have agreed that
this James, the brother of Jesus, is the ascribed author of the text—
though whether he is the actual author is a question we will explore
further below.

   Jewish historian Josephus (37–100) attests to the importance
of this James in the earliest decades of the Jesus movement in his
Antiquities of the Jews. According to Josephus, during a brief period
without a Roman ruler present in Palestine, the high priest in Jerusalem brought to trial "a man named James, the brother of Jesus who
was called the Christ, along with certain others."[12] The priest, who

11. Penner, *The Epistle of James and Eschatology,* 281.
12. Johnson, *The Letter of James,* 99.

was a Sadducee, accused the group of transgressing the law and condemned them to death by stoning, a punishment consistent with cases of blasphemy. The Pharisees apparently protested this action to the next Roman procurator. This brief account confirms that James was generally known as the brother of Jesus, and that he was an important leader of the Jerusalem community of those who called Jesus "the Christ." It also provides a clear date for his death (62 CE). Later Christian writers elaborated on James's martyrdom; Eusebius, for instance, cites Clement of Alexandria, who says that James was "thrown down from the pinnacle of the temple and beaten to death with a fuller's club."[13] Because of this legend, later iconography of James often portrays him with a club, recalling this alleged mode of his death.

Christian interpreters until the modern era commonly assumed that James, the brother of Jesus, named in Acts and named in the writings of Josephus and Eusebius, did indeed write this letter. In modern times, however, there has been serious debate about whether James actually wrote the letter or whether it was composed by someone writing in his name. Beginning in the sixteenth century with Erasmus, Cajetan, and Luther, biblical interpreters began to challenge the apostolic authorship of James.[14] In the nineteenth century, with the advent of the historical-critical method, biblical scholars settled into two basic camps: those who defended the traditional early dating of James (whether written by the brother of Jesus or pseudonymous) and those who argued that it was a late pseudonymous writing of the late first, second, or perhaps even early third century. Those two basic opinions continue to the present, but the preponderance of scholarly opinion has shifted, first toward the later dating and more recently to renewed arguments for early dating of James. However, scholars on both sides concur that it is difficult to make definitive claims about the historical context of the letter. As Luke Timothy Johnson puts it, judgments about authorship are based on "the cumulative force of probabilities rather than of mathematical demonstration."[15]

---

13. Eusebius, *Historia Ecclesiastica* II, 1, 5, quoted in Johnson, *The Letter of James*, 99.
14. Johnson, *The Letter of James*, 140–41.
15. Ibid., 92.

Over the course of the twentieth century, most New Testament scholars came to argue that the book of James was not written by the historical James but is a later pseudonymous writing. Martin Dibelius was an influential earlier proponent of this interpretation, and Dale Allison represents one of the most distinguished representatives of this view today.[16] Arguments for late dating include the following:

— The letter was not mentioned or accepted into the canon until late: Origen in the third century is the first to refer to the letter as Scripture, and it was not officially received into the canon in the West until the Synod of Hippo in 393.[17]

— The writer seems to be arguing against Paul himself, or against followers of Paul who have misunderstood his "faith alone" emphasis, which would place the writer at least a generation after Paul.

— The writing consists of general moralizing without a definite train of thought, a genre which belongs to (at least) a late first-century church.

— It seems unlikely that one who grew up in Nazareth as the son of a carpenter would have been able to write in such accomplished Greek.

In the 1980s, several scholars began to reconsider the dating and the significance of James, suggesting that it may have been composed in the mid-first century after all, and perhaps even by the brother of Jesus. Luke Timothy Johnson summarizes the arguments in favor of early dating:[18]

---

16. For detailed arguments, see Dibelius, *James,* 11–21 and Dale C. Allison Jr., *A Critical and Exegetical Commentary on the Epistle of James,* International Critical Commentary (New York: Bloomsbury, 2013), 3–32. Gay Byron argues that "it was most likely written around the end of the first century or early in the second century by a pseudonymous author who lived in either Syria, Egypt, or Rome" (Gay Byron, "James," in *The Women's Bible Commentary,* 3rd ed., ed. Carol A. Newsom, Sharon H. Ringe, and Jacqueline Lapsley [Louisville: Westminster John Knox Press, 2012], 613).

17. See Allison's review of this history in his *A Critical and Exegetical Commentary on the Epistle of James,* 13–18; cf. Keenan, *The Wisdom of James,* 8.

18. See Johnson, *The Letter of James,* 118–21. See also Margaret Aymer, *James: Diaspora Rhetoric of a Friend of God,* Phoenix Guides to the New Testament (Sheffield: Sheffield Phoenix Press, 2015), 4–13, 16, and Maynard-Reid, *Poverty and Wealth in James,* 6–7.

— James shows none of the "classic signs of late, pseudonymous authorship," such as elaboration of the author's identity, discussion of the delayed Parousia, or defense of a tradition to be handed on.

— The letter suggests social realities that fit a movement at the early stages of development: description of oppression from outside forces, a clear sense of imminent judgment, no concern about internal social structures (such as marriage or sexual relations), and overall emphasis on intimate social solidarity rather than developed institutional life.

— The letter clearly draws on Jesus' teachings in ways that resemble the hypothetical Q source and early Palestinian Christianity.

— James's writing in many ways resembles the "earliest datable Christian writer, Paul," in language, allegiance to Torah, and influence of Greco-Roman moral traditions. Rather than seeing James as a later response to Paul, it makes more sense to see these writings as contemporaneous.

— Several incidental details in the text suggest a Palestinian context (e.g., the use of the term "gehenna" in 3:6 and the reference to "the early and the late rains" in 5:7).

Though the questions of dating and authorship cannot be settled conclusively, the historical debates can have theological implications. Those who argue for late pseudonymous authorship of James, particularly those who follow the interpretation of Dibelius, tend to downplay this letter's theological significance, relegating it to the margins of the canon. Those who argue for an earlier date, however, contend that James gives us a glimpse of Palestinian Christianity in its earliest generation, a form of emerging Jewish Christianity whose teachings are closely linked to the Law/Torah and to Jesus' own sayings.

This commentary will not attempt to resolve the historical debates. Readers who wish to wrestle further with the arguments will benefit from turning to the fine works of Dale Allison and Luke Timothy Johnson, among others. Instead, I will follow the lead of Elsa Tamez, who says, "what matters is not so much the true identity

of this man, but rather his message for us today."[19] Whoever originally wrote the letter, it offers a perspective that enriches the choir
of voices in the New Testament canon, balancing Paul and amplify-
ing some themes we also hear in the Gospel accounts of Jesus. For
James, to be a Christian is to be a Jew, to be a follower of Jesus is to be
a follower of the Law, and to hear the word truly is to do it.

Is James the "brother of Jesus"? We cannot know if this is true
biologically, but it is true theologically. The writer of this letter shares
with Jesus a deep reverence for Jewish tradition as a living word for
his community that is poised at the turning of a messianic age. In this
commentary, I refer to the author as "James" for ease of reference
and out of respect for the author's own self-identification, while
acknowledging that the authorship cannot be known for certain.

Lutheran Scorn of James

Another reason to spend so many words on James is because of its
particular history of interpretation, especially among Protestants
influenced by Martin Luther. In his preface to the New Testament,
Luther ascribed to several books of the New Testament different
degrees of doctrinal value:

> "St. John's Gospel and his first Epistle, St. Paul's Epistles,
> especially those to the Romans, Galatians, Ephesians, and
> St. Peter's Epistle—these are the books which show to thee
> Christ, and teach everything that is necessary and blessed for
> thee to know, even if you were never to see or hear any other
> book of doctrine. Therefore, St. James's Epistle is a perfect
> straw-epistle compared with them, for it has in it nothing of
> an evangelic kind."[20]

According to Luther, there is a contradiction between James and other
parts of the New Testament, especially Paul. The major sixteenth-
century Protestant emphasis on justification by "grace alone"
through "faith alone" seemed to be contradicted by James's assertion

19. Tamez, *The Scandalous Message of James*, 7.
20. Martin Luther, "Preface to the New Testament" in *Martin Luther's Basic Theological Writings*,
    3rd ed. (Fortress, 2012), 112–17.

that "a person is justified by works and not by faith alone" (2:24). To talk of "justification by works" was anathema to Luther and his followers, so even though Luther did cite other parts of James approvingly in his writings, his scathing dismissal of the book overall as a "perfect straw-epistle" has had lasting influence on biblical interpretation of this book.

Well into the twentieth century, the majority of Protestant New Testament scholarship continued to dismiss or marginalize James as a puzzling addition to the canon without any particularly Christian theology or coherent message. One striking example of this is Rudolf Bultmann's almost complete lack of engagement with James in his influential two-volume *Theology of the New Testament*.[21] Several recent prominent New Testament introductions have scarcely mentioned James at all, revealing the lingering assumption that James does not fit well into the canon, which is so centered on a certain reading of Paul.[22]

More troubling is the way that James's deeply Jewish character has presented a problem for many earlier New Testament interpreters. As Penner says, a text so strongly rooted in Judaism does not fare well "in a world of scholarship that can still herald early Christianity as that which through the gift of spirit-enthusiasm brought about the early Christian recognition of Greek universalism, leading to the supersession of Judaism."[23] If Christianity is by definition opposed to Judaism, then a text that blurs those boundaries is itself likely to be ruled out of bounds.

As I suggested earlier, new scholarly developments starting in the late 1980s have inspired fresh interest in this book, challenging old assumptions and seeing in James a significant window on early Jewish Christianity. This commentary takes its cue from such recent scholarship, approaching James differently from Luther and his heirs, without presupposing that "the gospel" is determined solely by Paul's presentation of it. In this commentary, I invite you to encounter James as a glimpse of another early proclamation of the gospel, one that is not opposed to Romans and Galatians (in

---

21. Rudolf Bultmann, *Theology of the New Testament*, trans. K. Grobel, 2 vols. (New York: Charles Scribner's Sons, 1951/1955).

22. Penner, "The Epistle of James in Current Research," 257–60.

23. Ibid., 258.

fact, there is much in common), but emerging from a different early Christian community with different questions and concerns. From James we hear challenging words like these:

> — "If any think they are religious, and do not bridle their tongues but deceive their hearts, their religion is worthless" (1:26).
> — "Has not God chosen the poor in the world to be rich in faith and to be heirs of the kingdom . . . ?" (2:5)
> — "Come now, you rich people, weep and wail for the miseries that are coming to you. Your riches have rotted, and your clothes are moth-eaten" (5:1–2).

In other words, James is challenging indeed, but challenging in the way that Jesus is challenging: inviting us to take seriously what it means to follow the law of God, which is the law of embodied, righteous love.

James's Timely Word to the Contemporary World

The third, and most important, reason to read and write about James is that this often neglected text offers remarkably timely wisdom for our world today. This letter is not just an historical artifact, but Scripture. Through these words, God not only spoke to a community long ago but also continues to speak to us now. The pages that follow will explore what God might be saying through the words of James in each particular passage. Taken as a whole, James offers five themes that connect directly to contemporary concerns.

First, as it is addressed to "the twelve tribes in the Dispersion (*diaspora*)" (1:1), the letter speaks with special force to a world of **migration and refugees.** Though we do not know exactly what community James was addressing, the author identifies his audience as those who are in diaspora, scattered from their homeland.[24] Framed

---

24. For further discussion of historical context of James, see commentary on 1:1 below. For fine discussion of the diaspora perspective, see Margaret Aymer, *James: Diaspora Rhetoric of a Friend of God.*

in this way, the letter's emphasis on rooting the identity of the community in the enduring word, while it is under stress from outside and divided within, takes on new significance. Margaret Aymer suggests that we might helpfully read James as a "migrant writing" whose primary strategy is separation from the surrounding culture. James encourages his readers not to assimilate to the "world" around them but to maintain their distinctive traditions, especially rooted in the Torah. But migration is not just a long-ago and far-away situation.: "International migration has more than tripled in size since 1960, rising from 77 million to almost 244 million in 2015."[25] In the United States, while immigration policies are hotly contested, demographic patterns clearly indicate that the nation's immigrant population continues to grow. Increasingly, today's readers of James are either themselves in diaspora or live near communities in diaspora. How might James speak to us if we understand that "it was intended to be read by migrants rather than by landed citizen readers"?[26] How might James help those who are landed citizens hear more clearly the voices of those struggling to live in places that are not "home"?

Second, the "theological" (more than explicitly christological) perspective of James speaks helpfully into our world of *religious diversity and conflict.* As we noted above, James says little about Jesus but a lot about the God of Israel and the law God gave to the covenant people. The letter emerged from a context in which "Jewish" and "Christian" were not opposed or even distinct categories. This makes it a particularly fruitful resource for pondering the relationship between contemporary Jews and Christians, not to forget the intervening centuries of division but to engage a New Testament witness to a form of Christianity that does not make Jews into religious "others." James's unique perspective also holds promise for Christian engagement with traditions besides Judaism. I do not mean to suggest that interreligious engagement ought only to seek common ground, ignoring the differences that make religious traditions distinctive. Some of the liveliest interreligious encounters today are precisely those that start with particularity rather than

25. Migration Policy Institute, https://www.migrationpolicy.org/programs/data-hub/charts /international-migrants-country-destination-1960-2015?width=1000&height=850&iframe=true.
26. Aymer, *James: Diaspora Rhetoric of a Friend of God,* 2.

universal principles. But James's emphases on the generosity and goodness of God and on God's call to justice and righteousness can foster cooperation and dialogue with religious communities for whom the christological starting point is a serious obstacle. For the same reason, James can engage people who are suspicious of any kind of religion at all. We live in an age when there is conflict and contention over what we mean by "religion" and whether it can play a helpful role in the world today. For James, true "religion" is not a bounded institutional category called "Judaism" or "Christianity" nor is it explicitly about a set of doctrines. Religion for James is just this: "to care for orphans and widows in their distress, and to keep oneself unstained by the world" (1:27). Such an ethical imperative might appeal to those who identify as "spiritual but not religious," opening up conversation about, for instance, what commitments drive our pursuit of righteousness in the world.

Third, James offers practical guidance on *living in community with others*, a topic that speaks to many people today who are seeking to nurture community in a variety of forms. Christian readers have valued this aspect of James for centuries. Apparently, this letter was a favorite Scripture for early monastic communities in Egypt, Palestine, and Constantinople, who appreciated James because of his focus on practical living out of Christian ideals.[27] His warnings against harsh speech (3:1–12) and against division caused by wealth and privilege (2:1–7, 5:1–6) are particularly timely in a world in which hate speech and economic disparity fuel social division and violence. Furthermore, James's observations on the destructive power of envy and friendship with the "world" can draw our attention to the ways our behavior today threatens not only social relations but also the earth itself. James gives close attention to the habits of the human heart that lead to such destructive behavior.

Fourth, James's repeated concern for the *poor and the sick, those at the margins of society and community,* should stimulate Christians to reflect on our own practices and on the practices of any society that neglects and isolates those who are not powerful. He contrasts the rich and the lowly in 1:9–11, emphasizes that religion

---

27. Ibid., 78–79.; cf. Luke Timothy Johnson, *Brother of Jesus, Friend of God: Studies in the Book of James* (Grand Rapids: Eerdmans, 2004), 72.

is about caring for orphans and widows in 1:27, condemns privileged treatment of the wealthy in 2:1–7, condemns the rich oppressors themselves in 5:1–6, and commends praying for the sick in 5:13–18. In these ways, the writer draws a stark contrast between the true wisdom of God, which summons us to care for all neighbors in distress, and the "earthly, unspiritual, devilish" (3:15) wisdom of the world, which cares only for its own wealth and privilege. Though this contrast is clear, commentators have responded to it in various ways. Elsa Tamez points out that in the global north, "many of the commentaries on James dedicate long pages to the rich, thus consciously or unconsciously attempting to relativize this contrasting picture that James paints." By contrast, a Latin American reading of this letter "fixes its gaze on the oppressed and dedicates long pages to them, their sufferings, complaints, oppression, hope, and praxis."[28] In these days of growing economic disparity, James offers a necessary critique of those in positions of power, and necessary hope for those who are oppressed.

Finally, in a time of anxiety and change, James emphasizes the **enduring word of God and our corresponding call to endurance.** Unlike the wisdom of the world, which is fleeting and unreliable, with God "there is no variation or shadow due to change" (1:17). God is consistent, and consistently generous and just. Since the word of this God has been implanted in us (1:21), we should bear fruit consistent with the seed. Persevere. Endure. "Be quick to listen, slow to speak, slow to anger" (1:19). Be "peaceable, gentle, willing to yield" (3:17). "The testing of your faith produces endurance," he says, calling the readers to "let endurance have its full effect" (1:3–4). Again, in the last chapter, he counsels, "Be patient, therefore, beloved, until the coming of the Lord," for "we call blessed those who showed endurance. You have heard of the endurance of Job . . ." (5:7, 11). These words were addressed to a community under pressure, witnessing social changes all around them, perhaps wondering where God was amid it all. The social changes and pressures today are different, but the anxiety is recognizable: Where is God in the

---

28. Tamez, *The Scandalous Message of James*, 21.

chaos? Is God reliable? How should we live when things around us are changing so quickly?

And James says: wait for the Lord. Be patient. Endure. "For your anger does not produce God's righteousness" (1:20). For all who are tempted to anxiety in the face of the rapid rate of change in our world, James reminds us to take the long view. Keep "doing the word," walking in the ways of justice and righteousness, and don't grow weary. Like the farmer who plants the crops and waits for the rains, "you also must be patient. Strengthen your hearts, for the coming of the Lord is near" (5:8).

1:1–15

Greetings to a Community Being Tested

1:1

"James" Greets the "Twelve Tribes"

"James, a servant of God and of the Lord Jesus Christ, To the twelve tribes in the Dispersion: Greetings."

This single opening verse both reveals and conceals, offers hints and at the same time refuses to answer some of the questions that the contemporary reader is most curious to learn: Who is this "James"? To whom is he writing? What is the relationship between the author and the original recipients of this . . . letter? (Is it even a letter?) What is the reason for the writing? And where do we, the contemporary readers, fit in?

To puzzle over these questions is to reveal our own peculiarly modern preoccupations with historical context and original authorial intent in Scripture. It is a good and worthy thing to ask such questions, to recognize the historical distance between ourselves and the original audience, to try and ferret out the assumptions of those hearers that might not be our own, and thereby to challenge our own interpretive authority. James, however, is not particularly interested in these questions. At least not directly. Instead, the author of the book of James is eager to deflect attention from himself in order to teach, challenge, and counsel those who will listen—whether in the first or the twenty-first century.

The opening verse does not tell us much, but it does reveal a few things worth noting. First, the author identifies himself simply as "James." As discussed in the introduction, biblical scholars disagree about the identity of this James: Was the book written by James the brother of Jesus or some other James? Was it a pseudonymous work from a later period, attributed to the early leader of the church in Jerusalem? The very fact that there is no further explanation of identity but simply the bare moniker "James" is suggestive in two ways. First, the identity and authority of the author are simply assumed. The writer does not spend time introducing himself or justifying his right to speak. He and his authority are simply known and do not need further attention. Second, the name "James" itself bears historical significance beyond the immediate author. In Greek, the name is *Jakōbos*: Jacob, the father of the original twelve tribes of Israel. The author does not develop this connection explicitly, but when we recognize the name, we cannot miss the web of associations that this would have carried for those who heard it in the first century.

Jacob, servant of God, addressing the twelve tribes. This opening image might have taken the original hearers all the way back to the patriarch Jacob's last words to his twelve sons in Genesis 49. But even more, in addressing the twelve tribes "in the Dispersion," this verse echoes Isaiah 49:1–6, a passage that also presents Jacob/Israel as the servant of the Lord, appointed to speak and to gather the scattered tribes—as well as proclaiming salvation "to the end of the earth."[1] In any case, this verse signals to us that the author is speaking in a distinctively Jewish context, to an audience for whom such scriptural allusions would have been woven into their worldview, subtly framing this particular address.

Though the biblical resonance of the name itself is profound, the only explicit self-identification that "James" provides in the entire book is here in the first verse: he is "a servant of God and of the Lord Jesus Christ." That is apparently all we need to know about the one who is addressing us. No fancy title, no lineage by blood or teaching. Just "servant"—or "slave." The word *doulos* can be translated either way in English.

Such terminology is complicated. On the one hand, a servant, or slave, is clearly in a submissive position in relation to the one called "Lord." Especially in the United States, it is impossible to hear the

---

1. See John P. Keenan, *The Wisdom of James: Parallels with Mahayana Buddhism* (New York: The Newman Press, 2005), 31–32.

term "slave" without recalling the history of chattel slavery—the horrors of the Middle Passage, the plantation system that thrived in the nineteenth century American South because of the traffic in black bodies, and the lasting political, social, and economic damage that this history has caused for African American communities until today. And other forms of slavery continue to infest our world. In the sex trade, in factories, in mines, on farms, millions of people are forced to work without pay under threat of violence. Contemporary readers should pause at this language of servant/slave and ask whether such a metaphor of slaveholding and bondage is necessary to our understanding of God today.

At the same time, "servant *of God*" was a common title in the Old Testament for those in special (though certainly subordinate) relationship with God. Jacob/Israel, Moses, David, and Daniel, among others, were all called "servant of the Lord." To be a servant/slave of God was to be an instrument, a mouthpiece, a trusted helper, a worshiper devoted only to the Most High. To serve the Lord was to recognize all other powers as relative and passing. Thus, though "slave" suggests oppression, the phrase "slave of the Lord/God" raised the status of the speaker in paradoxical ways.[2]

Conjunctions do not usually merit great attention in biblical texts, but this verse contains a conjunction that is tantalizing in its ambiguity. James calls himself "a servant of God *and* of the Lord Jesus Christ." It is striking, first, for a letter that purports to be written by the brother of Jesus that the author never calls himself "brother" but "servant" of Jesus. He does not presume on any family relationship for his authority but places himself in a subordinate position.

Beyond that observation, this little word "and" raises a question about the relationship between the two terms "God" and "Lord Jesus Christ." Is this a relationship of loose connection or close identification? James does not elaborate on how we are to understand the relation between the two (indeed, he says little about Jesus explicitly at all, only mentioning him by name in 1:1 and 2:1). Not

---

2. Margaret Aymer, *James: Diaspora Rhetoric of a Friend of God,* Phoenix Guides to the New Testament (Sheffield: Sheffield Phoenix Press, 2015), 20; cf. Luke Timothy Johnson, *The Letter of James: A New Translation with Introduction and Commentary,* Anchor Yale Bible (New Haven, CT: Yale University Press, 1995), 167.

for several centuries do church leaders find it necessary to clearly specify the implications of this "and," at the Council of Nicaea in 325. Clearly, however, the "and" signals that there is agreement, not tension, between the two terms. All we need to know, for now, is that there is continuity between serving God and serving Jesus. The way of God and the way of Jesus are one and the same. Such simple and undefined Christology might offer us a gift today, inviting us to suspend any attachment or allergy to the theologically freighted term "one substance." Instead, consider the wisdom of James, for whom the point is not whether Jesus is of the same ontological "substance" as God but that his way of life aligns with the wise and merciful way of God.

So far, we have reflected on this "James" and his relationship as servant of God and of Jesus. But to whom is he writing, and why? The opening verse offers a clue, addressing "the twelve tribes in the Dispersion." Only James 1:1 and 1 Peter 1:1 in the New Testament use this term "Dispersion" to refer to Christians.[3] Such an unusual designation invites us to look both back and forward: to the scattered peoples of Israel whom Jesus came to restore, to the scattered Christian communities of the first century who quickly spread across the Mediterranean basin, and to all those today who live in exile from their original homeland. Into all of these situations of displacement, James speaks a word of hope.

The reference to "the twelve tribes in the Dispersion" (or Diaspora) first of all refers to the Jewish communities that had been scattered from the land of Israel because of conquest by foreign powers. "From 323 to 63 BCE—that is, from the conquest of the land by Alexander the Great to that of Pompey—fully two hundred military campaigns are fought on the territory once ruled by King David. Great numbers of people emigrate or are carried away into slavery."[4] Because of this scattering, Jewish communities by the time of Jesus had already flourished around the Mediterranean for centuries, at some distance from the center in Jerusalem. Indeed, by

---

3. See also occurrence of this term in John 7:35 to ask if Jesus is going to "the diaspora among the Greeks."

4. E. Elizabeth Johnson, "The Church as Israel" in *Ecclesiology in the New Testament*, Core Biblical Studies (Nashville: Abingdon, forthcoming).

the first century CE, there are more Jews living outside Palestine than living inside it. Perhaps James was addressing the Christ followers in these previously dispersed Jewish communities. Or perhaps he was speaking primarily to the (also Jewish) Christ followers who scattered from Jerusalem after the stoning of Stephen. There was a new wave of migration of early Christians who fled after the martyrdom of this leader, as described in Acts 6–7. Whether James was targeting one or both of these scattered peoples, he identifies his audience as displaced, not at home. They are in exile in another empire.[6]

In speaking to "the twelve tribes" without further specification, James also signals that he is writing at a time when the borders between "Christian" and "Jewish" communities had not yet become fixed. The establishment of the twelve tribes of Israel constituted the beginning of Israel's history as a nation, and in the first century CE, expectation of the restoration of the twelve tribes permeated Jewish as well as emerging Christian hopes for redemption. Jesus' calling of twelve disciples clearly signaled this hope for the restoration of the tribes as a part of the messianic age (as we see, for instance, in Matt. 10). To what extent does James bear hope for the restoration of the twelve tribes as a sign of redemption? We cannot tell, but this allusion in the opening verse does tell us that he does not feel the need to distinguish between Jewish and Christian self-understanding.

How might such an address to people in diaspora speak today, in an age of unprecedented migrations of people across borders because of war or economic hardship? There are 65.6 million people in the world today who have been forcibly displaced from their homes, of whom 22.5 million are classified as refugees.[7] In our contemporary context, most of those displaced persons are from Afghanistan, Syria, and South Sudan. In addition to this recent and unprecedented escalation in forcible migrations, we must also acknowledge the millions of descendants of the transatlantic slave trade.

5. Aymer, *James: Diaspora Rhetoric of a Friend of God*, 20.
6. Elsa Tamez, *The Scandalous Message of James: Faith without Works Is Dead*, rev. ed. (New York: Crossroad, 2002), 18.
7. The United Nations High Commissioner for Refugees, http://www.unhcr.org/en-us/figures -at-a-glance.html.

The word "diaspora" is also used to describe the millions of Africans who are scattered and dispersed throughout various parts of North and South America, the Caribbean, and other areas of the world as a result of the transatlantic slave trade. This dispersion brought with it a number of problems and hardships for those in the African diaspora, especially among African Americans, the effects of which are still being felt today. But many are now beginning to understand that those in the diaspora need not focus only on pain, hardship, and despair. The African diaspora is a rich collection of many persons who are an integral part of this rapidly changing world. As Psalm 147 indicates, those in the diaspora are sometimes best positioned to experience the mercy and power of God.

Gay Byron, *True to Our Native Land: An African American New Testament Commentary*, ed. Cain Hope Felder, Clarice J. Martin, and Emerson B. Powery (Minneapolis: Fortress, 2007), 463.

James uniquely in the New Testament speaks to those in dispersion without specifying which communities he is addressing. For this reason, James might speak in a particularly compelling way to all those today who find themselves exiled from their homeland, in situations of suffering caused by displacement. Margaret Aymer reads James from this diaspora perspective, discerning in this book a particular strategy for negotiating the relationship of a "home culture" (in this case, Jewish identity) to "host culture" (wherever James' audience may be scattered in the Greek-speaking Roman Empire). As she says, the book of James "proposes to its audience a subject positionality of withdrawal from the 'world'. It melds tradition and host culture in a kind of syncretism, and then claims that its particular blend of culture marks it as 'unstained by the world' (1.27)."[8] We will see this strategy unfold in the chapters to come. For now, it is enough to hear James's address to those "in diaspora" as an invitation to all diasporic peoples today to listen for the word from this servant of God.

And what is the first word he offers to the scattered people? "Greetings!" or literally, "may joy be with you." It is another uncommon phrase in the New Testament, used among Greeks rather than the common Jewish greeting *shalom*. Luke also uses this conventional Greek greeting in Acts 15:23, at the beginning of the

8. Aymer, *James: Diaspora Rhetoric of a Friend of God*, 79.

letter from the council of Jerusalem to Paul and Barnabas. The term signals James's mastery of Greek (the word also connects with "joy", in the following verse) but also underscores the theme of joy and hope that James offers to those in oppression.[9]

1:2–8
Faith and Wisdom in the Midst of Trials

After the brief greeting, James offers his audience advice that will trouble some contemporary readers: "whenever you face trials of any kind, consider it nothing but joy." We might want to ask James: Really? Trials *of any kind*? Is all suffering to be regarded as good for us, a reason to rejoice because it leads to our maturity?

Some Christian thinkers through the ages have said precisely this. John Calvin, for instance, regards the trials and temptations of this life as "a test of our obedience to God."[10] In his commentary on James, Calvin teaches that God afflicts us in various ways in order to produce the good fruit of patience. For that reason, we should rejoice when we face any kind of trial, because it provides an opportunity to mature in such patience. In a similar way, John Wesley also regards God as the "Author of all [our] suffering." In a sermon on patience, Wesley calls his listeners to consider God as the one who sends suffering, not in order to punish but in order to practice the patience that enables us to "be partakers of his holiness."[11] These two well-known theologians agree wholeheartedly with James that suffering produces endurance, which leads to spiritual maturity—and this means that the suffering itself must be sent by God.

This idea of suffering as redemptive is deeply rooted in Christian faith, but in recent decades it has also been challenged on several fronts. Christian and Jewish theologians since the Holocaust, for

---

9. Tamez, *The Scandalous Message of James*, 29.
10. John Calvin, *A Harmony of the Gospels Matthew, Mark, and Luke, Vol. III, and the Epistles of James and Jude*, trans. A. W. Morrison, ed. David W. Torrance and Thomas F. Torrance (Grand Rapids: Eerdmans, 1972), 261.
11. John Wesley, "On Patience," (Sermon 83, 1872); Global Ministries, The United Methodist Church, http://www.umcmission.org/Find-Resources/John-Wesley-Sermons/Sermon-83-On-Patience.

instance, have pointed out that it is simply demonic to imply that the horrors of Auschwitz are in any way redemptive. Surely, we would never say to those murdered in the gas chambers that they should regard their sufferings as joy that leads to mature faith. Likewise, this charge could only deepen the pain of someone trapped in an abusive relationship. Such a person needs to be empowered to leave such a relationship, not to be told to endure for the sake of her faith and maturity.

Yet many who have suffered also recognize wisdom in James's words here—that a strong endurance (rather than passive suffering) can indeed strengthen faith in God and fuel the pursuit of righteousness. New Testament scholar Elsa Tamez translates "endurance" as "patience," but she emphasizes that this is a strong, not a passive stance. The Greek term *hypomonē* comes originally from a military context, and by extension portrays the struggles of life as active battles. "Here to be patient means to persevere, to resist, to be constant, unbreakable, immoveable. . . . This is a militant patience that arises from the roots of oppression; it is an active, working patience."[12] More, perhaps, than Calvin or Wesley, Tamez helps us to see that when James calls his audience to face trials with joy, this does not mean sitting back, but stepping forward.

Many who have worked and suffered for reform of the church have looked to these words from James for strength and consolation. The Czech reformer Jan Hus (1369–1415), for instance, sharply criticized the luxurious living of church leaders in his day, and he was excommunicated and eventually killed for it. He compared his own trials—and the trials of others sympathetic to his reformist teachings—to the trials named by James here. In a letter written after his excommunication, he wrote, "Dearly beloved, I am now beginning to be tested; but I regard it as a joy that for the sake of the gospel I am called a heretic and am excommunicated as a malefactor and disobedient."[13] Like Tamez centuries later, Hus heard James's

---

12. Tamez, *The Scandalous Message of James,* 43–44. For other occurrences of this term, see 1:12 and 5:11.

13. Jan Hus, letter to John Barbatus and the people of Krumlov (1411), in *The Letters of John Hus,* trans. Matthew Spinka (Manchester: Manchester University Press, 1972), 50. Cited in David B. Gowler, *James through the Centuries* (Chichester: Wiley Blackwell, 2014), 68.

Surely it is difficult to rejoice without perturbation, and to esteem it all joy in various temptations. It is easy to talk about it and to expound it, but difficult to fulfil it. Even the most patient and valiant soldier, knowing that on the third day He would rise, conquering by His death the enemies and redeeming the elect from damnation, after the Last Supper was troubled in spirit. . . . O most kind Christ, draw us weaklings after Thyself, for unless Thou draw us, we cannot follow Thee! Give us a courageous spirit that it may be ready; and if the flesh is weak, may Thy grace go before, now, as well as subsequently. For without Thee we can do nothing, and particularly to go to a cruel death for Thy sake. Give us a valiant spirit, a fearless heart, the right faith, a firm hope, and perfect love, that we may offer our lives for Thy sake with the greatest patience and joy.

Jan Hus, from a letter written just prior to his being burned at the stake. In *The Letters of John Hus*, trans. Matthew Spinka (Manchester: Manchester University Press, 1972), 186–87.

words as a call to action, to endure resolutely in the face of struggle and even death.

The key to hearing these difficult words lies in the way James addresses his hearers: as "brothers and sisters." Not "you over there" but more "we together." The key for James, as for us, is the stance of the person who is calling for endurance of suffering (as well as the nature of that suffering). Is this suffering a suffering that the speaker also knows? Does the one calling for faithful endurance speak from experience?

When the call to strong endurance comes from one who has herself endured, it comes with greater authority. Hus and Tamez are good examples of this. So too is Calvin, who himself endured physical illness, personal loss, and a life of exile from his homeland, though he does not write directly about any of this. In a more recent example, the early twenty-first-century hymn writer Ruth Duck composed a text calling for strength and endurance out of her own struggle with disabling migraines. This hymn wrestles with the reality of suffering in the light of the faithful presence of God:

> When we must bear persistent pain
> and suffer with no cure in sight,
> come, Holy Presence, breathe your peace
> with gifts of warmth and healing light.

Support us as we learn new ways
to care for bodies newly frail.
Help us endure, and live and love.
Hear our complaint when patience fails.

. . . .

In ease or pain, in life and death,
to you our fragile lives belong,
and so we trust you in all things.
You are our hope, our health, our song.[14]

Duck here reframes James's exhortation as a prayer ("help us endure") while acknowledging that patience will fail amid persistent pain.

In another example, Martin Luther King Jr. modeled and called others to model the endurance of suffering for the sake of social change. For King, suffering was redemptive, not for its own sake, but because it can lead to individual and social healing. This conviction for King was rooted in the cross and resurrection: Jesus was willing to suffer and die on the cross as the result of his struggle for righteousness, but the cross was not the end of the story. His resurrection shows that such struggle, such suffering is not in vain. So too, "[a]ccording to King, as surely as Jesus achieved our salvation through suffering, we must be willing also to suffer in our struggle to be free and transform our society."[15] Whether or not James had Jesus' cross and resurrection in mind, the logic of his exhortation resembles that of Dr. King: suffering is not God's intention, but through it God accomplishes something greater: maturity, wholeness, salvation.

And what are the "trials" about which James is speaking? This too makes a difference in how we receive this teaching. Genocide and massive destruction do not count as "trials" or "testing." Some evils cannot and should not be endured; they must simply be condemned. No, James here addresses sufferings that are serious but not annihilating. Are these individual cases of physical or

14. "When We Must Bear Persistent Pain," text by Ruth Duck. Text © 2005 GIA Publications, Inc. All rights reserved. Used by permission.

15. Frederick L. Ware, *African American Theology: An Introduction* (Louisville, KY: Westminster John Knox Press, 2016), 136. See also Martin Luther King Jr., *A Testament of Hope: The Essential Writings and Speeches of Martin Luther King, Jr.* (New York: HarperOne, 2003), 41–42.

psychological suffering? Unjust treatment of the community by those outside? Unjust relations within the community itself? James does not specify here what difficulties the community is facing, but over the course of the book we glimpse some of the trials that he may have in mind, and they include all of the above: wrongful desires that lead to sin and death (1:14–15); favoritism in the church (2:2–6); the dangers of envy that can lead even to murder (4:1–2); economic injustice (4:3, 13; 5:2–5); and physical illness (5:14–16).[16] Nor are these trials disconnected from each other. James is likely speaking to a community that is itself economically marginal but that has some members or contacts with those who are more powerful. This contributes to dissension within the community: preferential treatment of the wealthy, and envy and backbiting among members. In the midst of this, some have fallen ill and are in danger of being ignored by others in the community. To all these trials, James says: such testing is not itself evil, but recognize it for what it is: an occasion for growth in faith.

The term "faith" itself appears here for the first time in James, and it will turn out to be a significant theme throughout the book. Famously, of course, James will eventually claim that "faith without works is . . . dead" (2:26)—the claim for which Luther condemned the book as a "perfect straw-epistle." Here, James presents faith as a quality that is developed over time, through encountering and enduring trials. Gay Byron argues that "faithfulness is at the heart of the letter of James,"[17] and already in these opening verses we glimpse how dynamic faith is for this author.

Verse 4 ends with a rousing exhortation: "let endurance have its full effect, so that you may be mature and complete, lacking in nothing." For the community facing trials, James reframes their suffering as opportunity for growth, a pathway to perfection. The author sounds like a coach here, or a drill sergeant, or a marching band conductor facing a sweaty bunch of recalcitrant teenagers after eight hours of practice. "Come on, people! I know your muscles are aching, but that's the only way to get better. Keep your eyes on the

---

16. Cf. Aymer, *James: Diaspora Rhetoric of a Friend of God*, 21.
17. Gay Byron, "James," in *The Women's Bible Commentary*, 3rd ed., ed. Carol A. Newsom, Sharon H. Ringe, and Jacqueline Lapsley (Louisville, KY: Westminster John Knox Press, 2012), 614.

prize!" Physical trainers teach us that strength and wholeness come through resistance, through endurance that builds muscles over time. This is true of bodies; it is also true of groups whose character is forged through active engagement and even conflict.

Elsa Tamez says that the fruit of active endurance of oppression is integrity. This is what she hears in James's teaching. When oppressed groups resist oppression, they experience wholeness and integrity here and now. "In the very process of resisting dehumanizing forces, the communities and their members are humanized."[18] Real, full humanity comes through asserting one's value against any forces that bring that into question.

The problem with James's teaching arises when we misunderstand the language of "mature and complete, lacking in nothing." James returns to this theme again and again. According to Tamez, "the word *teleios*, 'perfect,' [NRSV: 'mature'] appears twenty times in the entire New Testament; five appear in James. Moreover he uses the verb *teleō* twice and the substantive *telos* once."[19] The first occurrence is here. What does such language mean? Can frail and fallible human beings really be perfect, lacking nothing?

In a context of perpetual workaholic striving, such a call to "perfection" can set us up for failure. When superhero physiques and Barbie bodies are held up as models, and when plastic surgery and endless dieting make those seem achievable, when success in work is measured by financial gain and when personal worth is tied to such financial "success," then we are in danger of hearing James's call to perfection as an endorsement of individual achievement as the ultimate goal. Furthermore, any call to perfection that "lacks nothing" sets us up to think that we can in fact be self-sufficient. In other words, such a call can lure us into thinking that we can and should be equivalent to God.

The good news is that James is not talking about this kind of

> "Perfect means shallow and unreal, and fatally uninteresting."
>
> Anne Lamott, *Bird by Bird: Some Instructions on Writing and Life* (New York: Anchor Books, 1995), 50.

---

18. Tamez, *The Scandalous Message of James*, 47.
19. Ibid., 67.

perfection. As Tamez notes, "*teleios* can be applied in its fullest sense only to God and Christ." For human beings, it means wholeness, consistency of purpose, "a person who has achieved maturity, an undivided totality of personality and behavior."[20] One who is mature ✓ and complete has a singleness of purpose that mirrors, but does not replace, the perfect wisdom of God. This is the maturity to which James is calling us.

Gay Byron emphasizes the communal aspect of this wholeness, saying, "Womanist interpreters argue for this type of wholeness through their commitment to the wholeness of the collective community, which transcends the boundaries of racism, sexism, heterosexism, classism, and able-ism."[21] The completeness to which James is calling us, understood in this way, may present the very opposite of individual achievements in beauty or financial gain. Instead, to be "mature, complete, lacking in nothing" applies to the entire community.

James has just assured his audience that if they welcome trials, this testing will increase their endurance, leading to a full maturity in which they lack nothing. Immediately, however, he acknowledges that they may feel as though they do lack something: wisdom. What are people to do when they recognize the limits of their wisdom? James's answer is simple: ask God in confidence, and you will receive.

Some contemporary readers may immediately want to challenge James's assertion with questions of their own, beginning with "really? Is it really just a matter of asking God for the gift of wisdom and we will automatically receive it?" Surely there is a theological problem with turning God into a cosmic vending machine: just insert request here and wait for the answer to drop into the bin below. Unwrap, consume, and return for more high-calorie low-cost offerings tomorrow. Furthermore, don't we all know of cases when someone has prayed fervently for a certain outcome—healing, the return of a loved one, an end to war—only to have that petition unanswered?

To read James's words in this way, however, is to misread the particularity of what is being asked for as well as James's vision of the fundamental relationship of human asking and God's generous

20. Ibid., 68.
21. Byron, in *The Women's Bible Commentary*, 615.

giving. First, James is addressing a specific need in this passage: the need for wisdom. He is not advising his audience to ask for gold, or jewels, or a new car. Later, in chapter 5, he will develop the theme of prayer further, encouraging prayers for healing for those who are sick. There too, he underscores the power of prayer to bring about positive change. Here, however, he focuses on wisdom. He says that if any in the community lack *wisdom,* all they must do is ask. Could James have been thinking of Solomon here, who prayed for wisdom and was praised for it (1 Kings 3:1–15; 2 Chr. 1:1–13)? Certainly, this encouragement to seek wisdom echoes the Israelite wisdom tradition in which God gives understanding/insight/wisdom to the faithful. In the book of Proverbs, for instance, the teacher says, "if you indeed cry out for insight, and raise your voice for understanding . . . then you will understand the fear of the LORD and find the knowledge of God. For the LORD gives wisdom . . ." (2:3, 5–6a). So too James urges his audience to ask earnestly for wisdom, and God will give it.

"If any of you is lacking in wisdom, ask God, who gives to all generously and ungrudgingly, and it will be given you." (1:5) This verse draws on the Israelite wisdom tradition, and it also clearly resonates with the words of Jesus in Matthew 7:7, in which Jesus says, "Ask, and it will be given you" (cf. Luke 11:9). Both Jesus and James emphasize that God does hear and respond to faithful asking. James, however, focuses on the need for *wisdom,* while Luke focuses on the gift of the Holy Spirit (11:13), and Matthew does not specify an object of our asking.

Augustine drew on this passage from James to argue that we need to rely on God's grace and not our own free will alone. Wisdom is a gift of God, and we must *ask* for it—it does not come from humans.[22] This does not mean that we have no free will; indeed, our active will is involved in the asking and in obedience. But wisdom is a gift "from above" (as James would say), and it reminds us that we are continually dependent on God's grace, not our own human effort.

What is the wisdom that James is commending? James does not offer a definition. In fact, the term *sophia* itself occurs only

22. Augustine, *On Nature and Grace,* ch. 17, http://www.ccel.org/ccel/schaff/npnf105.xix
.iv.xlvi.html?

once more in the book, in 3:13–18, where the author compares two kinds of wisdom. Unlike Proverbs 8, wisdom in James is not personified, and unlike some other early Christian writings, it has no explicit christological connection. Yet wisdom is an important underlying theme throughout the book, deeply interwoven with the concepts of law and the word of God. Overall, wisdom for the writer of James means the capacity to recognize and the strength to follow the life-giving ways of God. William Brosend sums up James's view of wisdom, saying that it is "mature, stable, 'quick to listen, slow to speak,' expressed in faithful practice."[23] "Double-mindedness," which James will condemn in 1:8, is the opposite of this: "immature, unstable, blessing and cursing from the same mouth, forgetting one's own appearance after turning from the mirror. . . ." This contrast between wisdom and double-mindedness constitutes a basic concern in James's writing and may suggest a problematic dynamic he discerns in his community. Perhaps some "brothers and sisters" are prone to act in anger, with quick tempers and inconsistent judgments. Certainly, we know that there is a tendency to harsh words, as we will see in chapter 3. When

> Grant us wisdom,
>   grant us courage,
> for the facing of this hour,
> for the facing of this hour.
>
> Harry Emerson Fosdick, "God of Grace and God of Glory," *Glory to God* (Louisville, KY: Westminster John Knox Press, 2013), 307.

James counsels his brothers and sisters to ask for wisdom, he may have these issues in mind, calling them to the slow and disciplined path of life in God.

What then does it mean to "Ask God"? This too can easily be misunderstood. God the cosmic vending machine, or God the cosmic Santa, is hardly what James has in mind when he counsels his audience to "ask in faith." Asking God for something is not just like inserting coins, or submitting one's wish list with naive confidence that the Creator of heaven and earth will scurry off to the divine warehouse to fulfill our demands. Just as wisdom is not a one-time gift but a capacity grounded in ongoing attentiveness to God that grows and deepens over time, so too the

23. William Brosend, *James and Jude* (Cambridge: Cambridge University Press, 2004), 39.

asking, and the giving, are not single events but ongoing activities.
Endurance, patience, stability: these are aspects of wisdom that James
seeks to cultivate in his audience. These qualities imply duration
over time. It would be odd indeed to say to God: "I want patience,
and I want it NOW!" "Asking God," then, is less about a single event
and more about the cultivation of a relationship in which one turns
continually to the Giver of all good gifts, who stands ever ready to
pour out those gifts on those whose eyes and hearts are open.

Asking "in faith" implies such a personal relationship between
God and the asker. *Pistis* names the basic trust that God does hear
and to which God will respond. James might as well say, "Seriously.
Stop worrying about it and just ask. It's the worrying that is getting
in the way of your receiving." (See further reflection on faith below.)

One of the most difficult theological issues for the modern reader
of James comes in his stark contrast between faith and doubt. "Ask in
faith, never doubting," he counsels. Yet the whole of modern Western philosophy and science is built on the presumption that doubt
is fundamental to the pursuit of sure and certain knowledge. Des-
cartes, after all, began his *Discourse on the Method* with the attempt
to doubt everything—including traditional teachings that had been
passed on by church authorities—in order to uncover what could
not be doubted. His famous conclusion, "I think, therefore I am" is
the outcome of such systematic doubting: the one thing that could
not be doubted was the existence of the doubter! Such careful and
consistent questioning of assumptions, requiring evidence and logi-
cal proof, has led to major developments in fields such as technology
and medicine that we take for granted.

Considering this important role of doubt in the modern world,
it is no surprise that many Western Christian thinkers since the
twentieth century have reinterpreted faith in a way that incorpo-
rates doubt. According to this approach, "faith" and "doubt" are not
opposites, but allies. Theologian Paul Tillich, for instance, claims
that "doubt is not the opposite of faith; it is an element of faith."[24]
Other writers keen to speak Christianly to the contemporary context have challenged any notion that "faith" is an intellectual stance

24. Paul Tillich, *Systematic Theology*, vol. 2 (Chicago: University of Chicago Press, 1975), 116.

that leaves no room for questions or uncertainty. Far from doubt being the opposite of faith, doubt has become essential to the ongoing vitality of faith.

Given this cultural context, what might it mean to have *faith without doubt*? James here is not talking about a purely intellectual stance that excludes questions. Nor is this writer imagining that his audience might doubt God's ability to give; this is a modern problem, not an ancient one.[25] He is emphasizing singleness of heart, the wholeness of ourselves turned toward the wholeness of God, who is unfailingly generous. *Haplōs* in verse 5 ("generously," freely, without second thoughts) is contrasted with *dipsychos* ("double-minded") in verse 8. James portrays a stark contrast between God's wholehearted generosity and our human tendency to be divided within ourselves. The problem is not that we might have cognitive questions about God; the problem is that we might not stand still long enough to receive God's gifts.

To doubt is to be internally conflicted, to have (at least) two competing views of the world operating at the same time: one in which God is the giver of all good gifts on whom we rely, and one in which humans are isolated individuals left to fend for themselves. This is why, for James, to doubt is to be "double-minded." For similar reason, in 3:9–12, James argues that the same tongue cannot both bless God and curse the neighbor, who is made in God's image. To speak contradictory words with the same mouth is to be divided, to be "double." And again, in chapter 4, James condemns the internal divide of those who want to be friends with God and "the world" at the same time (4:4). Throughout, James seeks to nurture singleness of purpose, unity of heart, against those who are divided within themselves, or against other members of the community.

Though the precise term that James uses here (*dipsychos*) may not be attested before this writing,[26] the theme of a divided self as the antithesis of the whole self is common in the Hebrew tradition as well as early Christian teaching. For instance, the psalmist prays,

---

25. Brosend, *James and Jude*, 39.
26. For the debate about the history of this term, see Dale C. Allison Jr., *A Critical and Exegetical Commentary on the Epistle of James*, International Critical Commentary (New York: Bloomsbury, 2013), 186–87.

"Teach me your way, O LORD, that I may walk in your truth; give
me *an undivided heart* to revere your name" (Ps. 86:11). By contrast,
throughout the Torah as well as the wisdom books, "anything of
'two kinds' (Deut. 22:9–11) represents lack of wholeness."[27] It is in
keeping with this call to wholeness that Jesus teaches his disciples to
"love the Lord your God with all your heart, and with *all your soul,*
and with *all your mind*, and with *all your strength*" (Mark 12:30; cf.
Matt. 22:37; Luke 10:27). Not divided. Not double. Not two, but
one. Like Jesus, James is urging his audience to integrity, to "put your
whole selves in," as the contemporary wisdom of the Hokey Pokey
has it.

The image of the conflicted "double-minded" or "double-souled"
person has continued to resonate with people through the centuries, appearing in such literary works as Goethe's *Faust*, in which the
main character says,

> Two souls cohabit in my breast,
>   Each one struggling to tear itself from the other!
> The one, like a coarse lover,
>   Clings to the earth with every sensual organ;
> The other struggles violently from the dust and
> Soars to the fields of the great departed spirits.[28]

Goethe depicts in dramatic terms what many ordinary human
beings sense about the human condition: that we are often divided
within ourselves, making it difficult to focus on one thing and pursue it. For Goethe, the better option is clearly to "soar to the fields of
the great departed spirits," leaving behind the "coarse lover" of earth.
Such stark dualism presents its own problems, presenting the soul
that clings to earth as less valuable than the soul that departs. In our
current context, it is vital to the health of our planet and the future
of humanity to take more tender care of the earth than Goethe
suggests. But the conflict between the "two souls" continues to be
recognizable.

27. Herbert Basser, "The Letter of James," in *The Jewish Annotated New Testament*, ed. Amy-Jill
    Levine and Marc Zvi Brettler (New York: Oxford University Press, 2011), 428.
28. Johann Wolfgang von Goethe, *Faust Part One and Part Two* (Hanover, NH: Smith and
    Kraus, 2004), 44–45.

Nineteenth-century Danish philosopher Søren Kierkegaard was captivated by James's emphasis on the wholehearted devotion to God, and its opposite, the double-minded or divided heart. His religious discourse *Purity of Heart Is to Will One Thing* takes James 4:8 as its text, but 1:5–8 is also deeply implicated. Like James, Kierkegaard taught that a person can only become whole through abandoning all double-mindedness, all internal conflict, and devoting oneself wholly to one thing. That "one thing," however, cannot just be any object. If we devote ourselves to an object that is not itself whole and good, then we cannot become whole, because such devotion will eventually lead us back into division. Only God, who is the whole and inclusive Good, is worthy of our heart's whole devotion. As he says, "Shall a man in truth will one thing, then this one thing that he wills must be such that it remains unaltered in all changes, so that by willing it he can win immutability. If it changes continually, then he himself becomes changeable, doubleminded, and unstable."[29] To be "altered" or unstable is to diverge from the stable and unchanging way of God, which is the way of love. As Kierkegaard elsewhere makes clear, and as we will see in James in later verses, single-minded devotion to God in prayer is connected with loving commitment to the neighbor, especially the neighbor in need. Gay Byron clarifies this point in her own discussion of James when she says, "*double-mindedness* is the act of wavering in one's faith commitment *and* wavering in one's tangible support of the oppressed."[30] Kierkegaard, Byron, and James are all singing the same tune here: single-minded devotion to God, the Giver of all good gifts, includes active works of love toward our neighbors.

The last word to explore here is, ironically, the first word of the passage. It is that little word "if." "If any of you is lacking in wisdom," opens James. In incredulity, we might ask, "is anyone NOT lacking in wisdom?" Notice, however, that James does not condemn this state of "lack," but he uses it as a springboard to discuss God's generosity and our need for wholehearted faith in God as giver. It is not

29. Søren Kierkegaard, *Purity of Heart Is to Will One Thing*, trans. Douglas V. Steere (New York: Harper & Row, 1956), 60.
30. Byron, in *The Women's Bible Commentary*, 614.

"If any of you lack wisdom?"

Now wasn't that a courteous way for James to put it? Wasn't that nice of James to put that "if" in there? Was there really any doubt in his mind about whether or not we lack wisdom? Wisdom to James did not mean learning or profundity of thought but the ability to use the trials of life—the ability to discern in life itself the will of God. Now, do we lack that? For all of our supposed learning . . . for all our big talk . . . do we lack wisdom? There is no hope really for us as long as we think that we're wise. As long as we keep on believing that wisdom was born with us and that understanding shall perish with our going. Only men who confuse themselves with God will dare to pretend in this anguished and troubled day that they know the exact route to the Promised Land. Only men who take upon themselves the omnipotence that belongs to the Lord God Almighty alone will believe that they have in their own mind this day every answer and every truth. . . .

We could spend the rest of this Lord's Day praying—for wisdom—for light—for understanding! We need light today, not heat. What we need today is not men with hot heads and big mouths, but men with cool heads and warm hearts . . . [God] promises wisdom if we ask for it, provided we ask in faith, nothing doubting. "Nothing 'wavering'" the Greek really says. . . . We must come dependent, wholly and completely dependent upon God's wisdom, God's mercy, God's providence.

Robert H. Walkup, "Not Race but Grace," preached in Mississippi on September 30, 1962, the day James Meredith enrolled as the first African American student at the University of Mississippi, quoted in Davis W. Houck and David E. Dixon, eds., *Rhetoric, Religion, and the Civil Rights Movement, 1954–1965* (Waco, TX: Baylor University Press, 2006), 469–71.

lack of wisdom that is the problem here, it is lack of faith in God to address that need.

In the end, in these verses, the mode of asking ("in faith"), the object of our asking ("wisdom"), and the One whom we ask ("God") have remarkably similar characteristics: stability, patience, consistency over time.

FURTHER REFLECTIONS
Faith

Faith is a significant theme in the book of James. In the opening verses, the writer describes the "trials" of his audience as "the testing of your faith," which produces endurance. A few verses later, he calls on them to "ask in faith, never doubting," (1:6), suggesting that faith is the opposite of doubt. And famously, in chapter 2 he claims that "faith by itself, if it has no works, is dead." (2:14, 17) But what is "faith"? This concept has long been at the center of Christian vocabulary and a hot topic of controversy.

Sometimes we think of faith as belief in a certain set of doctrinal statements. We might imagine, for instance, that someone with deep faith is able to recite one of the historic creeds from memory, with full understanding and conviction. And surely "faith" does involve our conscious minds. To have faith in God is not just generic good feeling; it means having some specific sense of who God is, by listening to and learning from what others have said about God over time, pondering those claims and making them our own. In the early church, people preparing for baptism (called catechumens) might spend weeks or months studying the Apostles' Creed, the summary of the church's Trinitarian faith. At times, this "symbol of the faith," as early church writers called it, was ritually "handed over" to the catechumens, as a sign of their receiving faith from the church. At the time of their baptism, the catechumens would then "hand back" the creed by reciting it before entering the water. Most churches today still include some statement of faith (whether corporate or individual) as part of the baptismal service. Entrance into the Christian faith involves affirming certain statements about this God made known in Jesus the Christ.

In the sixteenth century, John Calvin too emphasized that faith involves believing certain things. Calvin, however, insisted that true faith is not just repeating what others say but having direct knowledge that "God is our merciful Father, because of reconciliation effected through Christ and that Christ has been given to us as righteousness, sanctification, and life."[31] In other words, faith in God involves knowledge of who God is and what God has done. Calvin argues against "implicit faith," or the acceptance of what the church teaches without understanding. If faith is simply trust in the church's authority, it can too easily become faith in the church rather than in God.

---

31. John Calvin, *Institutes of the Christian Religion*, ed. John T. McNeill, trans. Ford Lewis Battles (Philadelphia: Westminster Press, 1960), 3.2.2, 545.

Calvin implies that though faith involves the mind, it is not simply intellectual knowledge. It is an orientation of the whole self toward the goodness of God. His brief definition of faith makes this clear: "Faith is a firm and certain knowledge of God's benevolence toward us, founded upon the truth of the freely given promise in Christ, both revealed in our minds and sealed upon our hearts through the Holy Spirit."[32] According to this view, faith involves both the mind's knowledge and the heart's trust that God is truly benevolent toward us. Faith is not fear and trembling, or blind assent, but trust that the creator of heaven and earth is gracious and merciful toward us, which we know because of what God has demonstrated in Jesus Christ.

This resonates with James's use of the term "faith." Though he does not have Calvin's developed Trinitarian theology, James too points toward God's benevolence in which we are to trust. "Ask in faith, never doubting" (1:6), he says. Faith for James implies tenacious trust in the goodness of God, despite evidence to the contrary. It is not enough to know something about God in the abstract; faith is not just knowledge *about* God but knowledge *of* God. Karl Barth, in the twentieth century, also emphasizes this aspect of faith in his little book *Dogmatics in Outline*. He describes faith as encounter with the triune God, an encounter in which we realize that we are not alone. Out of free love, God has come to us to be in relationship with us—not because it was owed to us or because we deserve it, but simply out of God's grace. We can trust that God is with us, and therefore we do not need to trust in ourselves or in any other authority. This is the content of faith.[33]

Faith is *propositional* (involving certain affirmations about God), and it is *personal* (implying a fundamental attitude of trust in the goodness of God). For James, however, faith is above all *practical*. Someone who simply says the right things or professes to believe the right things but does not act on them does not have real faith. This is why James says that "faith without works is dead"— not because faith requires the addition of works but because any notion of faith that does not *produce* works is not real faith. Much of the Christian tradition has concurred with this view. Barth, for

32. Ibid., 3.2.2, 551.
33. Karl Barth, *Dogmatics in Outline* (New York: Philosophical Library, 1949), 17–18.

instance, concludes his discussion of faith in *Dogmatics in Outline* with a similar insight, which he calls "faith as confession." Faith is a decision—it is something undertaken in history by humans. Faith is not only God's initiative in meeting and illuminating humans; faith also involves the human active response. As Barth puts it, "Faith without this tendency to public life, faith that avoids this difficulty, has become in itself unbelief, wrong belief, superstition. For faith that believes in God the Father, the Son and the Holy Spirit cannot refuse to become public."[34] Faith as knowledge, as trust, and as confession—or as propositional, personal, and practical— these three dimensions together can help Christians avoid narrow understandings of what we mean by "faith."

1:9–11

Poor and Rich

In the previous passage, James addressed those in the community who feel that they lack wisdom, telling them simply to ask God in faith. In this passage, he addresses those "believers" (*adelphoi*, elsewhere translated "brothers and sisters," referring to members of the Christian community) who are "lowly," reassuring them that they will be "raised up." Reassurance abounds for those who need it in this letter, but there is a shadow side: just as those without faith will not receive wisdom (vv. 7–8), so here those who are rich will be brought low. Grace is free, but it is not cheap. Judgment comes on those who place their trust not in God, but in the quantifiable treasures of earthly life.

The writer of James sounds a lot like Mary here, when she rejoices in the hymn popularly called the "Magnificat": "[God] has brought down the powerful from their thrones, and lifted up the lowly; [God] has filled the hungry with good things, and sent the rich away empty" (Luke 1:52–53). Mary, of course, is herself echoing an older song: that of Hannah, who sings when she is pregnant with Samuel,

My heart exults in the LORD;

---

34. Ibid., 29.

my strength is exalted in my God.
· ·
The LORD makes poor and makes rich;
    he brings low, he also exalts.
He raises up the poor from the dust;
    he lifts the needy from the ash heap,
to make them sit with princes
    and inherit a seat of honor.
1 Sam. 2:1, 7–8a

God exalts the humble ones, those "of low degree," who are on "the ash heap." James also sounds here a lot like Jesus, who says, "All who exalt themselves will be humbled, and those who humble themselves will be exalted" (see Matt. 23:12; Luke 14:11; 18:14). Here with James, as with Jesus, as with Mary and Hannah, we rejoice that God makes great those whom the world regards as nothing; God magnifies those who are marginalized. It's God up to her old tricks again: making a way out of no way, a people out of no people, a whole world out of nothing.

We might pause and imagine a real family conversation in the deep background of these words. Imagine Mary (in the Hebrew, Miriam) and her sons Jesus (that is, Joshua) and James (Jacob), perhaps with other children gathered as well, sharing a simple meal— bread, diluted wine, a small fish netted by the boys—in their home. Some of the children are hungry, complaining that there is not more. "Those merchants we saw in the market today—I bet they have a lot more to eat," one grumbles. And Miriam, with a glint in her eye, reminds them that people who have power and plenty now will not always be so comfortable. God has a habit of overturning the power schemes of those who take advantage of the poor, she says. Remember Egypt? Remember our ancestors, even in Jerusalem, who were sent into exile because they did not care for the poor and needy? "Adonai has brought down the powerful from their thrones, and lifted up the lowly; he has filled the hungry with good things, and sent the rich away empty," she reminds them, and then sings another familiar tune: "Every valley shall be lifted up, and every mountain and hill be made low; the uneven ground shall become level, and the rough places a plain. Then the glory of the LORD shall be revealed!" (Isa. 40:4–5).

Perhaps when those sons grew up, they echoed their mother's words in their own teachings. "All who exalt themselves will be humbled, and those who humble themselves will be exalted" (Matt. 23:12). "Let the believer who is lowly boast in being raised up, and the rich in being brought low" (Jas. 1:9–10). Jacob and Joshua glance at each other across the table again with a smile and share the subversive hope of their mother.

James is echoing here what biblical scholar Carol Newsom calls an "iconic narrative" of Israel's history, a story that discloses the fundamental order of reality, even when there appears to be much evidence to the contrary.[35] An iconic narrative offers a basic window to interpret the world and to guide action in it. It is like a core myth of a given culture, depicting values most central to its identity. For instance, Newsom describes the "iconic narrative of entrepreneurial capitalism," the American story of "the individual who turns a creative idea into a flourishing business." Think of Steve Jobs or Bill Gates or Henry Ford. No matter that most new business ventures do not actually succeed, and no matter that these individuals could not themselves have succeeded without strong networks of support. The power of an iconic narrative is not that it describes each specific case but that it embodies fundamental values of a society, both interpreting and empowering practices of that society toward a shared end. In the case of the entrepreneurial narrative, the business practices such as "identifying a need, developing a business plan, raising capital, training workers, arranging a distribution network, [and] advertising" all "make sense only in the context of the iconic narrative."[36] The practices drive toward the end described in the iconic narrative, and the narrative gives meaning to the individual practices of the society.

James is offering an iconic narrative not of entrepreneurial success but of the reversal of fortune, in which those with power and wealth will pass away, and those who are poor and lowly will be exalted. It is

---

35. See Carol Newsom, *The Book of Job: A Contest of Moral Imaginations* (Oxford: Oxford University Press, 2003), 122–25.
36. Ibid., 123.

a narrative deeply rooted in Israel's prophetic and wisdom literature, connected to the story of the exodus and to its most ancient of songs, in which the original Miriam rejoiced with the rhythmic chime of her tambourine, "Sing to the Lord, for he has triumphed gloriously; horse and rider he has thrown into the sea" (Exod. 15:21). It is the story of the lowly raised up, captives freed, the least of these being invited to places of honor. James and Jesus, Mary and Hannah—do they see this triumphant overturning every day, in every instance? Hardly. This is not sunny optimism, but stubborn hope shaped by a narrative that insists on God's fundamental righteousness that does and will guide the world to its ultimate end. Their visions are attuned to this, their confidence deeply rooted in centuries of song, storytelling, and ritual practice, so that they glimpse the true moral structure of the world behind the shiny surfaces of success.

This iconic narrative, as expressed in James, has continued to resonate down through the centuries with biblical interpreters particularly attentive to social and economic injustice. In the nineteenth century, American theologian and leader of the social gospel movement Walter Rauschenbusch called James "one of the most democratic books of the New Testament."[37] He praised James, with an eye on passages like this one, for being an example of Jewish Christianity, which he described as "the radical social wing of the primitive church." More recently, Costa Rican theologian Elsa Tamez has called attention to the theme of reversal throughout James, beginning here. God will raise up the poor, she affirms, and this affirmation brings genuine hope even today to those who are oppressed, particularly in Latin America. Tamez also notes that James does not necessarily promise economic gain to the "believer who is lowly," but promises that the lowly will be "raised up"/ "exalted"—that is, "raised up to the dignified level of a human person and recognized as a preferred creature of God."[38] Such a narrative offers powerful hope to any who feel beaten down by economic systems and who see the wealthy taking pride in their material goods. Mary and Hannah, Jesus and James offer a song to empower

37. Walter Rauschenbusch, *Christianity and the Social Crisis* (originally published 1907; reprinted Louisville, KY: Westminster John Knox Press, 1991), 98.
38. Tamez, *The Scandalous Message of James*, 34.

resistance, to remind the faithful that it will not always be so, and therefore it is right and just to work in keeping with God's plan for the raising up of the lowly even now.

Key to this narrative is the conviction that riches are not permanent, and thus rich people, who invest themselves in accumulation of wealth, will themselves "disappear like a flower in the field" (1:10). Wealth does not bring permanent security but will eventually fade. Here, James draws on imagery common in the Hebrew Bible, comparing the mortality of humanity to fleeting and fragile vegetation. Perhaps he is still humming that song he learned from his mother, the one about the valleys being lifted up and the rough places plain, and continuing with the next verses from Isaiah 40:

> All people are grass,
>> their constancy is like the flower of the field.
> The grass withers, the flower fades,
>> when the breath of the LORD blows upon it;
>> surely the people are grass.
> The grass withers, the flower fades;
>> but the word of our God will stand forever.[39]

These verses resound powerfully with James's teaching here. More particularly, he is echoing several passages in Job and Psalms that describe the fleeting nature of wealth or power or those whose lives are defined by those things. So, for instance, Job 24:24: "[the mighty] are exalted a little while, and then are gone; they wither and fade like the mallow; they are cut off like the heads of grain."[40] James, in other words, is not inventing new imagery or ideas here but working out of the ancient wisdom he has inherited to speak to his own new situation.

Though we have little specific information about James's context, his repeated discussions of rich and poor suggest that the situation

---

39. Isa. 40:6–8; Cf. Job 14:2; Ps. 90:5–6; 103:15–16.
40. Cf. Job 27:19, 21: "They go to bed with wealth, but will do so no more; they open their eyes, and it is gone . . . the east wind lifts them up and they are gone; it sweeps them out of their place." Cf. Ps. 49:16–17: "Do not be afraid when some become rich, when the wealth of their houses increases. For when they die they will carry nothing away; their wealth will not go down after them." Ps. 37:2: "[the wicked] will soon fade like the grass, and wither like the green herb."

included some kind of tension between social classes.[41] This is the
first time that he speaks of "the rich," and he returns to the contrast
between rich and poor in 2:1–7 and 4:13–5:6. Interpreters of James
debate about whether the term "believer/brother" (*adelphos*) in 1:9
also applies to the "rich" in 1:10. In other words, are "the rich" part
of the Christian community, or are they outside the community?
We cannot tell for sure. In chapter 2, the writer describes tension
within the community about unequal treatment of rich and poor;
it may be that the brothers and sisters are seeking favor from
those who have resources, or it may be that some members of
the community themselves have economic means that gain them
privileged treatment. Either way, James cautions his audience that
those who have riches now should not be deceived into thinking
that wealth puts them permanently at the right hand of God. Riches
wither and fade. God alone endures. This plays on the basic contrast
discussed in the previous passage, between God's ways and God's
wisdom that endure and the fleeting nature of the world, which is
variously associated with the wicked, the wealthy, the unwise, and
the "double-minded." Hope lies not in binding oneself to riches but
in binding oneself to God.

Do riches here necessarily mean literal economic wealth? This
too is a matter for debate among interpreters. For instance, John
Calvin reads this passage as reassurance to the lowly that they
have been adopted as the children of God, while the rich likewise
should rejoice that they have the very same status. Both classes
are no more and no less than beloved children of God. Therefore,
Calvin concludes, the poor should be "content with their humble
and depressed condition; while the [rich] are to have their pride
checked."[42] Contemporary readers may wish to challenge Calvin on
his counsel to accept the given social order as the will of God; don't
unjust economic systems need to be challenged rather than simply
accepted? Yet his insight regarding the adoption of "the poor" into
God's family remains powerful. If a child born into poverty is taught
from the beginning that she is somebody, that she has worth and

41. Tamez, *The Scandalous Message of James*, 22.
42. Calvin, *A Harmony of the Gospels Matthew, Mark, and Luke, Vol. III, and the Epistles of James and Jude*, 266.

dignity in the eyes of God, then she is far more likely to walk tall and look confidently into the eyes of the world around her. Even if her actual economic condition does not change, she knows that her value as a person does not depend on material goods but on what Calvin calls "joining the assembly of the angels."[43]

Meanwhile, other interpreters read James as a clear critique of actual economic inequity. Pedrito Maynard-Reid, for instance, examines the phrase *en tais poreiais,* translated by the NRSV as "in the midst of a busy life" and argues that the term *poreia* refers not to generic "ways" (the basic meaning behind the NRSV's expression) but to literal commercial travel by merchants in first-century Palestine, also described in chapter 4:13–15.[44] According to this reading, James is implicitly challenging the merchants of his day, those who spend their lives in business class, who risk forgetting that such a life does not last forever. The warning that "the rich will disappear like a flower in the field" is no abstract observation that all wealth eventually vanishes but a targeted social critique of those caravans crossing the deserts bearing silks and spices, assuming that their material goods will preserve them from mortality.

Pheme Perkins, while acknowledging that "rich" and "poor" have economic implications, interprets "the poor" as a reference to "membership in a community of the pious who remain faithful to God despite the adversity caused by the wicked," a reading similar to the Dead Sea Scrolls' use of the term.[45] Reading the references to "the lowly" in the context of postexilic Jewish traditions, she suggests that this term is primarily about the Israelites who are oppressed by external ruling powers. In this reading, the lifting up of the lowly and the deposing of the rich reinforces communal identity against a threatening and alien political power—whether Babylon, Rome, or any contemporary empire.

In truth, James's declaration that the lowly will be lifted up and the rich brought low presents an eschatological hope deeply rooted in prophetic and wisdom literature that weaves together both economic

---

43. Ibid.

44. Pedrito Maynard-Reid, *Poverty and Wealth in James* (Maryknoll, NY: Orbis, 1987), 47.

45. Pheme Perkins, *First and Second Peter, James, and Jude,* Interpretation: A Bible Commentary for Teaching and Preaching (Louisville, KY: John Knox Press, 1995), 91.

and political dimensions.[46] When we hear James resonating with Jesus, Mary and Hannah, Isaiah and the psalmist, we recognize that this theme of reversal emerges from a particular history of an oppressed people and voices a firm hope that God is about to do a new thing in overturning the human power schemes that harm God's beloved chosen ones. The question for a contemporary reader, then, is how this promise to a particular people with a particular history also speaks into a new context. Are we called to identify the lowly and work to raise them up? Are we invited to nurture the self-worth of people in economic hardship, to help them bear their condition with dignity? Are we ourselves the lowly ones, hearing with joy the promise that we will be lifted up? Are we the rich, wrestling with the truth that we and our wealth will soon wither away?

There is a final danger to beware here, and it comes from the sharp distinction between "the lowly" and "the rich." If these are simply economic categories, that is one thing; the passage then reads as a clear affirmation that God works for the overturning of unjust economic disparity. But some scholars suggest that these categories are more communal than economic, in which case their words can carry danger as well as liberation. If "the lowly" refers to the community of the faithful, chosen and favored by God, and "the rich" refers to all outside forces, then this passage is exalting the chosen community over any who might oppose it. Liberation of the few then comes at the expense of destruction of those deemed unworthy of God's care. As we teach and discuss this provocative text, do we need to be cautious about hardening communal lines between insiders (termed "lowly") and outsiders (deemed "rich")?[47]

In eighth-century England, Bede ("the Venerable") connects James's teaching here with Jesus' parable in Luke of the rich man and Lazarus.[48] The parable depicts literally what James says about the believer being "raised up" and the rich being "brought low":

> There was a rich man who was dressed in purple and fine linen

---

46. For full discussion, see Todd Penner, *The Epistle of James and Eschatology: Re-Reading an Ancient Christian Letter*, Journal for the Study of the New Testament Supplement Series 121 (Sheffield: Sheffield Academic, 1996), 162–70.

47. See Todd Penner's caution in ibid., 271–72.

48. Bede the Venerable, *Commentary on the Seven Catholic Epistles*, trans. David Hurst (Kalamazoo, MI: Cistercian, 1985), 11–13.

and who feasted sumptuously every day. And at his gate lay a poor man named Lazarus, covered with sores, who longed to satisfy his hunger with what fell from the rich man's table; even the dogs would come and lick his sores. The poor man died and was carried away by the angels to be with Abraham. The rich man also died and was buried. In Hades, where he was being tormented, he looked up and saw Abraham far away with Lazarus by his side (Luke 16:19–23).

Bede says, "let [the rich man] remember that his glory, in which he takes pride about his wealth and looks down on or even oppresses the poor, must come to an end, that having been humbled he may perish for ever with that rich man in purple who looked down upon the needy Lazarus."[49] In connecting these two passages, Bede highlights the ironic twist in the meaning of "down": from "oppressed socioeconomic status" to "placed in eternal torment." Reading James in the company of Bede helps us to laugh at our common assumptions about what really lasts. Beware of looking "down" on anyone, Jesus and James remind us, because soon enough others may quite literally be looking down on you.

> To all, life thou givest,
>   to both great and small.
> In all life thou livest,
>   the true life of all.
> We blossom and flourish
>   like leaves on the tree,
> then wither and perish;
>   but naught changeth thee.
>
> Walter Chalmers Smith, "Immortal, Invisible, God Only Wise," *Glory to God*, 12.

1:12–15

Enduring Temptation

Here James circles back to the theme of endurance, which set the tone at the beginning of the book, in 1:2–4. Clearly the audience is struggling with trials and temptations, and James seeks to boost their strength to resist anything that would lead them away from the just and generous ways of God.

49. Ibid., 11.

"Blessed is anyone who endures temptation. Such a one has stood the test and will receive the crown of life that the Lord has promised to those who love him" (1:12). This is another passage (like 1:9–11) in which James echoes Jesus' own teachings, especially the Beatitudes of Matthew 5:3–12 and Luke 6:20–22. These *macarisms* (so named because of the Greek word *makarios*, translated here "blessed") are themselves rooted in patterns from the Israelite wisdom tradition that both James and Jesus knew so well. For instance, the very first verse of the very first psalm begins, "Happy [or blessed] are those who do not follow the advice of the wicked . . ." (Ps. 1:1; see also Prov. 8:34; Job 5:17). To be blessed, for the psalmist and other wisdom literature, is to be happy and to be in alignment with God's law. The blessed one is satisfied with her life because she is rooted in the abiding ways of God. James, himself rooted in this tradition, affirms here that true happiness emerges for those who "endure temptation," which would presumably lead away from the path of God. In addition to this wisdom, James echoes the Jewish apocalyptic confidence that God will bless the faithful who endure suffering: so, for instance, the book of Daniel concludes, "Happy are those who persevere and attain the thousand three hundred thirty-five days. But you, go on your way, and rest; you shall rise for your reward at the end of the days" (Dan. 12:12–13; see also 4 Macc. 7:22). So here, James promises a "crown of life" to those who continue to love God.

It is nevertheless a puzzling kind of blessing that James reiterates: the blessing that comes through sadness, poverty, persecution, suffering? The words of Jesus' Sermon on the Mount have become so familiar to many Christians that we recite them without choking on what we are saying. But James may help us here to pause and savor the strangeness. Notice that James is not identifying blessedness with the experience of testing. He is not celebrating emotional or physical hardship itself as a sign of God's favor—indeed he explicitly denies it, insisting that God "tempts no one" (1:13). Rather, blessedness is the result of enduring that hardship and coming out on the other side.

There are two ways to think about blessing that comes from endurance. One approach is to emphasize the intrinsic relationship between endurance and blessing: facing hardship can and does build character. This is more in keeping with the wisdom tradition, which offers moral instruction for this present life. At the simplest level, we recognize the way that athletic training makes muscles sore, but enduring such pain really does make the body stronger. So too with working for positive social change: shifts in public policy or any kind of injustice requires long, slow, often frustrating effort; but those who endure often see the results of their labor.

This is consistent with what James describes in 1:3–4, where the writer affirms that testing produces endurance, and endurance leads to maturity, or wholeness. As noted there, we need to exercise caution in prescribing all endurance as worthwhile for building

---

Above all, trust in the slow work of God.
  We are quite naturally impatient in everything
  to reach the end without delay.
  We should like to skip the intermediate stages.
  We are impatient of being on the way to something
  unknown, something new.
  And yet it is the law of all progress
  that it is made by passing through
  some stages of instability—
  and that it may take a very long time.
And so I think it is with you;
  your ideas mature gradually—let them grow,
  let them shape themselves, without undue haste.
  Don't try to force them on,
  as though you could be today what time
  (that is to say, grace and circumstances
  acting on your own good will)
  will make of you tomorrow.
Only God could say what this new spirit
  gradually forming within you will be.
  Give our Lord the benefit of believing
  that his hand is leading you,
  and accept the anxiety of feeling yourself
  in suspense and incomplete.

—Pierre Teilhard de Chardin, SJ, in *Hearts on Fire: Praying with Jesuits*, ed. Michael Harter, SJ (Chestnut Hill, MA: Institute of Jesuit Sources, 1993), 58.

up whole human beings. After all, some situations (like any form of domestic violence) should not be endured but vehemently condemned. Yet in this passage, James does not counsel endurance of every suffering; he proclaims that "anyone who endures *temptation*" is blessed. Calvin emphasizes this interpretation of endurance and blessing, saying, "I consider that [James's] praise is for fortitude in the face of adversity, making the paradox that the blessed are not those commonly so called (who get everything to suit them) but those who are not crushed by their troubles."[50]

A second way to interpret the relationship of hardship and blessing is to see blessing as the extrinsic reward from God for endurance, a vindication of God's righteousness. This is the eschatological confidence that we noted in Daniel 12:12–13 above, promising that even if the righteous receive no reward in this life, God is not done yet. Justice and mercy will finally prevail. Jan Hus represents this approach, citing James 1:12 when he was preparing for his own execution, connecting his suffering with the suffering of Jesus and with the crown of life that lies ahead: "That crown, I firmly hope, the Lord will allow me to share along with you, most fervent lovers of the truth, and along with all who firmly and steadfastly love the Lord Jesus Christ, Who suffered for us, leaving us an example that we should follow in his steps."[51] More recently, Elsa Tamez describes this verse as an "apocalyptic blessing" for the oppressed who will be saved and participate in the world to come because of their steadfastness of faith.[52] The promise of the "crown of life" infuses hope into readers who are suffering, promising a future in which the crushed will be crowned.

James's teaching about the blessing that comes from endurance includes both of these facets—the present and the future, the intrinsic and the extrinsic, the wisdom and the eschatological perspective. Furthermore, though James makes no direct reference to Jesus' temptation and endurance, it is enlightening to stand with other interpreters through the ages and read James's words with an eye

---

50. Calvin, *A Harmony of the Gospels Matthew, Mark, and Luke, Vol. III, and the Epistles of James and Jude*, 267.
51. Jan Hus, in *The Letters of John Hus*, 186–87.
52. Tamez, *The Scandalous Message of James*, 31-33.

to Jesus' own story. If we do this, we can also see both aspects of James 1:12 embodied there. For instance, "Blessed is anyone who endures temptation" calls to mind the temptation narrative in Mark 1:12–13 (cf. Matt. 4:1–11 and Luke 4:1–13), at the beginning of Jesus' ministry. The Gospel narratives certainly imply that by enduring this season of temptation, Jesus demonstrated and honed his authority, launching the teaching and healing ministry in which he was recognized as blessed. In this way, Jesus demonstrates the intrinsic relationship between endurance and blessing in James's teaching: by standing firm in the face of temptation, Jesus himself is blessed.

On the other hand, reading James 1:12 with an eye to Jesus' story also illumines the eschatological thrust of the passage: "Such a one has stood the test and will receive the crown of life that the Lord has promised to those who love him." Jesus truly endured till the end, remaining faithful to God even when it led to the cross. Yet Jesus' resurrection fulfilled the promise of divine vindication on the far side of death, the "crown of life" that James names here. As with Jesus, so too with those who follow him: endurance of temptation will lead to fullness of life, both now and in God's promised future.

Having affirmed the importance of enduring temptation, James immediately heads off a possible misunderstanding: "No one, when tempted, should say, 'I am being tempted by God'; for God cannot be tempted by evil and he himself tempts no one" (1:13). James does not want anyone to hear him saying that God is the source of temptation, because God is only and ever the giver of good gifts (see 1:5 and 1:17). The problem is that this claim seems to contradict other passages in the Bible. Wasn't God testing Abraham in commanding the patriarch to sacrifice his son Isaac in Genesis 22? What about Moses' warning regarding false prophets, in which he says, "the LORD your God is testing you, to know whether you indeed love the LORD your God with all your heart and soul" (Deut. 13:3)? What about the explicit petition of the psalmist, "Prove me, O Lord, and try me; test my heart and mind" (Ps. 26:2)? Finally, why would Jesus teach his disciples to pray "lead us not into temptation," if God, by definition, "tempts no one"?[53]

---

53. See Allison, *A Critical and Exegetical Commentary on the Epistle of James*, 237, for more examples.

We see in James an effort shared by many post-exilic texts, and
further developed by ideas from the Hellenistic world, to completely
disassociate God from all evil.[54] Temptation can lead people away
from goodness, and surely a good God cannot be responsible for
any departure from the good. The Greek-speaking Jewish/Christian
world in which James was written affirmed that God is good *all the
time*—an affirmation that most Christian interpreters through the
ages have likewise adopted. Yet how do we hold together this view
with older Scriptures that link God's hand with at least some of the
suffering endured by people?

Many interpreters have wrestled with this apparent inconsistency
between James and earlier biblical claims that God does send testing.
One approach is to emphasize two kinds of human response to
temptation: enduring it (like Jesus and Abraham) and succumbing
to it. Dionysius of Alexandria in the third century and John Cassian in
the late fourth and early fifth, for instance, take this angle. Temptation
itself, for these writers, comes from the devil, not from God. Cassian
writes, "Abraham was tempted, Joseph was tempted, but neither
of them was led into temptation for neither of them yielded his
consent to the tempter."[55] Another approach is to emphasize two
different sources of temptation: the kind from God, which proves
faith and is therefore good, and the kind that leads astray.[56] Whether
focusing on the source of temptation or the human response to it,
anyone attempting to teach or preach on James in the context of the
wider canon needs to acknowledge the tension between trust in the
goodness of God and the human experience of temptation, which
does not feel very good—and yet sometimes produces an outcome
more good than it would have been otherwise.

What is tempting the readers of James? He does not give specifics
here. But unlike the earlier verses, which suggest external threats to
be endured, the focus here is internal.[57] The temptation is "one's own

54. Ibid., 238, 242–43.
55. David B. Gowler, *James through the Centuries*, 104.
56. See, e.g., Augustine, *Lectures or Tractates on the Gospel according to St. John*, trans. John Gibb
    and James Innes, tractate XLIII: chapter VIII.48–59, paras, 5–6), http://www.ccel.org/ccel
    /schaff/npnf107.iii.xliv.html
57. For similar interpretations of internal and external kinds of temptation, see Bede,
    Commentary on the Seven Catholic Epistles, 15, and Calvin, *A Harmony of the Gospels Matthew,
    Mark, and Luke, Vol. III, and the Epistles of James and Jude*, 267–68.

desire" (1:14). This desire within is like a hungry animal, lured by food into a trap or onto a hook. The ways of desire are hard to resist, according to James, but they must be endured to receive "the crown of life."

The concept of "desire" has a complex history in Jewish as well as Christian theological reflection. James's negative view has much in common with the rabbinic notion of the "evil desire," which leads one away from the ways of God. It also plays into the negative view of desire embodied in much Christian teaching since Augustine. Yet other Hebrew wisdom literature uses "desire" in a positive sense, and many ancient writers—including Augustine—also see wisdom as driven by desire, not opposed to it. Philosophers and theologians since Plato have often explored desire as a driving force of human nature that can lead not only to possession of things, and not solely to human relationships, but ultimately to relationship with God. The Bible itself speaks about the relationship between God and humanity in terms of desire: "As a deer longs for flowing streams, so my soul longs for you, O God" (Ps. 42). In Hosea, God speaks about Israel as a desiring (and betrayed) husband speaks about his wife: "I will now allure her, and bring her into the wilderness, and speak tenderly to her. From there I will give her her vineyards, and make the Valley of Achor a door of hope. There she shall respond as in the days of her youth, as at the time when she came out of the land of Egypt" (2:14–15).

It is easy for a contemporary reader to oversimplify James's point here, to read the danger of "desire" as a condemnation of sexual desire, and then either to focus single-mindedly on the need to avoid specific kinds of sexual activity, or to dismiss the teaching as an outdated concern of another age. To be sure, James's description of desire is both negative and implicitly sexual. "Desire" is personified as a woman who lures the listener into a sexual encounter, giving birth to a child named "sin," who then bears a grandchild named "death." James's original audience would surely have heard the parallels here to the "foolish woman" of Proverbs, who was similarly described (see, e.g., Prov. 5:1–23; 6:20–35; 7:1–27). Those who explore this teaching today need to exercise caution about simply passing on such ancient embedded stereotypes of women as dangerous temptresses intent on seducing upright men from the paths of righteousness. This portrayal damages women and undermines healthy relationships between women and men. But given the rest of James's teaching, sexual activity itself does not seem to be his concern. The condemnation of "one's own desire" has more to do with the destruction that follows when we are driven by our own immediate self-gratification rather than the slow and steady work of growing in wisdom and faith.

Notice the contrasting images that have already begun to emerge in this letter: between the one who endures and becomes mature (1:4) and the one who doubts and is tossed about like a wave on the sea (1:6); between the lowly believer who is raised up (1:9) and the "rich" who disappear and are taken away "in the midst of a busy life" (1:11); between one who endures temptation and one who is lured away to sin and death. James plays throughout this writing

---

Thou wast their rock, their fortress, and their might;
 thou, Lord, their captain in the well-fought fight;
 thou, in the darkness drear, their one true light.
. . . .
And when the strife is fierce, the warfare long,
 steals on the ear the distant triumph song,
 and hearts are brave again, and arms are strong.

Alleluia! Alleluia!

William Walsham How, "For All the Saints," *Glory to God*, 326.

---

with the difference between wisdom, which is slow and steady and patient, enduring trials and rooted in the deeply implanted word of God, and ways of life that are more fitful and erratic, craving bright shiny riches, which do not last. The contrast here is between the endurance of "those who love [God]," who will receive a crown of life, and those who are driven by more immediate "desire," who are "deceived." Anyone who is enticed by immediate satisfaction has lost sight of the more profound blessing that can only be gained over time, by endurance.

1:16–27

The Living Word of Truth

1:16–18

Being Born of the Word

In these verses, James offers us an alternate birth narrative, contrasting with the preceding passage. In verses 14–15, human desire gives birth to sin, which gives birth to death—a disturbing genealogy, which any contemporary teacher or preacher should handle with care, attentive to the ways that this image could retraumatize listeners who have experienced stillbirths or miscarriages. In verses 16–18, however, the image is full of life: God gives birth to us by the word of truth, so that we can become the "first fruits of his creatures." Later, James makes it clear that if we tend this seed of truth implanted in us, we also become fruitful—by "doing the word."

Who is the "us" to whom God gives life? This is presumably identical with "my beloved (brothers and sisters)," whom James is addressing. Who are they—and are we, the contemporary readers included? The answer to this question is closely related to how we interpret the "word of truth" which "gave *us* birth" (1:18).

There are three traditions of interpretation here.[1] One possibility is that the "word of truth" is an echo of creation in Genesis 1, in which God creates heavens and earth by speaking words: "Let there be light.... Let there be a dome in the midst of the waters ... let the dry land appear," and eventually, "Let us make humankind in our

---

1. For more detailed discussion of these three approaches, see Dale C. Allison Jr., *A Critical and Exegetical Commentary on the Epistle of James*, International Critical Commentary (New York: Bloomsbury, 2013), 255–56, 280–85.

image." Other Old Testament passages also describe God creating by "the word"; so, for instance, "By the word of the LORD the heavens were made, and all their host by the breath of his mouth" (Ps. 33:6). According to this interpretation, James is evoking God's cosmic creativity, inviting every possible reader to recognize God as the good and gracious source of life. Certainly "Father of lights" is a term that depicts God as author of the sun, moon, and stars, recalling God's role as creator of all things. The "us" then could be universal—all of us can trace our birth ultimately to the "Father of lights." To describe humanity as "first fruits," in this reading, is to highlight the place of humans as the highest among creatures, like the best part of the sacrifices offered to God (as in 1 Sam. 2:29 and 15:21, where the same word is translated as the best things to be sacrificed). All of us are born of the word, all of us are called to lives of grateful response, perhaps by claiming our role as the "first fruits" and tending the rest of God's good creation.

Another interpretation, favored by many recent interpreters, reads the "word of truth" not as creation generally, but as the law, by which God gives birth to the people of Israel. The law, or the commandments, is called "word of truth" in several places, especially Psalm 119, which says, "Do not take the word of truth utterly out of my mouth, for my hope is in your ordinances" (Ps. 119:43). The giving of the law at Sinai is closely associated with the birth of Israel as a people. Furthermore, when the Hebrew Bible portrays God giving birth, this metaphor always refers specifically to the people of Israel, not to humanity in general (see, e.g., Num. 11:12, in which Moses yells at God, "Did I conceive all this people? Did I give birth to them . . . ?" and Deut. 32:18, in which Moses chastises the people, "You were unmindful of the Rock that bore you; you forgot the God who gave you birth"). The "us," according to this approach, is the Israelite people, who are also called "first fruits" in biblical texts like Jeremiah 2:3: "Israel was holy to the LORD, the first fruits of his harvest." This reading underscores the Jewish/Christian identity of James's primary audience and their reliance on the life-giving power of the law, which gives them a distinct place among the nations.

The most popular Christian interpretation from at least the early medieval period until the twentieth century adopts a christological lens that is not explicit in James, but which may be developed from interaction with other portions of the New Testament. This approach interprets the "word of truth" as the word of the gospel, or Christ himself, in keeping with the prologue to the Gospel according to John: "In the beginning was the Word, and the Word was with God, and the Word was God. . . . All things came into being through him" (John 1:1, 3a). In this reading, the "us" refers to the new community that comes into being because of the Word made flesh, the community of the baptized who are reborn by their union with Christ. We "first fruits" are the eschatological community, those who, with Christ, participate in God's new reign that is dawning. Paul uses the phrase "first fruits" in this way, to speak both of Christ (1 Cor. 15:20) and of converts to the way of Christ (Rom. 16:5; 1 Cor. 16:15; 2 Thess. 2:13). Reading James in conjunction with Paul and John can shape such a christological approach, which we see for instance in Bede: "God has changed us from being children of darkness into being children of light, not because of any merits of ours but by his own will, through the water of regeneration . . . we have become 'the first fruits of his creatures,' which means that we have been exalted over the rest of creation."[2]

I think that contemporary readers can savor the richness of all three lines of interpretation, rather than choosing only one. To be sure, the christological reading is almost certainly not James's original intent, but a later canonical interpretation. James himself offers very little explicit Christology, such as we see in the later Johannine literature which so shaped the development of Nicene orthodoxy. It is important in reading this passage not to practice a replacement theology that completely supplants the Torah with Christ as the "word of truth." But appreciating the multivalence of this passage might help address precisely this problem, by calling attention to the coherence of God's word through the ages. The word of creation, Sinai, and Jesus Christ, in whom is the new community, is the same Word: Love. The word is "let there be light" and "I am the Lord your

---

2. Bede, "Concerning the Epistle of St. James," in A. Hammann, ed., *Patrologia Latinae Supplementum* (Paris: Garnier Frères, 1963), 3:67, cited in *Ancient Christian Commentary on Scripture: New Testament*, vol. 11: James, 1–2 Peter, 1–3 John, Jude (Downers Grove, IL: InterVarsity Press, 2000), 16.

God" and "love the Lord your God and love your neighbor as yourself." Light and law and love—these are all one complex life-giving
Word. Because the readers are already "first fruits," they are not to be
lured and enticed by self-serving evil desires (1:13–15), but to live
out of the ever-generative word that has given them birth. This is the
word that James, a few verses later, will call us to "do."

Before we can receive the charge to be "doers of the word," however, James calls our attention to its source: the unchanging and
generous God: "Every generous act of giving, with every perfect
gift, is from above, coming down from the Father of lights, with
whom there is no variation or shadow due to change" (1:17). In
contrast to the negative theological statement of 1:13 ("God cannot be tempted"), this passage describes God positively, as source
of all good things. This single verse has been one of the most quoted
verses of James over the centuries, and has been particularly popular
in Eastern Christianity.

Many Orthodox Christians still hear this verse each week,
because it appears in the Divine Liturgy of Saint John Chrysostom.
Following the celebration of the Eucharist, the priest prays this portion of the Litany of Thanksgiving:

> Lord, bless those who praise You and sanctify those who trust
> in You. Save Your people and bless Your inheritance. Protect
> the whole body of Your Church. Sanctify those who love the
> beauty of Your house. Glorify them in return by Your divine
> power, and do not forsake us who hope in You. Grant peace to
> Your world, to Your churches, to the clergy, to those in public
> service, to the armed forces, and to all Your people. *For every
> good and perfect gift is from above, coming from You, the Father of
> lights.* To You we give glory, thanksgiving, and worship, to the
> Father and the Son and the Holy Spirit, now and forever and
> to the ages of ages.[3]

This liturgical text gives thanks for God's good gifts and prays for
God's continuing generosity, particularly toward the church. It
includes, however, a petition for peace for "Thy world"—presumably

3. "The Divine Liturgy of Saint John Chrysostom," a New Translation by Members of the
Faculty of Hellenic College/Holy Cross Greek Orthodox School of Theology (Brookline,
MA: Holy Cross Orthodox Press, 1985), 35.

the whole world, calling attention to the wideness of God's generosity.

Such a focus on divine generosity is one of two main aspects of this verse. "Every generous act of giving, with every perfect gift, is from above, coming down from the Father of lights." God is a generous giver, the source of every single act of giving, and of every single gift we receive in this world. The reiteration of "every" (act of giving and perfect gift) invites reflection on the wideness of God's generosity: "each little flower that opens, each little bird that sings," as the old hymn "All Things Bright and Beautiful" has it, and also each person we encounter in our daily lives, each meal shared, each insight gained, even each difficulty we encounter that enables us to learn patience and mercy. "Every generous act of giving and every perfect gift" can also include good gifts outside the realm of Christian faith, including Shakespeare, art, and other religious traditions.[4] Furthermore, God is the giver not only of external gifts but also of those things in us that are good, such as our desire to keep the law, our capacity to care for one another, and our faith in God.[5] The overflowing generosity of "the Father of lights" is on full display in this passage, inspiring readers to refer all good things in our lives to their source, and inviting us to look for the goodness in all things in our lives.

> All good gifts around us
> are sent from heaven above.
> Then thank the Lord, O thank the Lord,
> for all his love.
>
> Matthias Claudius, "We Plough the Fields and Scatter," trans. Jane M. Campbell, *Trinity Psalter Hymnal* (Willow Grove, PA: Trinity Psalter Hymnal Joint Venture, 2018), 551.

God is a bountiful giver. This is the first divine attribute James celebrates in this verse. The second key divine attribute in James's theological vision is that God is utterly dependable: "the Father of lights, with whom there is no variation or shadow due to change." As "Father of lights," the one who created the heavenly lights, God's ways are even more dependable and fixed than the (apparently) fixed patterns of the stars' movement. And unlike the shifting shadows on

---

4. See Allison, *A Critical and Exegetical Commentary on the Epistle of James*, 257–58.
5. See Gowler's discussion of Cassian's and Luther's interpretations of this verse in *James through the Centuries* (Chichester: Wiley Blackwell, 2014), 116–18.

the ground caused by the changing position of the sun, God has no shadow to shift. Some Christian interpreters, especially in early centuries, used this verse to emphasize that God's nature is simple and unchanging, unlike everything we see around us that is constantly in flux. There is a fundamental difference between the nature of creation and the nature of the Creator, and change belongs to this created world, not to the One who created it.

This theological claim that God by definition cannot change influenced early christological and Trinitarian reflection. In the fourth century, for instance, Athanasius employed James 1:17 in his argument against Arian teaching. God is a simple and unchanging essence, contended Athanasius, and there can be no variability in God's nature. If Jesus is one with God, as he says in the Gospel of John ("I and the Father are one"), then this must be a permanent and unchanging reality—and therefore "the Son's relation to the Father [is] essential, not merely ethical."[6] Athanasius and his colleagues in Alexandria were deeply concerned about any hint of separation between God and Christ. Jesus and God must be absolutely united in essence, in order for our humanity to be truly united to God. In other words, our salvation depended on the oneness of Father and Son. In the context of this commitment, James 1:17 played an important role in underscoring the eternal unchanging nature of God, always essentially united.

For many contemporary readers, the real force of this affirmation that God does not change is moral, not metaphysical. The point is that God is faithful and steadfast in all God's purposes.[7] We can therefore trust that though the mountains shake and fall into the sea, and though the waters roar and foam (which they will), God remains steady.

This affirmation that God is the dependable giver of all good gifts, to whom we should give thanks in every circumstance, is fundamental to the theology of nineteenth century Danish philosopher Søren Kierkegaard. He explores verse 1:17 in four

6. Gowler, *James through the Centuries*, 114.
7. See discussions of this popular modern view in Richard Bauckham, *James: Wisdom of James, Disciple of Jesus the Sage* (London and New York: Routledge, 1999), 168; and Allison, *A Critical and Exegetical Commentary on the Epistle of James*, 259.

complete discourses over the course of his lifetime, calling attention
again and again to the affirmation that "every good and every perfect
gift is from above."[8] Kierkegaard helps us to see that this is no easy or
naive celebration, but a hard calling to receive all of life as a gift and
thank God for it—no matter what life brings.

> When you had doubts about what came from God or about
> what was a good and a perfect gift, did you risk the venture?
> And when the light sparkle of joy beckoned you, did you
> thank God for it? And when you were so strong that you felt
> you needed no help, did you then thank God? And when your
> allotted portion was little, did you thank God? And when your
> allotted portion was sufferings, did you thank God? And when
> your wish was denied, did you thank God? And when you
> yourself had to deny your wish, did you thank God? And when
> people wronged you and insulted you, did you thank God? We
> are not saying that the wrong thereby ceased to be wrong—
> what would be the use of such pernicious and foolish talk!
> It is up to you to decide whether it was wrong; but have you
> taken the wrong and insult to God and by your thanksgiving
> received it from his hand as a good and a perfect gift? . . . It
> is beautiful that a person prays, and many a promise is given
> to the one who prays without ceasing, but it is more blessed
> always to give thanks. Then you have worthily interpreted
> those apostolic words more gloriously than if all the angels
> spoke in flaming tongues.[9]

glorious

For Kierkegaard, the declaration that every act of giving and every
perfect gift comes "from above" should shape our view of everything
that happens in life. Even suffering is transformed when we receive
it as a gift, because we place it in relation to our ever-generous God,
whose purpose is always life.

The vision of God's relationship to the cosmos in these verses is a
dynamic interaction that is begun but not concluded. Though God
does not change, everything else in this passage does: lights, gifts,
us. Gifts are even now "coming down" from above. In the past, God

8. See Bauckham, *James: Wisdom of James, Disciple of Jesus the Sage*, 169–70, for concise
exploration of Kierkegaard's interpretation of this verse.
9. Søren Kierkegaard, "Every Good and Every Perfect Gift," in *Eighteen Upbuilding Discourses*, ed.
Howard V. Hong and Edna H. Hong (Princeton, NJ: Princeton University Press, 1990), 43.

> Great is thy faithfulness, O God my Father;
> there is no shadow of turning with thee.
> Thou changest not; thy compassions they fail not.
> As thou hast been thou forever wilt be.
> Great is thy faithfulness! Great is thy faithfulness!
> Morning by morning, new mercies I see.
> All I have needed thy hand hath provided.
> Great is thy faithfulness, Lord unto me!
>

"gave us birth," and this birth has a purpose that may or may not already be accomplished: "so that we would become a kind of first fruits." Luther cited this verse in support of his view that in this life, a beginning is made in us so that in this life we may grow, and after death be perfected. His version of this verse reads, "God has given us birth through his word, out of his sheer gracious will, without our merit, that we should be a first fruit of his work, or creatures."[10] Perhaps James is offering a charge to his audience, reminding them of the purpose that stems from their creation: "you were created to be first fruits—so now act like it!"

FURTHER REFLECTIONS
Divine Immutability

In 1:17, James claims that "there is no variation or shadow due to change" with God. This verse has often been used as a major support for the doctrine of divine immutability, the teaching that God does not and cannot change. Many early church teachers, including Athanasius and Cyril of Alexandria, Augustine, and John of Damascus, affirmed that God's essence is intrinsically immutable. In this way, God is fundamentally different from the world around us, which is susceptible to change, decay, and death. This early emphasis on the unchanging stability of God was informed partly by Greek

---

10. Martin Luther, "Defense and Explanation of All the Articles" in *Luther's Works*, American edition, vol. 32, ed. George W. Forell (Philadelphia: Muhlenberg Press, 1958), 24.

philosophy, which also tended to portray the eternal divine realm as beyond change. Yet the affirmation that God does not change also rests on biblical affirmations that God is a stable refuge in the face of instability (e.g., Ps. 46). Both Greek philosophy and biblical faith, then, combined in the early development of the doctrine of God's essential immutability.

The Fourth Lateran Council in 1215 offers this classical statement of the doctrine of God, including the affirmation that God is unchangeable:

> We firmly believe and confess without reservation that there is only one true God, eternal, infinite and unchangeable, incomprehensible, almighty, and ineffable, the Father and the Son and the Holy Spirit; three persons indeed, but one essence, substance or nature entirely simple.[11]

A few years later, Thomas Aquinas offers a clear defense of God's immutability in his *Summa Theologiae*, defining change as movement. He acknowledges that Scripture speaks of God moving, but he argues that God is in fact immutable, that is, not moving or changing in any way. He gives three reasons:

1. God is pure act, without any potentiality. For God to have potentiality would mean that God changes, which cannot be true.
2. Everything that moves remains in part and "passes away" in part. God cannot pass away, so God cannot move.
3. Everything that moves acquires something in its movement, but God already comprehends everything in himself and cannot acquire anything new.[12]

For all of these reasons, Aquinas argues, God does not change.

The 1647 Westminster Confession of Faith includes a very similar statement about the nature of God, beginning with these words:

> There is but one only living and true God, who is infinite in being and perfection, a most pure spirit, invisible, without

---

11. Lateran Council IV, cited in *Catechism of the Catholic Church* (1992), par. 202, http://www .vatican.va/archive/ENG0015/__P16.HTM.
12. *Summa Theologiae* Pt. 1, Q 9, art. 1. See second and revised edition, 1920, literally translated by Fathers of the English Dominican Province, http://www.newadvent.org/summa/1009.htm.

body, parts, or passions, immutable, immense, eternal, incomprehensible, almighty; most wise, most holy, most free, most absolute....[13]

Protestants and Catholics alike affirmed God's immutability in these terms until the twentieth century.

Beginning early in the century, philosophers and theologians began to attack the classical doctrine of immutability for several reasons. One challenge came from the emerging field of process thought, which proposed a new metaphysical account of reality in which God is not separate from creation but is deeply implicated in it. Charles Hartshorne formulated the notion of "dipolar theism," in which God is both eternal in essence and open to change in concrete actuality. God knows everything that is knowable at any one time, but new things are always emerging, which are new also to God. In this way, process thought accounts for God being open to change, while also having an element of unchangeability. Hartshorne (and other process theologians, such as John Cobb) also argues that if God is love, then God must be open to change in some way. Love means that one is sympathetically moved by the condition of another; if this is true of God, then God must really be susceptible to movement and change in God's own being. In this way, process theologians reject classical arguments about divine immutability.

Another critique of divine immutability has come from liberation theologians, who observe that a classical understanding of God as incapable of change or response to earthly reality is no help to people who are oppressed. To say that God is immutable seems to suggest that God is purely amoral, without concern for actual people and situations in history.[14] Early feminist theologian Mary Daly challenges the traditional view of an all-powerful, transcendent God as a figment of male imagination. God sitting in supreme isolation from the world, self-sufficient and invulnerable to change,

13. Westminster Confession of Faith, in *The Constitution of the Presbyterian Church (U.S.A.)*, Part 1, *Book of Confessions* (Louisville, KY: Office of the General Assembly, Presbyterian Church (U.S.A.), 2014), 6.011.
14. James Cone, *A Black Theology of Liberation*, 20th anniversary edition (Maryknoll, NY: Orbis, 1990), 74–76.

she judges to be the worst kind of projection—one that has served to bolster male power in the world and oppress women.[15]

In addition to these philosophical and ethical objections, some theologians have begun to challenge the classical doctrine of immutability based on the biblical witness. Daniel Migliore, for instance, argues that it is particularly important to ground our understanding of God in the revelation of God in Christ crucified. The cross challenges any notion of a God who is untouched by human suffering. Migliore suggests that if we understand God as impassible, immutable, and so forth, this can contribute to ways of thinking and behaving that are insensitive to the suffering of others.[16] As a result, following Karl Barth's pattern of naming the divine attributes in dialectical pairs, Migliore reinterprets the notion of immutability in terms of "constancy and ever-changing actions." God is constant in purpose: that is, God always turns toward the world in redeeming love, yet that redeeming love expresses itself in new and different ways each day. As Migliore puts it, this is to honor the biblical witness which affirms both "Jesus Christ is the same yesterday and today and forever" (Heb. 13:8) and God's love is "new every morning."

1:19–27
Hearing and Doing the Word

In these verses James seeks to cultivate in the listener an appreciation for slowness, for listening, as opposed to the quick fire of self-righteous anger. We have already begun to discern this basic contrast in earlier verses: the restlessness of the wave as opposed to the stability of God's generosity, those who are lured away by their own selfish desires as opposed to the steady endurance of those who love the Lord. James keeps tracing the contours of difference between change and patience, between impulsiveness and rootedness, between one's

15. Mary Daly, *Beyond God the Father: Toward a Philosophy of Women's Liberation* (Boston: Beacon Press, 1973).

16. Daniel L. Migliore, *Faith Seeking Understanding: An Introduction to Christian Theology*, 3rd ed. (Grand Rapids: Eerdmans, 2014), 83.

It sometimes seems to me that our days are poisoned with too many words. Words said and not meant. Words said *and* meant. Words divorced from feeling. Wounding words. Words that conceal. Words that reduce. Dead words.

If only words were a kind of fluid that collects in the ears, if only they turned into the visible chemical equivalent of their true value, an acid, or something curative—then we might be more careful. Words do collect in us anyway. They collect in the blood, in the soul, and either transform or poison people's lives. Bitter or thoughtless words poured into the ears of the young have blighted many lives in advance. We all know people whose unhappy lives twist on a set of words uttered to them on a certain unforgotten day at school, in childhood, or at university.

We seem to think that words aren't things. A bump on the head may pass away, but a cutting remark grows with the mind. But then it is possible that we know all too well the awesome power of words—which is why we use them with such deadly and accurate cruelty.

Ben Okri, *Birds of Heaven* (London: Phoenix, 1996), 3–5.

own isolated self-interest and the wise righteousness of God. He is trying to coax his listeners to stop, look, and listen first, before issuing judgments.

It is easy to rush to judgment, to publish one's opinion quickly, to make it clear where you stand. And our society rewards it. Harder in these days is to follow the wisdom of James: "be quick ... to *listen* ... slow to speak, slow to anger. ..."

Nor is it only our age that has struggled with this tendency to rush to judgment. It seems to be a persistent problem in human societies, including Christian communities. Over the centuries, interpreters both early and modern have used this passage from James to caution those in power not to judge too quickly. For instance, Gregory the Great in the sixth century writes to Rechared, the king of Spain, "Care also is to be taken that wrath creep not in, lest whatever is lawful to be done be done too hastily. For wrath, even when it prosecutes the faults of delinquents, ought not to go before the mind as a mistress, but attend as a handmaid behind the back of reason, that it may come to the front when bidden."[17] Other interpreters have taken

17. Gregory the Great, letter to Rechared (Epistle CXXII), http://www.ccel.org/ccel/schaff
/npnf213.ii.v.lvii.html?highlight=gregory,the,great,letter,to,rechared.

James's advice as particularly helpful for teachers; Bede cites James in his advice to refrain from teaching what you have recently learned, in order to reach maturity of wisdom.[18] When considering those in positions of power, whether political, ecclesial, or academic, James's words offer much-needed caution about the use of words without due consideration.

But is this advice always wise? Does not this counsel to "be slow to speak, slow to anger" lead to passivity in the face of injustice? Aren't there reasons—good reasons—to raise voices against real evils in the world? Aren't there good reasons to be angry? Taking James's counsel out of context could indeed lead to an overly cautious temperament, as we see mocked in the fawning character of Polonius in *Hamlet*, who offers this advice to his son Laertes:

> Give thy thoughts no tongue,
> Nor any unproportioned thought his act.
> . . . Beware
> Of entrance to a quarrel, but being in,
> Bear't that the opposed may beware of thee.
> Give every man thy ear, but few thy voice;
> Take each man's censure, but reserve thy judgment.[19]

Shakespeare is certainly not offering Polonius as a figure to be imitated, but as a man so anxious to avoid conflict or offense that he is utterly useless to anyone.

If we continue to listen to James, however, it becomes clear that he is not advocating passivity. Indeed, he lifts his own voice against injustices that he sees in the community—the rich being treated with greater honor than the poor, members of the community succumbing to envy and ambition. His own words can sound pretty angry at times: "Come now, you rich people, weep and wail for the miseries that are coming to you. Your riches have rotted, and your clothes are moth-eaten . . ." (5:1–2). The point is not to avoid all speech or

18. Bede the Venerable, *Commentary on the Seven Catholic Epistles*, trans. David Hurst (Kalamazoo, MI: Cistercian, 1985), 11–13.
19. William Shakespeare, *Hamlet*, act 1, scene 3, in *The Riverside Shakespeare* (Boston: Houghton Mifflin Co., 1974), 1147.

all judgment but to consider whether our words and our judgment arise from ourselves or from the "implanted word" of God.

I once had an eager student who wrote impressively long papers and exams, and who was always the first to raise his hand in class in answer to a question. When he graduated from seminary, he invited me to offer the charge at his ordination service. I offered him these three words: *Stop. Look. Listen.* Usually offered as advice for what to do when you approach a railroad crossing, these three verbs seemed appropriate guidance for this new minister, and they are in keeping with James's advice to all members of the community in this passage. *Stop* before rushing to judgment and potentially stepping into the path of an oncoming train. "Your anger does not produce God's righteousness." Or to put it another way: God is the source of true righteousness. Not you. Then: *Look.* Try to discern where God is at work before madly leaping in to destroy what you judge to be "rank growth of wickedness." Above all, James exhorts his audience to *listen.* This is a wise reminder in any case to listen to others, to treat others with respect rather than always dominating the conversation with your own views. For James, however, this listening is especially connected with the "implanted word."

James weaves the theme of the "word" through the larger passage of 1:16–27, and it is helpful to see this progression as a whole:

— The word of truth, which is from God, gives us life (1:18).
— This word is implanted in us (1:21).
— We are called to be "doers of the word"—so this word bears fruit (1:22–23).

First, as we saw in 1:16–18, God is the one who has birthed us by the word of truth. *Already* we have been given this word, which is life. As we saw in the previous passage, the "word" could refer to creation, or to law, or to Jesus Christ, and contemporary interpreters will do well to hold all these interpretations together. "Let there be light," says God in the beginning. And there was light. "In the beginning was the Word," says John, "and the Word was with God and the Word was God. . . . What has come into being in him was life, and the life was the light of all people." This is the life-giving Word: that God has from the beginning *already* been shining into the darkness, that in Jesus Christ, God has *already* walked in the darkest places. Before we speak any words ourselves, God has already spoken. Grace precedes us.

Second, here in this passage, the word is planted within us. James says, "welcome with meekness the implanted word that has the power to save your souls" (1:21b). The word that is life, and light, does not just remain outside of us, but by God's grace it settles deep within us. Here, James evokes the internalized law of Jeremiah, who speaks for God, saying, "I will put my law within them, and I will write it on their hearts; and I will be their God, and they will be my people" (Jer. 31:33). Indeed, in verses 22–25, James clearly equates the "word" with "the perfect law, the law of liberty." The word implanted within us is that same "law" inscribed on our hearts, that word that says, "you are my beloved people. Do not fear. I am with you. Come with me."

How do we nurture such a word so that it takes root in our lives? It takes space, and time. It takes suspending our own quick tempers and judgments and clearing space together to listen. "Be quick to listen," says James, "and slow to speak, slow to anger. For your anger does not produce God's righteousness."

Nurturing the word requires us to "rid yourselves of all sordidness." "Rid yourselves" here is an idiom often used for removing clothes, and "sordidness" is the same word used in 2:2 for dirty clothes. One implied image, then, is that our habits of verbal abuse are like the stained clothes that we need to wash. They are not an intrinsic part of who we are. We need to strip them off, do the laundry, and start again.

Doing laundry is one operative image in James's wise counsel. Another is that of a patient gardener. Even the most forgetful and haphazard gardeners know what James is talking about. Lots of things grow quickly in a garden, and the most enthusiastic plants that appear and multiply and take over are usually weeds. If we do not watch and tend, clearing away what James calls the "rank growth," then the tomatoes and squash and okra will get choked out. We will never get our gumbo or our squash casserole.

John Calvin takes James's advice in this direction, emphasizing the connection between refraining from speech and listening to God's word. Calvin does not think that James is calling for silence simply to cultivate patience and wisdom on our own. Instead, Calvin calls us to suspend our words to make room for God's word. He envisions the world as God's schoolhouse, in which we need to listen well to the teacher: "Hush, the apostle says to us, no-one will ever be a good student of God, if he will not listen to Him in silence . . . it is only a check on our impatience, to stop us (as we usually do) from interrupting God out of turn. As long as His sacred lips are open towards us, our minds and ears are to be open towards Him, and we are not to seize the conversation for ourselves."[20] That word has been given to us, and is being given to us, but we need to pay attention in order to recognize and understand it.

The word brings us life. That same word is planted within us, so that we may welcome and tend it. But in the end, we are summoned to be more than listeners. In the next passage, James calls us to be "doers of the word." It is important that this is third. We cannot do the word unless we first listen and tend it. But then we do—and we must—act in keeping with the word, to bear God's life and light into the world that so desperately needs it.

In verses 19–21, James's message seems to have been basically: Stop. Look. Listen. Be "quick to listen" to the word of God, to be sure that your own reactions are of God, not from your own self-righteous anger. Attend to the "implanted word that has the power to save your souls" (v. 21).

Simply remaining in a listening posture, however, is not enough. At this point the writer recognizes that his audience might think that he is calling them to inaction, and he hastens to head off that misunderstanding. Listening deeply to the word does not mean refusing to act. It means rooting our action in the words and ways of God. And as we will soon see, God's words and ways have everything to do with caring for victims of unjust economic and political systems.

"Be doers of the word," calls James, "and not merely hearers who deceive themselves." Though James says little directly about Jesus,

---

20. John Calvin, *A Harmony of the Gospels Matthew, Mark, and Luke, Vol. III, and the Epistles of James and Jude*, trans. A. W. Morrison, ed. David W. Torrance and Thomas F. Torrance (Grand Rapids: Eerdmans, 1972), 271.

this is one of many places where he echoes Jesus' teaching: "Blessed . . . are those who hear the word of God and obey it" (Luke 11:28). He sounds even more like Paul, when Paul writes to the Romans: "For it is not the hearers of the law who are righteous in God's sight, but the doers of the law who will be justified" (Rom. 2:13). To be sure, Paul goes on to argue that no one is able to keep the law perfectly, that all have sinned and fallen short, so that justification comes by faith, and not by works. Yet Paul continues to proclaim the goodness of the law itself, affirming that "the law is holy, and the commandment is holy and just and good" (Rom. 7:12). It is especially helpful to see this convergence of James and Paul on the importance of "doing the word/law," given the historical perception that the two writers present fundamentally different interpretations of Christian teaching.

"Doers of the word." It is worth pausing and pondering the meaning of this phrase. Clearly James, like Jesus and especially Paul, intends it as a contrast with being "merely hearers." But what exactly does it mean to "do the word"? Scholars have pointed out that this is a Semitic phrase, because the usual Greek use of this term would mean "poet"—someone who does things *with* words.[21] As one Jewish commentator on this text states, "for Jews, 'doers [of the word]' refers to performing Torah."[22] We see the same phrase, for instance, in the Greek version of Psalm 103:20 (the version of the Scriptures available to the writer of James). That psalm verse speaks literally of "doing [God's] word and hearing the voice of his words." (Notice that for the psalmist, hearing and doing are complementary, while James here draws a contrast between them!) We today might hear "word-doer" as an image of a person who works with words externally. But in keeping with the tradition of the psalmist, the word is not external to James. He cannot do something *with* it; it does something with him. He calls on his audience to allow the word to take root and grow in them so that their lives are outworkings of its power. To be a word-doer is to live from the "word of truth" by which God gave us birth (1:18); it is to nurture the seed that was

---

21. Luke Timothy Johnson, *The Letter of James,* Anchor Yale Bible (New Haven, CT: Yale University Press, 1995), 206.
22. Herbert Basser, "The Letter of James," in *The Jewish Annotated New Testament,* ed. Amy-Jill Levine and Marc Zvi Brettler (New York: Oxford University Press, 2011), 430.

planted in us (1:21) so that we are a kind of "first fruits" of God's creatures (1:18). The grounding metaphor here is that of a garden, in which God is the master gardener, and we are seedlings growing, reaching for the light.

From the garden, James then shifts to another metaphor familiar to moral teachers in the Greek world: that of the mirror.[23] Those who only hear the word are "like those who look at themselves in a mirror; for they look at themselves and, on going away, immediately forget what they were like" (1:23–24). Writers in the first century often used the mirror as a metaphor for self-improvement: literally, it gave the viewer a chance to examine her reflection and fix any visible imperfections. By extension, it could provide a model for proper behavior; gazing into the mirror of self-reflection could enable one to become morally better. James is drawing on this use of the metaphor here, to suggest that the one who goes away and forgets has not properly used the mirror for self-improvement by turning hearing into deeds. This image also lays the groundwork for the specific models from the mirror of the law that James later invites the reader to imitate: Abraham and Rahab (2:21–25), Job (5:11), and Elijah (5:17–18). All these figures exemplify faith translated into deeds, in language drawn from the mirror metaphor.

The image of the mirror, like that of the garden, underscores James's recurring theme of endurance vs. distraction. Here, he draws a contrast between the momentary glance at the self and the pro-longed gaze into the law of God. Both the patient tending of the garden and the long gaze into the law are presented as positive images, emphasizing endurance rather than flightiness, deep rootedness over time rather than quickness that arises and immediately dies away.

This counsel to be "doers of the word" rather than "merely hearers" has over the past century often been directed against those who spend their time in intellectual understanding of the faith, rather than more public ethical activity. For some of us, such a critique hits uncomfortably close to home, which is probably why we still need to hear it. For instance, Scottish Baptist minister Alexander Maclaren preached a sermon on James 1:25 in 1900 that includes this caution:

---

23. See Luke Timothy Johnson, "The Mirror of Remembrance: James 1:22–25," in *Brother of Jesus, Friend of God: Studies in the Book of James* (Grand Rapids: Eerdmans, 2004), 168–81.

> No word of the New Testament is given us in order that we may know truth, but all in order that we may do it. Every part of it palpitates with life, and is meant to regulate conduct. . . . This thought gives the necessary counterpoise to the tendency to substitute the mere intellectual grasp of Christian truth for the practical doing of it. There will be plenty of orthodox Christians and theological professors and students who will find themselves, to their very great surprise, among the goats at last.[24]

Study and action are not, of course, polar opposites; the writer of James would not have made such an oversimplification, and neither should we. Study is itself an activity, and ethical action is always shaped by our understanding that needs ongoing engagement. Yet Maclaren's point remains worthwhile. Those of us who spend much time studying need regular reminders that study alone could make us "merely hearers," ever on the sidelines of the action weighing the arguments and counterarguments, without ever wading in to do the hard and loving work of God.

Christians have a long-standing argument over the meaning and value of the "law," a term that James uses for the first time in this passage, alluding to "the perfect law, the law of liberty" (1:25). For James, "law" (*nomos*) is synonymous with the "word" (*logos*) that we are called to do. Like the description of the law in Psalm 19:7, so too for James, the "law of the Lord is perfect," leading to freedom and life. Sometimes Christians hear the term "law" as restrictive, an endless series of "thou shalt nots," the opposite of the good news of the gospel. Martin Luther is particularly prone to such an oppositional view of law and gospel, influenced as he is by his reading of Romans in his specific historical era. Not so for James, who presents the law as the word of God without apology or defense.

This simple identification of law and word of God offers both danger and gift. The danger enters if we reduce "law" to a set of instructions that, if we just follow them, will automatically produce God's favor. Do this, don't do that, and, voilà! You will be blessed. Such a portrayal of the law misunderstands it as a static set of regulations rather than a living embodiment of a covenant

---

24. Andrew Maclaren, in *The Sermon Bible* (New York: Funk & Wagnalls, 1900), 351.

We confess and acknowledge that the law of God is most just, equal, holy, and perfect, commanding those things which, when perfectly done, can give life and bring man to eternal felicity; but our nature is so corrupt, weak, and imperfect, that we are never able perfectly to fulfill the works of the law. Even after we are reborn, if we say that we have no sin, we deceive ourselves and the truth of God is not in us. It is therefore essential for us to lay hold on Christ Jesus, in his righteousness and his atonement, since he is the end and consummation of the Law and since it is by him that we are set at liberty so that the curse of God may not fall upon us, even though we do not fulfill the Law in all points.

Scots Confession, in *The Constitution of the Presbyterian Church (U.S.A.)*, Part 1, *Book of Confession* (Louisville, KY: Office of the General Assemby, Presbyterian Church (U.S.A.), 2016), 3.15.

relationship. It overlooks the stamina required and the internal transformation over time that James envisions from living in the word. If we read "law" simply as list of rules, then we can easily fall into either self-righteousness because we keep the rules so well, or into despair because we cannot. This is the danger that Luther sees so very clearly; no one has ever or can ever actually keep the commandments perfectly, and therefore the law alone can only ever show us how far we fall short. We need something more—the word enlivened by the Spirit and received by the gift of faith—to know and love God truly.[25]

On the other hand, James's vision of law as word of God can offer a gift to contemporary readers who are tempted to dismiss "law" as irrelevant or counter to the gospel of Jesus. By straightforward identification of the law with God's word, James invites us to reclaim the ways that Jesus himself comes "not to abolish" the law "but to fulfill" it (Matt. 5:17). This law, for James as for Jesus, is not a static set of rules, but a guiding commitment to the "royal law" of love that James names in 2:8 (recalling Jesus in Matt. 22:34–40, and its parallels in Mark and Luke): "You shall love your neighbor as yourself." Can we keep this perfectly? Indeed not, but absolute perfection of human observance is not James's point here; it is the perfection of the law itself, which is given as a life-giving word to guide our every action. Paradoxically, those who follow the law steadfastly in their daily

25. See Luther, commentary on Galatians 3:2, in *Luther's Works*, American edition, vol. 26, ed. Jaroslav Pelikan (Saint Louis: Concordia Publishing House, 1963), 203–4.

lives, according to James, are truly free, because they are grounded in the ways of God who created us.

Reclaiming the value of the law as God's word can also help address any sneaking anti-Jewish tendencies that continue to haunt too much Christian teaching and preaching. An unfortunate side effect of the old law/gospel contrast is that Judaism past and present comes to be associated with the "law" while Christianity embodies the "gospel." From that association, it is a quick step to judge Jewish adherence to the Torah as a preoccupation with static regulations rather than the life-giving word of God we see in Jesus. James provides an early Christian perspective that offers no room for such a judgment. The Law, the Torah, simply is the word of God, and there is no tension between that conviction and James's belief in "our glorious Lord Jesus Christ" (2:1).

James affirms that those who look into the law, and do it, will be "blessed." We encountered this same term in 1:12, where the writer adopts a speech pattern familiar to both Jesus and Israelite wisdom literature: "Blessed is anyone who . . ." We will encounter it a third time toward the end of the book, in 5:11. To be "blessed," for the psalmist and other wisdom literature, is not to be free of all pain, but to be happy because of being in alignment with God's law. The blessed one is satisfied with her life because she is rooted in the abiding ways of God. James, himself rooted in this tradition, affirms here that true happiness emerges for those who "do the word" rather than merely hearing it. Each time he uses the term, James emphasizes that blessing is a state that comes from endurance over time: endurance of temptation (1:12), perseverance in enacting the word (1:25), and endurance of suffering (5:11). How vital to hear this interpretation of "blessing" in a world which tempts us to associate that term with material goods or isolated moments of happiness. James invites us to notice blessing that emerges precisely in and through the struggles of life.

In the last two verses of this passage, James addresses the question of what constitutes true religion. As in earlier passages, so too here, his discussion presents readers with a stark contrast: between "worthless" religion, characterized by self-deception and an unbridled tongue, and religion that is "pure and undefiled," which manifests itself in care for the vulnerable and remaining "unstained by the world." The critique of those who do not "bridle their tongues" returns to a theme introduced in 1:19, and which James develops at length in 3:1–12, where he brings back the image of the bridle to call his audience to tame their tongues. Calvin suggests that James is identifying a particular problem among those who think themselves religious: the tendency to judge others. "When people shed their grosser sins, they are extremely vulnerable to contract this complaint. A man will steer clear of adultery, of stealing, of drunkenness, in fact he will be a shining light of outward religious observance—and yet will revel in destroying the character of others; under the pretext of zeal, naturally, but it is a lust for vilification."[26] Calvin's observation in the sixteenth century remains relevant today; how often do we see in others and in ourselves the tendency to equate religious fervor with self-righteous judgment of others? Instead of such false religion, James describes the elements of true religion: "to care for orphans and widows in their distress, and to keep oneself unstained by the world" (1:27).

This is not the only time that James voices concern for social and economic inequality. He has already drawn a contrast between the "lowly" and the rich in 1:9–11, and in the next chapter he sharply critiques those who treat the wealthy and well-dressed with more favor than those who are poor. Though interpreters differ in their assessment of whether there are wealthy people in James's own Christian community (see discussion at 1:9–11), there is no doubt that concern for economically marginalized people, and critique of the rich, is at the center of James's understanding of God's word. In this, he echoes a major theme in the Hebrew Bible (particularly the prophetic tradition) and in Jesus' teachings (e.g., Matt. 25; Mark 12:40–44). Scholars note that in referring to widows and orphans, James is highlighting the systemic social oppression of these disadvantaged groups. The call to care for such classes of people, then, is not simply urging members of the community to send charitable gifts to individuals, important though that is. "Pure and undefiled religion" is also working to change the systems themselves that keep people in situations of poverty.[27]

---

26. Calvin, *A Harmony of the Gospels Matthew, Mark, and Luke, Vol. III, and the Epistles of James and Jude*, 274.
27. Elsa Tamez, *The Scandalous Message of James: Faith without Works Is Dead*, rev. ed. (New York: Crossroad, 2002), 18.

The description of right religion as "pure and undefiled" in this passage contrasts with the "sordidness and wickedness" of 1:21. Such terminology deserves attention, since our ears may import meanings that James himself did not intend. For many contemporary readers, language of purity is associated with individual moral behavior, particularly restrictions on certain kinds of sexual and drug-related activity. "Purity tests" and "purity rings" are just two examples of such use of purity language in recent American culture. Such associations are not alien to James, but they do not convey the fullness of what the writer is saying and what we may need to hear. The language of purity in the first century was particularly associated with communal identity and cultic activity. Who is inside and who is outside the community? Who is permitted inside the temple and who is not? Purity was linked to the ancient concept of "miasma," the contagious pollution that needs to be kept apart from the sacred. As compared to others in his own historical context, James seems to care little about ritual dimensions of purity, but he cares a great deal about ethical behavior in the community. As compared to our own historical context, though James is also concerned with individual aspects of moral purity that distinguishes the followers of Jesus from "the world," he is much more focused on group identity and the behaviors that threaten its cohesion (envy, backbiting, economic injustice).[28]

> The orphans and the widows . . . represent the oppressed and exploited, and the world responsible for their being oppressed represents the institutions, the structures, the value system that promote injustice or are indifferent toward it.
>
> Elsa Tamez, *The Scandalous Message of James*, 51.

Such a focus on the social ethical interpretation of purity resonates with Jesus' teaching in Mark 7:14–23, in which he says, "there is nothing outside a person that by going in can defile, but the things that come out are what defile" (Mark 7:15). Like Jesus, so too James focuses on the intentions and activities that come from within a person that damage the fundamental law of God to love the neighbor.

To be a "word-doer" is simply to love those whom the world

28. Gowler, *James through the Centuries*, 136.

The church of this country is not only indifferent to the wrongs of the slave, it actually takes sides with the oppressors. It has made itself the bulwark of American slavery, and the shield of American slave-hunters. Many of its most eloquent Divines, who stand as the very lights of the church, have shamelessly given the sanction of religion and the Bible to the whole slave system.

They have taught that man may, properly, be a slave; that the relation of master and slave is ordained of God; that to send back an escaped bondman to his master is clearly the duty of all the followers of the Lord Jesus Christ; and this horrible blasphemy is palmed off upon the world for Christianity. . . . These ministers make religion a cold and flinty-hearted thing, having neither principles of right action, nor bowels of compassion.

They strip the love of God of its beauty, and leave the throne of religion a huge, horrible, repulsive form. It is a religion of oppressors, tyrants, man-stealers, and thugs. It is not that "pure and undefiled religion" which is from above, and which is "first pure, then peaceable, easy to be entreated, full of mercy and good fruits, without partiality, and without hypocrisy." But a religion which favors the rich against the poor; which exalts the proud above the humble; which divides mankind into two classes, tyrants and slaves; which says to the man in chains, stay there; and to the oppressor, oppress on; it is a religion which may be professed and enjoyed by all the robbers and enslavers of mankind; it makes God a respecter of persons, denies his fatherhood of the race, and tramples in the dust the great truth of the brotherhood of man.

Frederick Douglass, "What to the Slave Is the Fourth of July?" (July 5, 1852), in *The Frederick Douglass Papers*, series 1, vol. 2: 1847–1854, ed. John W. Blassingame (New Haven: Yale University Press, 1982), 377–78.

has treated as unlovable. It is to look for the ones who are the most crushed by systems of power and oppression (widows and orphans, in James's day) and care for them. Rather than following the cynical and power-hungry ways of the world, to be word-doers who embody "pure religion" is to place ourselves as beacons of light in the darkness, even as God has shone light into the weary darkness of the world.

FURTHER REFLECTIONS
Religion

James wades into the thorny topic of "religion" at the end of the first chapter: "If any think that they are religious, and do not bridle their tongues but deceive their hearts, their religion is worthless. Religion that is pure and undefiled before God the Father, is this: to care for orphans and widows in their distress, and to keep oneself unstained by the world" (1:26–27). This is the first and last time that James broaches the issue of religion; but given the controversial nature of this topic in our current world, it deserves a brief pause for reflection.

What do we mean by "religion"? The term that James uses here, *thréskeia,* can refer to both ritual and moral purity, and it is likely that the writer means both. He is criticizing those who claim to be either ritually observant or morally pure but who do not attend to their words or to those who are economically oppressed. In this way, the writer reiterates the point from the preceding verses: we are to be doers of the word, and not just hearers. True religion involves care for those at the margins of society, not just talking about it.

In the contemporary English-speaking context, "religion" often has negative connotations. This comes from at least three overlapping sources: the spiritual but not religious (SBNR) movement, the critique of religion by the new atheists who see religion as antithetical to science, and postcolonial critiques of religion as a Western imperial construction that privileges white Western Christianity as the highest form of human religion. Each of these movements deserves attention if we have any hope of hearing James's call for "religion that is pure and undefiled" today.

Since about 2000, the term "spiritual but not religious" has become a common term in Western culture to name a growing number of people who shy away from religious institutions but who seek relationship with the divine in more individualistic ways. In this way of speaking, someone who is "religious" might go to church and identify with a particular denomination, while someone who is "spiritual" might practice yoga and read prayers at home, without officially belonging to a community. The contrast of "spiritual" and "religious" in this phrase reveals a perception that "religion" names something formal, organized, and institutional, while "spiritual" refers to an aspect of life that is more individual and interior. Over the course of history, these terms have sometimes been synonymous, but common English usage today tends to differentiate them.

The new atheists, such as Richard Dawkins, Christopher Hitchens, and Sam Harris, are more scathing in their critiques of religion.[29] Rather than contrasting religion with spirituality, these writers contrast religion with natural science, which in their view is sufficient to provide meaning and order in the universe. They tend to equate "religion" with faith in a transcendent God who is the omnipotent creator and guide of history. According to these thinkers, however, there is no God of any kind. Everything that happens can be explained based on scientific reason, usually in evolutionary terms. Nature is self-originating, not created by an outside force or being. In addition to these "scientific" objections to religion, the new atheists offer sharp moral critique: faith in God directly causes many evils in the world and should therefore be eradicated. This argument became particularly popular in the aftermath of September 11, 2001, which called attention to the dangers of religious fundamentalism. People do not need faith in God to behave morally, argue Hitchens, Dawkins, and Harris. In fact, people behave better without religion than with it. Sam Harris, for instance, argues that faith causes so much destruction in the world because to have faith is to reject any appeal to reason. To have faith in a god—any god—is to believe in something for which there is no evidence, which is inherently dangerous. It is better to trust in reason, which relies on empirical, scientifically testable claims.

Both of these critiques of religion are worth hearing and deserve response from those who (like this writer) still find value in Christian writings and Christian communities. Notice, however, that their definitions of "religion" differ. While the SBNRs portray religion as organized external practice (rather than internal spirituality), the new atheists focus on religion as (blind, irrational) faith—which is first of all an internal worldview, and only secondarily a matter of external practice.

Finally, many scholars today are challenging the concept of "religion" because of its historical alliance with Western colonial

---

29. See, e.g., Richard Dawkins, *The God Delusion* (New York: Houghton Mifflin Harcourt, 2006); Sam Harris, *Letter to a Christian Nation* (New York: Knopf, 2006); and Christopher Hitchens, *God Is Not Great: How Religion Poisons Everything* (New York: Twelve Books, 2007).

power.[30] The study of religion developed in the eighteenth and nineteenth centuries at the same time as the development of evolutionary theory and the expansion of Western power, and it was used to map and control differences among various peoples of the world. The concept of "religion" was defined by Western Christian scholars and then applied to people who had not used this concept before. Gradually, through complex subtle mechanisms, peoples in many places came to think of themselves as having single, clearly defined religious identities, such as "Hindu" and "Buddhist." Certain "religions" then came to be defined as "world religions," characterized by a set of parallel characteristics (such as Scriptures) that made it possible for scholars to compare and order them according to their development. This historical analysis has led many analysts to wonder about whether the concept of "religion" is useful anymore, or whether it obscures more than it reveals.

James speaks to a different world than the one in which we live. Even so, his call for a religion that guards the tongue, tends to the poor, and refuses to be drawn into the destructive power schemes of the world just might open up interesting conversations with all those who criticize the idea of "religion" today.

30. See, e.g., Tomoko Masuzawa, *The Invention of World Religions* (Chicago: The University of Chicago Press, 2005); Paulo Gonçalves, "Religious 'Worlds' and their Alien Invaders," in *Difference in Philosophy of Religion*, ed. Philip Goodchild (Burlington, VT: Ashgate, 2003), 115–34; Arvind Mandair, "The Repetition of Past Imperialisms: Hegel, Historical Difference, and the Theorization of Indic Religions," *History of Religions* 44, no. 4 (2005); and "What If *Religio* Remained Untranslatable?" in *Difference in Philosophy of Religion*, ed. Philip Goodchild (Burlington, VT: Ashgate, 2003): 87–100.

2:1–13

Playing Favorites

For several years, I served on the "Examinations Commission" of the presbytery (the regional association of churches) where I live. Our job was to interview ministers coming into the presbytery, to engage them on questions related to Bible, theology, worship and sacraments, and polity, as a way of holding each other accountable for ongoing reflection on these important matters. One question we often asked in those conversations was "if you could throw out one book of the Bible, which one would it be and why?" The most common answer: Leviticus.

Not surprising, perhaps. Leviticus has a bad reputation among many contemporary American Christians, who regard it as obscure and harsh and legalistic, more concerned with sexual purity than mercy and justice. But James loved Leviticus, at least particular parts of it. And James can help us to recover an appreciation for the mercy and justice in this much-maligned book.

James seems to have the scroll of Leviticus before him as he begins this passage, with its sharp critique of those who show preferential treatment to the privileged. Leviticus 19:15 says, "You shall not render an unjust judgment; you shall not be partial to the poor or defer to the great: with justice you shall judge your neighbor." James resonates deeply: "My brothers and sisters, do you with your acts of favoritism really believe in our glorious Lord Jesus Christ?" (2:1). In the Septuagint (the Greek version of the Old Testament that the writer of James knew), the term "defer to the great" is the same word that James uses here, which the NRSV translates as "show favoritism." These two passages share the same underlying concern: those who profess to worship the generous and just God have no business treating wealthy, well-dressed people with greater favor.

Leviticus is not the only Scripture that informs James's sharp advice here. While Leviticus criticizes all who treat the rich better than the poor, Deuteronomy offers the following guidance for judges in particular: "You must not distort justice; you must not show partiality; and you must not accept bribes, for a bribe blinds the eyes of the wise and subverts the cause of those who are in the right" (Deut. 16:19). One rabbinic text comments on this verse in words reminiscent of James: "Do not say this one is rich while this one is poor . . . this one [qualified yet destitute] should sit beneath [me], and do not have it that the poor stand and that the rich sit . . . God stands with the poor and not with those who oppress them."[1] The writer of James is part of a larger world in which many religious leaders are wrestling with issues of economic injustice in light of the clear Torah guidance to pursue justice for all, not just for those who can afford to pay.

The religious world of James is one in which there is not yet a clear divide between "Jews" and "Christians." This fluidity is evident in the opening verses of chapter 2, through implicit appeal to the Torah side by side with invocation of "our glorious Lord Jesus Christ" (2:1). There is no hint that belief in Jesus supersedes, or replaces, Torah teaching; they are of a piece. Unified Jewish-Christian identity is also evident in the use of both "synagogue" (translated as "assembly" in 2:2) and *ekklēsia* (translated as "church" in 5:14) to name gatherings familiar to James's audience, showing no tension between synagogue and church. This glimpse of early Jewish Christianity invites reflection on contemporary Christian-Jewish relations, which have warmed in recent decades but are still fraught by centuries of Christian anti-Judaism as well as ongoing political turmoil in Israel/Palestine. While we cannot erase the historical differences between the two religious communities, with our distinctive practices of messianic expectation, Scripture interpretation, and ritual observance, we can see in James the original unity

---

1. Midrash Tannaim on Deut. 16:19; cited in Herbert Basser, "The Letter of James," in *The Jewish Annotated New Testament*, ed. Amy-Jill Levine and Marc Zvi Brettler (New York: Oxford University Press, 2011), 430.

of these sibling traditions. Passages like this might invite Christians into deeper mutual reflection with our Jewish neighbors on the dangers of economic disparity within our respective communities and in the wider society that we share.

Followers of Jesus have from the very beginning struggled with issues of favoritism. How do we live in a way that truly honors all people equally as beloved children of God? Jesus spoke frequently, especially in the Gospel of Luke, about the importance of honoring the poor rather than favoring the rich. He gave these instructions, for instance, to someone who had invited him to dinner:

> When you give a luncheon or a dinner, do not invite your friends or your brothers or your relatives or your rich neighbors, in case they may invite you in return, and you would be repaid. But when you give a banquet, invite the poor, the crippled, the lame, and the blind. And you will be blessed, because they cannot repay you, for you will be repaid at the resurrection of the righteous (14:12–14).

James in this passage is echoing Jesus' teaching again, calling those who profess to believe in "our glorious Lord Jesus Christ" to live out the teachings of their rabbi.

"Our glorious Lord Jesus Christ" is a rare and sudden appeal to Jesus in this book. The explicit name of Jesus occurs only twice in James: here (2:1) and in 1:1. Although the name "Jesus Christ" may not have been originally included, but inserted in a later generation of the text, the version that we have inherited since at least the third century includes this name, and therefore it deserves our attention. This passage addresses people for whom the name of Jesus is connected to faith. But what is the relationship between faith and the name of Jesus? Translators disagree, and the debate has been a major one in New Testament scholarship of the past few decades. The NRSV translates *pistis christou* here as "faith *in* . . . Christ." In this translation, Jesus Christ is the object of faith, the one in whom we place our trust. Others argue that this phrase is better translated "have the faith *of* Jesus Christ." This version makes Christ the subject of faith, the one whose faith we are called to receive and imitate. It is a significant theological difference, one which affects how we understand the activity of God in Christ in relation to human activity. Does faith originate with us, directed to Jesus? Or does faith originate in Jesus' attitude of trust in God, an attitude into which we are invited to participate? The grammatical form could be read either way. Some interpreters argue that this ambiguity is intentional, since both insights have value.[2] Perhaps James (as well as Paul, who uses this phrase three times) intended readers to ponder both directions of faith. What is clear, however, is that James sees a contradiction between faith in Jesus—or the faith of Jesus—and acts of favoritism. Those who share in Jesus' faith cannot dishonor those who are poor.

Such critique of economic injustice offers a fresh variation on the same theme with which James concluded chapter one. What constitutes "pure and undefiled" religion (1:27)? Care for "orphans and widows," who are the most economically vulnerable members of society. Those who do God's word notice the people at the margins and take care of them. Similarly, in his critique of favoritism in this passage, James calls his audience to notice the people in dirty clothes, and to treat them with greater honor than those who wear gold rings.

Interpreters differ in their assessment of the economic status of James's own Christian community (see discussion at 1:9–11), but there is no doubt that concern for "the poor," and critique of "the rich," is at the center of James's understanding of God's word. In this, he echoes a major theme in the Hebrew Bible (particularly the prophetic tradition) and in Jesus' teachings (e.g., Matt. 25; Mark 12:40–44).

Do riches here necessarily mean literal economic wealth, and are "the poor" simply those who lack economic resources? On this point, too, interpreters disagree. Some biblical scholars argue that the rich person depicted in the scenario is specifically a person of the Roman equestrian class, signified by a gold ring, fine clothing, and seating privileges, all of which are included in this verse.[3] Perhaps the person is running for public office (signified by the Greek

---

2. For discussion of this interpretive issue, see Richard Hays, *The Faith of Jesus Christ: The Narrative Substructure of Galatians 3:1–4:11*, 2nd ed. (Grand Rapids: Eerdmans, 2002).

3. Ingeborg Mongstad-Kvammen, *Toward a Postcolonial Reading of the Epistle of James: James 2:1–13 in Its Imperial Context* (Leiden: Brill, 2013), 85; cf. Elsa Tamez, *The Scandalous Message of James: Faith without Works Is Dead,* rev. ed. (New York: Crossroad, 2002), 23.

term for "fine clothes," the equivalent of the Latin *toga candida*, which candidates running for election would wear).[4] If this is the intention, then we can discern not only economic privilege, but imperial political power present—and challenged—in the text. Other scholars do not see such specificity in the depiction of the rich person; instead, James may be portraying the struggle of an early Christian community to earn favor from a wealthy patron who can sponsor and protect their gatherings.

Although this is a relatively minor disagreement about the specific identity of the well-dressed person in 2:2–3, there is deeper disagreement about who "the poor" are in this scene. Based on historical analysis of the term "the poor" in Israelite literature, some scholars interpret poverty in James as a religious, not just an economic concept.[5] The exile of Israel led to a description of the entire dispossessed nation as "the poor," so some prophets describe the whole people as needy (see, e.g., Isa. 41:17; 49:13). Later, a distinction emerges between rich and poor in the nation itself, and prophets come to denounce the powerful leaders of Israel as those who wrong the poor and are therefore responsible for the downfall of the people. Eventually the "poor" become identified with the pious followers of the law; this group may well have been economically disadvantaged, but economic status is not primarily the issue here. From this perspective, "the pious thought of themselves as the poor because poverty had become a religious concept."[6]

David Edgar concurs with the importance of reading the historical development of the term "the poor" in Israelite literature, but he focuses more on the concrete social context which James is addressing in the early Christian era. He interprets James 2:5–6, depicting the unequal treatment of two visitors to a local assembly as the center of the entire book. According to Edgar, the main problem in James is that the audience is honoring "the rich" by trusting in their economic support as potential patrons of the community rather than trusting in God, who is the provider of all good gifts

---

4. Mongstad-Kvammen, *Toward a Postcolonial Reading of the Epistle of James,* 127–28.
5. See, e.g., Martin Dibelius, *James,* 5th ed., translated from the 1964 German ed. (Philadelphia: Fortress, 1976), 39–42.
6. Ibid., 40.

(1:17). Edgar interprets "the poor" as a group of radical wandering charismatic followers of Jesus—people who are economically marginal, but with great respect in the Christian community. The community that professes faith in "our glorious Lord Jesus Christ" should honor these poor ones, but instead they honor the rich, who possess the false glory of gold rings and fine clothing. The main issue is misplaced trust, not simply the economic conditions themselves.[7]

Craig Blomberg discerns a different specific social situation behind James 2:1–7. He argues that James is calling for care specifically for the poor in the Christian community, who may have been day laborers suffering from increasing debt at the hands of absentee landlords.[8] It is not a generic call to care for all those in economic hardship, though certainly Christians should be concerned for believing and non-believing persons in poverty. James's question "has not God chosen the poor in the world to be rich in faith?" according to Blomberg, calls attention to the responsibility of other Christians to care for the poor *who have faith.*

Several other interpreters argue that "the poor" refers simply and directly to those who are economically deprived. When James exhorts his readers to honor the poor, he means all the poor—not just those in the Christian community, and not just those of Israelite descent. Economic oppression was widespread in Roman-occupied Palestine, and James, like Jesus, is prophetically denouncing the mistreatment of the poor as counter to God's kingdom. Elsa Tamez offers a clear summary of this view: "Here the poor are the *ptōchoi,* those who have absolutely nothing, not even a job; they depend on alms. It is not true that James is here thinking of the poor as the devout or pious, as certain late rabbinic literature would have it."[9] Tamez also points out how the perspective of the reader shapes interpretation of James's discussions of poverty and wealth. Those who highlight the religious rather than the economic identity of the "poor" tend to be in positions of privilege, while those who are more

---

7. David Edgar, *Has God Not Chosen the Poor? The Social Setting of the Epistle of James* (Sheffield: Sheffield Academic, 2001), 112–25.
8. Craig L. Blomberg, *Neither Poverty nor Riches: A Biblical Theology of Material Possessions* (Grand Rapids: Eerdmans, 1999), 151–54.
9. Tamez, *The Scandalous Message of James,* 36.

politically and economically oppressed hear James's words directly addressed to their own economic condition. She goes on:

> Interestingly enough, many of the commentaries on James dedicate long pages to the rich, thus consciously or unconsciously attempting to relativize this contrasting picture that James paints. . . . We should note that many of the points made in these commentaries are accurate enough; what is striking is simply the angle of the perspective and the special concern for the rich. A Latin American reading of the epistle, on the other hand, fixes its gaze on the oppressed and dedicates long pages to them, their sufferings, complaints, oppression, hope, and praxis.[10]

Where do we stand in this text? Do we automatically identify with the rich visitors to the assembly, and therefore worry about our place in the kingdom? Do we identify with the poor ones in shabby clothing, and therefore give thanks that we are welcome? For instance, the late medieval English reforming group known as the "Lollards" strongly identified with "the poor" of this verse (2:5), and they therefore heard it as good news. In a sermon on Luke 2, they point out that Jesus chose the poor (like the Lollards themselves) for his friends rather than the rich, in contrast to the "lofty clergy and intellectuals" of their day.[11] What is our immediate response to the scenario James describes here, and what does this reveal about our own social and economic power? Teachers and preachers exploring this text with others would do well to begin with self-reflection on these issues and then invite others to do the same.

Many Christian groups over the centuries have shared James's concern for unequal treatment of people in church based on their clothes. Groups such as Amish, Mennonites, Moravians, and Conservative Quakers have practiced "plain dress" in order to preserve humility and communal identity. This usually includes modest design, avoidance of ornamentation like ruffles or showy buttons, and a fairly uniform style within a community. Part of the rationale is recognition that ostentatious or fashion-conscious

---

10. Ibid., 21.
11. In Andrew Bradstock and Christopher C. Rowland, eds., *Radical Christian Writings* (Oxford: Blackwell, 2002), 56–58.

dress draws attention to the self and can lead to division within the community. John Wesley and early Methodists shared this concern as well. In his sermon "On Dress," Wesley said, "Nothing is more natural than to think ourselves better because we are dressed in better clothes; and it is scarce possible for a man to wear costly apparel, without, in some measure, valuing himself upon it."[12] Whatever the original context of James's cautionary tale, Christians past and present easily recognize the way that distinctions in outward dress affect the way we perceive and treat one another, turning "beloved brothers and sisters" into "judges with evil thoughts."

> Full many people go to church,
> As everybody knows;
> Some go to close their eyes,
> and some to eye their clothes.
>
> *Doran's Ministers Manual: A Study and Pulpit Guide for the Calendar Year* (New York: Harper and Brothers, 1942) on "The Harm of Showy Dress in the Church."

James does not only criticize his audience for showing favoritism toward the rich; even more sharply, he criticizes the rich themselves, who dishonor the poor and oppress the readers ("beloved brothers and sisters") by dragging them into court. The term translated in the NRSV as "oppress" (*katadunasteuo*) is particularly significant, because it is the same word used by the prophets in the Greek version of the Old Testament for the oppressive actions of the rich against the poor, aliens, widows, and orphans (see Jer. 7:6; Ezek. 18:12; Amos 8:4). James 2:6 also resonates closely with language in Proverbs about dishonoring the poor and God's threat to take the offenders to court (e.g., Prov. 14:31; 17:5a; 22:23–24). In all these passages, *katadunasteuo* is a strong word with violent implications. "It is also significant that in the only other place the word is used in the New Testament, the 'devil' is the subject (Acts 10:38)."[13] By using this language, James clearly reminds his readers of what they should already know: that their own prophets and sages denounced those who abuse their power to harm the poor. Rather than being attracted to their fine

---

12. John Wesley, Sermon 88, "On Dress," http://wesley.nnu.edu/john-wesley/the-sermons-of -john-wesley-1872-edition/sermon-88-on-dress/.
13. Pedrito Maynard-Reid, *Poverty and Wealth in James* (Maryknoll, NY: Orbis, 1987), 63.

clothes, the brothers and sisters should be noticing the shabby behavior of these rich people.

The primary form of oppression named here is that the rich "drag you into court" (2:6). The legal action is unspecified, but it could be over financial matters, given the theme of economic injustice that predominates in this passage. We see a specific reference to unjust treatment of laborers in 5:4, and historians attest to the poor being taken to court for failure to pay their debts. Is the reference to the human legal system here subtly contrasting with the perfect Law/Torah to which the audience is supposed to be loyal? There is certainly an implicit contrast between these two forms of "law," but James draws a sharp explicit contrast between the honor being shown to the rich and the honor that God shows to the poor. The writer seeks to shame his readers with such a contrast, calling them to consider what counts as the true Law, and where they should be directing their honor.

For contemporary American readers, it is difficult to read this passage in James and not think of the economic inequities in our own criminal justice system, where people who grow up in situations of poverty are disproportionately represented in jails and prisons. The reasons for this are complex, of course, having to do with racism, education, and changes in the labor market, among other things. Part of the problem, however, is that being poor has not only economic and social but also legal disadvantages: people with little or no income cannot pay for legal representation and frequently suffer greater penalties as a result. In addition, someone who is unable to pay legal fines, fees, or back taxes in many states can be incarcerated for failure to pay—a modern form of debtors' prison. In linking poverty with legal injustice, James calls us to confront the ugly reality of this connection in our own day.

> We have a system of justice in this country that treats you much better if you're rich and guilty than if you're poor and innocent. Wealth, not culpability, shapes outcomes.
>
> Bryan Stevenson, "We Need to Talk about an Injustice," TED talk, March 2012, https://www.ted.com/talks/bryan_stevenson_we_need_to_talk_about_an_injustice?language=en.

Within Christian communities, despite the best efforts of James and Jesus, practices of "favoritism" have persisted, taking new and creative forms in each age. In nineteenth-century England and the United States, it became common to rent pews in Anglican, Catholic, and Presbyterian churches to support the church work and to ensure that wealthy members contributed to the communities. This practice of pew rental, however, led to abuse: wealthy members of congregations were guaranteed the best seats, while poorer members had to sit in the back. Joseph Mayor calls on James as he laments this practice around 1897:

> It is to be feared that, if St. James were to visit our English churches, he would not find much improvement upon the state of things which existed in the congregations of his time. ... The poor are at any rate not to be at a disadvantage in the House of God. The free and open seats should at least be as good as the paying seats, and it should not be in the power of a seat-holder to prevent any unoccupied sitting from being used.[14]

A century later, partiality manifested itself in a more demonic form in South African apartheid, and James again was summoned as part of the critique. South African Reformed theologian Dirk Smit pointed this out in 1990:

> In many South African churches one will find the same kind of problem to which James refers in his example, namely that the church—in spite of the fact that they are poor, oppressed, powerless, "black," themselves—pay much more respect and honour to the rich and powerful, than to the poor, the women, the widows, the orphans, the children, among their own members. There are many and understandable reasons for this—in the light of the norms that are accepted in society at large and the possible advantages—but in the church it remains sin, a denial of God's own actions, of Jesus Christ, the Lord of glory, and a transgression of the will of God.[15]

In response to apartheid, after decades of growing protest, the

14. Joseph B. Mayor, *The Epistle of St. James.* 3rd ed., reprinted (Minneapolis: Klock & Klock Christian Publishers, 1977), 211.
15. D. J. Smit, "'Show no partiality ...' (James 2:1–13)," *Journal of Theology for Southern Africa* 71 (1990): 66.

Dutch Reformed Mission Church, with the leadership of Allan Boesak, drafted a confession declaring the separation of races to be a sin against God's reconciling work in Christ. This Confession of Belhar, now adopted as an official confessional document by several Reformed Protestant churches around the world, appeals to James in its call for justice and peace.

We believe

— that God has revealed God's self as the one who wishes to bring about justice and true peace among people;

— that God, in a world full of injustice and enmity, is in a special way the God of the destitute, the poor and the wronged

— that God calls the church to follow God in this; for God brings justice to the oppressed and gives bread to the hungry;

— that God frees the prisoner and restores sight to the blind;

— that God supports the downtrodden, protects the stranger, helps orphans and widows and blocks the path of the ungodly; . . .

— that the church as the possession of God must stand where the Lord stands, namely against injustice and with the wronged; that in following Christ the church must witness against all the powerful and privileged who selfishly seek their own interests and thus control and harm others.

Therefore, we reject any ideology

— which would legitimate forms of injustice and any doctrine which is unwilling to resist such an ideology in the name of the gospel.

—Confession of Belhar in *The Constitution of the Presbyterian Church (U.S.A.)*, Part 1, *Book of Confessions: Study Edition Revised* (Louisville, KY: Office of the General Assembly, Presbyterian Church (U.S.A.), 2017), 10.7-10.8.

Teachers and preachers engaging James today might reflect on what "acts of favoritism" in our own society demand attention. When have we also judged people based on their appearance? If someone walked into our church wearing a Hugo Boss suit and Gucci shoes, would we treat them the same as someone who entered wearing secondhand clothes from the clothing closet? What about the justice system—are all people equally well treated, equally well represented, no matter their economic status? Hardly. As Gay

Byron argues, James calls his audience in this passage to notice our participation in systems of economic injustice and to amend our ways. The writer "is appealing to all in his global community (*diaspora*) to assume responsible economic relationships—that is, to seek ways to redistribute the imbalance of wealth, to acknowledge fraudulent activities, to pay more equitable wages, to welcome (even honor) the poor, and to renounce arrogance, greed, and gluttony."[16] James, with the scroll of Leviticus in his hand and the words of Jesus echoing in his ears, speaks uncomfortable truth to us wherever we are, challenging us to reflect on ways that we ourselves have shown favoritism, and inviting us to do better.

Amid critique and challenge, the good news in this passage comes in 2:5: "Listen, my beloved brothers and sisters. Has not God chosen the poor in the world to be rich in faith and to be heirs of the kingdom that he has promised to those who love him?" In contrast to the favoritism that James condemns in 2:1, and unlike the oppression and blasphemy displayed by the rich in 2:6–7, "brothers and sisters" emphasizes a relationship of equal siblings, a beloved community. And what do these brothers and sisters need to hear so urgently? That God has chosen the poor. James clearly expects his audience to know this and to nod (perhaps with embarrassment) in affirmation, remembering God's preference for "the poor."

Because God has chosen the poor, so we too should love God by loving those whom God has chosen. These marginalized ones are the true "heirs of the kingdom." Such a title stands in stark relief if it is addressed to people who are "poverty-stricken exiles in diaspora."[17] The most destitute are the subjects in a new empire coming into the world.

In verses 8–13, James continues what he began in the preceding verses: reminding his audience of the problems that arise from playing favorites, especially favoring the wealthy and well-dressed over the poor. This is an ongoing concern for the writer of James, which suggests that the community was struggling to treat all people

16. Gay Byron, "James," in *The Women's Bible Commentary*, 3rd ed., ed. Carol A. Newsom, Sharon H. Ringe, and Jacqueline Lapsley (Louisville, KY: Westminster John Knox Press, 2012), 614.
17. Margaret Aymer, *James: Diaspora Rhetoric of a Friend of God* (Sheffield: Sheffield Phoenix, 2015), 61.

equally, regardless of social class. The teaching of Leviticus was in the background before now, but in verse 8, James quotes it explicitly, referring to the "royal law" to "love your neighbor as yourself" (Lev. 19:18b). In effect, James is saying, "you may think that you are faithfully displaying love by treating the wealthy so well, but you are just deceiving yourselves. If you really want to love your neighbor as yourself, you will not favor those who can repay you, but you will show mercy to those who have no ability to pay you back."

Here we glimpse the insidious way that we can all deceive ourselves when we treat others well. It is always possible to say, "I am just loving my neighbor!" But James invites us to hold up a mirror and ask ourselves the difficult question: in "loving" one person, are we in fact failing to love someone else fully? In our acts of kindness to a person who can be kind to us in return, are we neglecting to show mercy to those who need it most? Are we really showing love, or are we trying to win favor with someone who can help us later?

My aunt Carol, who was a Montessori teacher for many years, used to say that those children who are the most unlovable are precisely the ones who most need love. She was observing the effects of emotional deprivation on children: those who tend to act out in preschool often do so because they have not been freely and generously loved at home. I wonder if James has some of this same wisdom, transposed into the economic realm: those who are the most economically deprived are those most in need of active, merciful love. It may be easy to "love" those who are beautiful. However, there are two potential problems with this: (1) Are they really the ones who most need it? And (2) is this really love, or is it self-promotion?

John Calvin sniffs out this danger, drawing attention to James's distinction in this passage between the *neighbors* we are to love and favoring *particular persons*. He says about this verse, "God bids us love our neighbours, not certain selected persons. Now the word *neighbour* is understood across the human race. . . . God expressly commends to us both the alien and the enemy, and all who in any sense might seem contemptible to us. Acceptance of persons [by which Calvin means partiality] is utterly opposed to this teaching."[18]

18. John Calvin, *A Harmony of the Gospels Matthew, Mark, and Luke, Vol. III, and the Epistles of James and Jude,* trans. A. W. Morrison, ed. David W. Torrance and Thomas F. Torrance (Grand Rapids: Eerdmans, 1972), 279.

[handwritten margin notes: "my impartially", "poorly summarizing their—not w/ JC is saying."]

Love of neighbors means love of all neighbors, Calvin emphasizes. To love just a few is not really to love at all.

James affirms, "You do well if you really fulfill the royal law according to the scripture, 'you shall love your neighbor as yourself'" (2:8). James elevates this command, as Jesus did, to the highest place in the entire Torah (along with loving God; see Matt. 22:34–40). At least one early rabbinic text, from about the third century, also elevates this commandment to the "supreme rule," served by all the rest of Scripture's tenets.[19] Many other rabbis in the first few centuries of the Common Era likewise focused on Leviticus 19:18 as the key commandment that should be used to interpret the rest of the law.[20] In citing this verse, James is not ignoring the rest of the Torah but, like many other teachers of the time, lifting up the love commandment as the norm to guide all other interpretations of God's word.

> [God] will bless you, if you show mercy to your neighbor. For the things which we wish to obtain from God, of those we ought first to impart to our neighbors. But if we deprive our neighbors of them, how can we wish to obtain them?
>
> John Chrysostom, Homily III on Philemon 1:17–19.

What does it mean to call this the "*royal* law"? Though the term is used in other Greco-Roman sources, we have no record of any Jewish or Christian author apart from James using this specific term for the command to love neighbor as self. Perhaps it is simply a way of underscoring the importance of this commandment. Perhaps it is a way of connecting it with God as king, or Jesus Christ as king, or with the kingdom of God that Jesus proclaimed. Whatever the original intent, naming the commandment to love one's neighbor as "royal" offers a challenge to any perception we might have of monarchy as authoritarian or tyrannical. To follow in the royal way is not to exercise power over, but to show love toward the other.

This "royal law" of neighbor-love serves as a guiding principle to

19. Midrash Sifra on Lev. 19:18, cited by Herbert Basser, "The Letter of James," in *The Jewish Annotated New Testament*, 431.
20. See "The Concept of Neighbor in Jewish and Christian Ethics," in *The Jewish Annotated New Testament*, ed. Amy-Jill Levine and Marc Zvi Brettler (New York: Oxford University Press, 2011), 540–43.

interpret the law of God. This does not lead to a narrowing of the law, however. James cautions his audience, "For whoever keeps the whole law but fails in one point has become accountable for all of it" (2:10). To focus on the main point does not mean we should jettison all the points that help support it. The whole law, with all its parts, is oriented toward neighbor-love, and if we forget that, we distort and misunderstand God's word. On this issue, James stands in the same tradition with Jesus and Paul, who make very similar arguments. In Matthew 5:19, for instance, Jesus says, "whoever breaks one of the least of these commandments, and teaches others to do the same, will be called least in the kingdom of heaven." In his letter to the Galatians, Paul emphasizes the wholeness of the law (see Gal. 3:10 and 5:3), and in Romans 13:9 he asserts, "The commandments 'You shall not commit adultery; You shall not murder; You shall not steal; You shall not covet'; and any other commandment, are summed up in this word, 'Love your neighbor as yourself.'" Many other first- and early second-century Christian writings also emphasize the wholeness of the law, with Leviticus 19:18 as the summary of the last four or five commandments, and rabbinic traditions of the same era say that all ten commandments can be found in Leviticus 19.[21] For all of these early writers, the commandment to love one's neighbor as oneself is the heart of the law, and the commandments to avoid adultery, murder, stealing, and coveting are all forbidden because they violate this central principle. James reiterates this theme but adapts it for his particular purpose by adding partiality/favoritism to the list of acts that violate love of neighbor.

Such an emphasis on the entire law, with the accompanying threat that failure to keep any part of the law makes us accountable for all of it, could well lead to despair. How can we possibly keep the whole

> Jesus Christ, the Son of God and Lord who humbled Himself to be a servant, is also the Son of Man exalted as this servant to be the Lord, the new and true and royal man. . . .
>
> Karl Barth, *Church Dogmatics* IV/2 (Edinburgh: T&T Clark, 1958), 3.

---

21. See Dale C. Allison Jr., *A Critical and Exegetical Commentary on the Epistle of James*, International Critical Commentary (New York: Bloomsbury, 2013), 407.

law? Despite our best efforts, surely no one is able to love every single neighbor as fully as we ought. We all get angry, lose our tempers, ignore those in need. Does James leave us with any hope? Several interpreters through the centuries have struggled with this very issue. Both Jerome and Augustine in the late fourth and early fifth centuries, for example, argue that humans cannot live without sin, so James cannot mean that it is possible for people to completely avoid transgressing the law. Yet this difficult sentence of James seems to say that anyone who violates any portion of the law is accountable for the whole. If we remember that the point of the law is love, according to Augustine, it can help; James is reminding us that any failure to love another person is a failure to keep the central point of the law. The intention is not to leave us in despair but to empower our own works of love. The hope comes when this verse is read in connection with what follows, when James affirms that our words and acts of mercy are important, and that "mercy triumphs over judgment."[22] Just as God's mercy triumphs over judgment, so too should our own. God's mercy should empower our own acts of mercy to others. This makes even more sense if we keep reading James: in the following passage, he goes on to argue for the importance of doing works of mercy, not resting in a passive form of faith.

> If the law of freedom is not fulfilled in its entirety, it is not fulfilled at all.
>
> Elsa Tamez, *The Scandalous Message of James*, 52.

Following his discussion of the entirety of the law, James offers another evocative phrase that provokes more puzzlement the longer we think about it: "So speak and so act as those who are to be judged by the law of *liberty*" (2:12). This "law of liberty" seems to be synonymous with the law of love in verse 8, but to connect law, love, and liberty so closely can strike a contemporary reader as odd. How can it be that the "law," which sounds restrictive, actually brings liberty? And how can liberty, which sounds like utter independence from any binding commitments, be synonymous with love? Furthermore,

---

22. Augustine, letter to Jerome CLXVII. See http://www.ccel.org/ccel/schaff/npnf101 .vii.1.CLXVII.html?highlight=augustine,letter,to,jerome,clxvii.

how can there be a *"law* of love" to begin with—can you actually command someone to love another?

The problem, of course, is not so much with James as with us. At least in modern Western societies, we tend to think of ourselves as isolated individuals who are most fully ourselves when left alone, not entangled with others or bound by the demands of culture or tradition. Love is an emotion that we individually feel and that we then act on. If we carry these (often unexamined) assumptions, then "law" sounds like a negative constraint on my own "liberty," and "love" is something I freely choose, without an external command forcing me into it. But our world is not the world of James—nor, for that matter, the world of Paul or the historical Jesus. For the Jews of the first century, God's law is clearly good news, rooted in the order of creation and offered as a gift to the people of the covenant whom God chose in love. The law is not primarily about "thou shalt not," but "love your neighbor." We are commanded to love not because it keeps us from being our best selves, but precisely because it enables us all to be our best selves together. Love is not first about warm emotional attachment, but about embodied acts of mercy. Such acts can indeed be "commanded," as we see here. The emotional, affective dimension of love may then emerge from the "doing." Loving one another knits the community together and faithfully reflects the love of God who first and freely reached out to us.

Biblical scholar Dale Allison points out that the connection of the law to liberty is not new to James, or Paul, or the Christian tradition, but is also attested in rabbinic and Stoic literature. James does not explain how the law brings freedom; it is simply assumed. Generations of Christian interpreters, however, have offered fuller discussions of the relationship of freedom and law, largely based on Pauline texts such as Romans and Galatians.

> For you were called to freedom, brothers and sisters; only do not use your freedom as an opportunity for self-indulgence, but through love become slaves to one another. For the whole law is summed up in a single commandment: "You shall love your neighbor as yourself."
>
> Galatians 5:13–14

Common Christian interpretations of freedom include: freedom
from sin, freedom from bondage to ceremonial law, freedom from the
rigor of moral law, and freedom from the wrath of God.[23] All of these
are framed as freedom *from* something external, whether it is sin or law
or divine wrath. Even more importantly, some Christian theologians
have elaborated on freedom as freedom *for*. This shift helps to clarify
how freedom/liberty, law, and love might be intimately connected.
Martin Luther, for instance, sums up the freedom of a Christian
in two paradoxical theses: "A Christian is a perfectly free lord of all,
subject to none. A Christian is a perfectly dutiful servant of all, subject
to all."[24] That is, a Christian is not subject to the dictates of worldly
powers, but as one who participates in the work of Christ who is king,
a Christian is free, not ultimately subject to any other human law.
At the same time, this freedom leads to perfect service to all in love.
This is freedom for the other, that is, freedom to fulfill the law rather
than being condemned by it. Luther is, of course, developing his
theology largely based on Paul. James does not have the same strong
Christological center in his theology of freedom and law. He does,
however, share Paul's (and Luther's) conviction that true freedom is
the freedom to love others, which is the heart of the law.

Building on Luther's insight, Karl Barth, in *The Humanity of
God*, argues that a proper understanding of human freedom begins
with a proper understanding of divine freedom. Divine freedom is
not essentially freedom *from* (although God is free from external
constraints), but freedom *for*. The character of God's freedom
is relationship, the ability to be completely for the other. God's
freedom is not utter independence, but unforced, gracious attention
to others. In particular, God is *for us*. God chooses to be for the
people of Israel, to make covenant with them and be their God.
Even more radically, God chooses to be for the whole world in Jesus
Christ. This is the content of the gospel.[25]

To be sure, there will be judgment: "So speak and so act as those
who are *to be judged* by the law of liberty" (2:12). Perhaps the

23. Allison, *A Critical and Exegetical Commentary on the Epistle of James*, 339.
24. Martin Luther, "On the Freedom of a Christian," in *Three Treatises*, 2nd rev. ed.
   (Minneapolis: Fortress, 1970), 277.
25. Karl Barth, *The Humanity of God* (Richmond, VA: John Knox Press, 1960), 72–73.

> God is who He is in the act of
> His revelation. God seeks and
> creates fellowship between
> Himself and us, and therefore
> He loves us. But He is this
> loving God without us as
> Father, Son and Holy Spirit, in
> the freedom of the Lord, who
> has His life from Himself.
>
> Karl Barth, *Church Dogmatics* II/1
> (Edinburgh: T&T Clark, 1957), 257.

language of "law of liberty" helps us to see what it means to love truly, and therefore to focus on the criterion by which we will be judged. To love freely is to love without expectation of return. To be judged by this law of liberty (which is the law of love) means that we will be judged by how well we demonstrate genuinely free mercy toward those who cannot offer us mercy in return.

Such an interpretation might also help us with the final puzzling, even paradoxical statement about judgment and mercy: "For judgment will be without mercy to anyone who has shown no mercy; mercy triumphs over judgment" (v. 13). The first half of the verse continues the theme that James has been developing for a while now: if you do not show mercy to those most in need, you have failed to follow God's law of love, and there will be consequences. God will judge you in the same way that you have judged others. In this teaching, James echoes (in reverse) Jesus in the Sermon on the Mount: "Blessed are the merciful, for they will receive mercy" (Matt. 5:7), and "if you do not forgive others, neither will your Father forgive your trespasses" (Matt. 6:15). This is not unique to Jesus and James; it is a traditional Jewish teaching of the time. To receive mercy from God requires showing mercy to others. It sounds as though God will judge us based on what we have done, whether we have showed mercy. It sounds even, and ominously, as though our salvation might depend on rightly following the law. The second half of verse 13, however, sounds like a complete reversal: "mercy triumphs over judgment." This sounds like grace is free; love wins. Despite our failures, God will nevertheless show mercy. Luther and Calvin both appeal to this affirmation to support their shared conviction that salvation depends solely on God's mercy, not on any work of ours.[26]

26. See Martin Luther, *Luther's Works*, ed. J. Pelikan and H. T. Lehman (Philadelphia: Muhlenberg, 1955–76), 19:47–48; and Calvin, *A Harmony of the Gospels Matthew, Mark, and Luke, Vol. III, and the Epistles of James and Jude*, 282.

One early interpreter offers a way of reading this statement that moves beyond paradox. John Cassian cites this verse in connection with the petition of the Lord's Prayer, "Forgive us our debts," explaining that those who have forgiven/offered mercy can ask with confidence for mercy and forgiveness from God, but if they have not forgiven, then such a prayer calls down judgment rather than forgiveness.[27] Perhaps this insight can help to hold the entire passage together. Those who genuinely show mercy understand the royal law, which is true freedom, and which "triumphs": that is, love your neighbors who are most in need, without expectation of return, and thus by your life you show the truth that mercy triumphs over judgment. "In other words, this is a wise observation about the rhythms of human life before God: those who show no mercy will not find mercy (either from others or from God), while those who live mercifully will experience the truth of God's abundant mercy. This is not a calculating quid pro quo: James the sage wants us to live according to the patterns God intends for human life, so that we may all flourish."[28]

> [God] tempers his judgment with the mercy which he shows in doing kindness even to the unworthy. And not only does this mercy follow his judgment but it also precedes it. For mercy with him is older than justice.
>
> Philo, "Quod Deterius Potiori insidiari solet" (The Worse Attacks the Better)

---

27. Cassian, Conference IX.22, http://www.ccel.org/ccel/cassian/conferences.ii.x.xxi.html.
28. With thanks to Amy Plantinga Pauw for this insight. Personal correspondence.

2:14–26

Faith without Works Is Dead

This passage, with its apparent rejection of the understanding that faith alone is the basis of justification, is the one that caused Luther so much heartburn. "Faith by itself, if it has no works, is dead." James here seems to be deliberately picking a fight.

It is possible, of course, that James was directly arguing with Paul. It is even more possible that he was arguing against a group of early Christians who had heard a version of Paul's teaching and were proclaiming the sole power of faith to save us, apart from any human action. Pheme Perkins, for instance, reads this passage as rejecting a "secondhand Paulinism that is put to quite a different use."[1] Whatever the original historical circumstance, it is important for contemporary readers of James not to read this passage through the filter of a faith-vs.-works theology. Instead, James offers here a vital glimpse of what it means to live truly out of the implanted word of God. In other words, this is a natural extension of the argument he has already made in the preceding chapter, in which he calls his listeners to "be doers of the word, and not merely hearers who deceive themselves" (1:22).

In the classic Broadway musical *My Fair Lady*, Eliza Doolittle sings in exasperation to her would-be suitor Freddy: "Don't talk of stars burning above, if you're in love, show me!"[2] Eliza and James could be singing a duet here. The point is this: true faith, like true love, simply *is* evident in what a person does. Eliza is fed up with

---

1. Pheme Perkins, *First and Second Peter, James, and Jude*; Interpretation: A Bible Commentary for Teaching and Preaching (Louisville, KY: John Knox Press, 1995), 112.
2. "Show Me," from Frederick Loewe, *My Fair Lady* (New York: Columbia, 1964).

> This whole passage of the Apostle is so cleere against justification or salvation by onely faith, damnably defended by the Protestants, and so evident for the necessitie, merite, & concurrence of good workes, that their first author Luther and such as exactly follow him, boldly (after the manner of Heretikes) shift nor false glose for the text, deny the booke to be Canonical Scripture.
>
> Commentary on James 2:14, in *The New Testament of Jesus Christ, Translated Faithfully into English out of the authentical Latin ... in the English College of Rhemes* (1582)

Freddy talking all the time, as if love were fully expressed in words alone. So too with James, who seems fed up with any claim that faith floats free of actual embodied deeds. What in the world would such faith mean?

It can help to substitute a different word for "works" here, to get away from the old Protestant assumption that "faith" and "works" are opposing terms. Consider replacing it with "deeds" (as does Luke Timothy Johnson), and recognize that the contrast is not between sheer trust in God's faithfulness and a conviction that our own actions can earn us God's favor. Instead, the contrast is between mere "belief" and fullness of response to God.

Early church interpreters Origen and Augustine saw no contradiction between Paul's emphasis on "faith alone" and James's emphasis on "faith and works" here. Writing in third-century Egypt, Origen says,

> we must keep in mind that we are judged at the divine tribunal not on our faith alone as if we did not have to answer for our conduct (cf. James 2:24), nor on our conduct alone as if our faith were not subject to examination. ... If then we wish to be saved, let us not, in our commitment to the faith, be negligent of our practical conduct, nor, conversely, be overconfident of our conduct.[3]

Faith and conduct together are judged by God. Similarly, in the early fifth century in what is now Algeria, Augustine repeatedly revisits the apparent tension between Paul and James on the topic of faith

3. Origen, "Dialogue of Origen with Heraclides and His Fellow Bishops on the Father, the Son, and the Soul," in *Treatise on the Passover and Dialogue of Origen with Heraclides and His Fellow Bishops on the Father, the Son, and the Soul*, trans. Robert J. Daly, SJ (New York: Paulist Press, 1992), 64.

and works. Consistently, the great North African theologian points out that the faith that saves is the faith that goes to work, as Paul says in Galatians 5:6: "For in Christ Jesus neither circumcision nor uncircumcision counts for anything; the only thing that counts is faith working through love ." Faith that does not work through love is not faith at all.[4]

Significantly, in spite of Luther's harsh critique of James, he too agrees that true faith bears fruit. "Faith is a work of God in us, which changes us and brings us to birth anew from God (cf. John 1). . . . It is impossible that faith ever stop doing good. . . . Whoever doesn't do such works is without faith; he gropes and searches about him for faith and good works but doesn't know what faith or good works are."[5] Even Luther concurs that faith properly understood leads to works of mercy.

It is this aspect of Luther's thinking that finally, in the last days of the twentieth century, contributed to a landmark ecumenical agreement between the Lutheran World Federation and the Vatican's office on ecumenical relations, the Pontifical Council for Promoting Christian Unity. After centuries of rancor and mutual condemnation over the key Reformation controversy about justification by faith, these two Christian bodies came together in 1999 to sign the "Joint Declaration on the Doctrine of Justification." At the center of the document is this statement: "Together we confess: By grace alone, in faith in Christ's saving work and not because of any merit on our part, we are accepted by God and receive the Holy Spirit, who renews our hearts while equipping and calling us to good works."[6] James, of course, was not working with developed Christian theological notions of "grace," "justification," and "merit," or with the concept of the Holy Spirit as a person of the triune God. Yet we now, reading James's strong call to the unity of faith and works, can appreciate the

---

4. See Augustine, *Enchiridion*, ch. 67: "Faith without Works Is Dead, and Cannot Save a Man," http://www.ccel.org/ccel/schaff/npnf103.iv.ii.lxix.html
5. Luther, "Preface to the Letter of St. Paul to the Romans," in *Luther's Works*, ed. Jaroslav Pelikan and Helmut T. Lehmann (Philadelphia: Muhlenberg, 1955–76).
6. Lutheran World Federation and the Catholic Church, "Joint Declaration on the Doctrine of Justification" (1999), par. 15, http://www.vatican.va/roman_curia/pontifical_councils /chrstuni/documents/rc_pc_chrstuni_doc_31101999_cath-luth-joint-declaration_en.html.

resonance of his teaching with the unity of faith and good works in the Joint Declaration.

James shows us what a cruel joke it can be to proclaim a thin view of faith divorced from action. Imagine that a beloved member of your community (a "brother or sister," he says) needs food and clothing. Would you just say, "you are fine—go get something to eat and something to wear," without offering to help? Would you defend your action by saying, "God will provide," and excuse yourself from participating in God's gracious act of provision? As James points out, such a view of faith is dead.

John Calvin, in his reading of this passage, affirms the importance of keeping faith and love together: "The point is that faith without love gives no profit, indeed it is sheer loss."[7] James is here arguing against people who use the word "faith" incorrectly, according to Calvin, suggesting that any so-called faith that does not lead to works of mercy is not faith at all, but mere pretense. A more recent interpreter, Elsa Tamez, likewise affirms James's integration of faith and works of mercy. She compares James's discussion of faith and works to John Wesley's understanding of sanctification. Sanctification (what Wesley often calls "perfection") is the process of continual growth that integrates faith and deeds, theory and practice.[8] Neither James nor Wesley denies justification by faith, she points out. Instead, these two Christian teachers, from the first and the eighteenth centuries, are emphasizing a different problem from the one that preoccupied Luther: the problem of "faith" that is theoretical, not lived.

> For that faith which bringeth not forth repentance but either evil works or no good works, is not a right pure and living faith, but a dead and devilish one.
>
> John Wesley, "Of the Salvation of Mankind" in *John Wesley*, ed. Albert C. Outler (New York: Oxford University Press, 1964), 128.

Important though it may be, the broad theological issue of faith and action should not distract us from the particularity of James's

7. Calvin, *A Harmony of the Gospels Matthew, Mark, and Luke, Vol. III, and the Epistles of James and Jude*, trans. A. W. Morrison, ed. David W. Torrance and Thomas F. Torrance (Grand Rapids: Eerdmans, 1972), 282.
8. See Elsa Tamez, *The Scandalous Message of James: Faith without Works Is Dead*, rev. ed. (New York: Crossroad, 2002), 54, 67.

example here. He draws readers' attention to the concrete reality that there are people—perhaps even people in the community itself—who need food and clothing. "If a brother or sister is naked and lacks daily food, and one of you says to them, 'Go in peace; keep warm and eat your fill,' and yet you do not supply their bodily needs, what is the good of that?" He is not just talking about "works" in the abstract, but calling his audience to specific works of mercy: caring for those who lack the basics to sustain human life. In this way, James echoes Jesus' specific attention to clothing the naked and feeding the hungry in the famous judgment scene in Matthew 25: "Then the king will say to those at his right hand, 'Come, you that are blessed by my Father, inherit the kingdom prepared for you from the foundation of the world; for I was hungry and you gave me food, I was thirsty and you gave me something to drink, I was a stranger and you welcomed me, I was naked and you gave me clothing, I was sick and you took care of me, I was in prison and you visited me'" (Matt. 25:34–36). For James, as for Jesus, true faith shows itself in caring for the actual hungry, cold, neglected bodies of our brothers and sisters.

When the poor ones who have nothing share with strangers,
when the thirsty water give unto us all,
when the crippled in their weakness strengthen others,
then we know that God still goes that road with us,
then we know that God still goes that road with us.

Miguel Manzano and José Antonio Olivar, "When the Poor Ones," stanza 1. Text © 1971 José A. Olivar. All rights reserved. Exclusive agent: OCP. All rights reserved. Used by permission.

In 2012, the Pew Research Center reported that the number of Americans who do not identify with any religion increased from 15 percent in 2007 to 20 percent in 2012. Among these "nones," many describe themselves as "spiritual but not religious." Though there is a good deal of variety among the folks in this movement, one critique of organized religion (especially Christianity) often surfaces: those who profess belief in Christian teaching do not seem to live out those beliefs in their behavior.[9] Christians profess faith in a God who is merciful and compassionate, but they do not show such mercy and compassion in their own lives. Therefore, their professions of faith remain false and unconvincing.

James offers resounding support to such people who criticize the gap between believing and behaving. He exclaims in exasperation, "Do you want to be shown, you senseless person, that faith apart from works is barren?" (2:20). In contemporary American speech, we might say, "don't you see that saying you believe something, without actually doing it, is meaningless?" He vigorously continues the theme from the preceding verses, concluding as he did there that faith without works is dead.

For James, however, such critique does not lead away from religion, or away from the law; it emerges from deep roots in the religion of Israel, with its faith in the Word/Law of God. As we have heard in earlier passages, James presents the word of God as enduring, and the source of endurance in times of trouble. A key portion of the law in Israelite tradition is the Shema: "Hear, O Israel: the Lord is our God, the Lord alone," also translated "The Lord our God, the Lord is one" (Deut. 6:4). God commands the people to recite these words to their children, to bind them on their hands and foreheads, and to write them on their doorposts—a commandment that observant Jews today embody in practices of attaching *mezuzot* to doorposts and binding tefillin to arms and forehead during prayer. The affirmation that God is one, alone, has been at the center of Israelite religion for a very long time.

The affirmation that "God is one" is surely central to the faith of the writer of James as well. Why then does he offer the snarky comment, "You believe that God is one; you do well. Even the demons believe—and shudder"? Is this statement "you do well" a genuine affirmation or a flash of sarcasm? Scholars disagree. What seems clear, however, is that James does not regard mere recitation of the words of the Shema as sufficient. Again, he is working out a contrast between a faith that says all the right things and a faith that actually

9. See, e.g. Linda Mercadante, *Belief without Borders: Inside the Minds of the Spiritual but Not Religious* (New York: Oxford University Press, 2014), 77–78.

lives out what it professes. Even demons can say "God is one," but merely saying it does not make it faith.

In the seventh and eighth centuries, English Christian scholar Bede "the Venerable" comments on these verses, offering a still-useful distinction between different kinds of belief that helps to clarify what James is saying: "For it is one thing to believe him (i.e., God), another to believe that he exists, another to believe in him."[10] Even the demons can believe the first two (to believe that what God says is true and to believe that God exists), but only those who are Christians believe *in* God, which is to love God. Those who love God show that love in their actions, "because without love faith is empty; with love it is the faith of a Christian, without love the faith of a demon." As we saw in 2:14–17, the integration of faith and love, belief and action, is crucial to James's vision.

James's deep roots in the word of God lead him on beyond the Shema, to two examples of Israelite ancestors who lived their faith through their actions: Abraham and Rahab. Abraham comes first: "Was not our ancestor Abraham justified by works when he offered his son Isaac on the altar?" (2:21) Appealing to *"our* ancestor" slightly softens the harsh insult "you senseless person" from the preceding verse. James calls on the audience to remember lessons from the history that binds them together in one common family.

Although it has a long and complex history of interpretation in Jewish and Christian literature, this is one of only two New Testament passages that alludes to the sacrifice of Isaac. The other is Hebrews 11:17: "By faith Abraham, when put to the test, offered up Isaac. He who had received the promises was ready to offer up his only son. . . ." This is part of the long litany in Hebrews of ancestors who received "approval" because of faith (Heb. 11:2). Hebrews, however, says nothing about the status of the "law" or "works" in this context, nor about justification. James is distinctive in claiming that in offering up his son, Abraham was "justified by works" and that therefore "a person is justified by works and not by faith alone" (Jas. 2:24).

The story of the near-sacrifice of Isaac (sometimes called the

10. Bede the Venerable, *Commentary on the Seven Catholic Epistles,* trans. David Hurst (Kalamazoo, MI: Cistercian, 1985), 29.

Akedah, the Hebrew word for "binding") is among the most contested passages in Jewish, Christian, and Muslim biblical interpretation. Some medieval Jewish interpreters read between the lines of Genesis 22 and glimpse Abraham's actual slaughter of Isaac, and God's resurrection of him from the dead.[11] Many Christian interpreters, particularly in the medieval period, also see hints of resurrection in this story. They frequently portray the offering of Isaac as a figure of Christ, foreshadowing the sacrifice of God's only son. For this reason, many artists have depicted this story in Christian sacred spaces, as for example, the sixth-century mosaics in the church of San Vitale in Ravenna, and Ghiberti's and Brunelleschi's competing original designs for the fifteenth-century "Gates of Paradise" on the baptistery in Florence, Italy. By juxtaposing this story with the story of the death and resurrection of Jesus Christ, Christians open up layers of figurative interpretation: Jesus as the ram who dies in the place of Isaac, Abraham as the father willing to offer his son,[12] the offering of Isaac as a parallel with our own offering of bread and wine in the Eucharist.

James, however, shows no hint of such christological interpretation. Like many interpreters, both Jewish and Christian, James praises Abraham for his wholehearted obedience to God's command, to be willing to give up his only son to death. This is in keeping with most Jewish interpretations of the first century. Abraham's active obedient commitment is a model for the community to follow in light of the coming judgment.[13]

Kierkegaard, in the nineteenth century, also praised the obedience of Abraham in this story, but he pressed the sense of "duty" beyond any comfortable sense of following the rules. In the terrifying event of Abraham's willingness to sacrifice Isaac, Kierkegaard sees the true nature of faith, which is obedience to God's will alone, even when it goes against the "ethical."

Other interpreters, especially in recent decades, point out that

---

11. See Shalom Spiegel, *The Last Trial: On the Legends and Lore of the Command to Abraham to Offer Isaac as a Sacrifice: The Akedah* (Philadelphia: The Jewish Publication Society of America, 1967).
12. Cf. Romans 8.
13. Robert J. Foster, *The Significance of Exemplars for the Interpretation of the Letter of James* (Tübingen: Mohr Siebeck, 2014), ch. 4 (59–103).

Abraham's situation is a kind of trial, a temptation. But what does that mean? What we usually call a temptation is something that keeps a person from carrying out a duty, but here the temptation is the ethical itself ("Thou shalt not kill") which would keep him from doing God's will. But what then is duty? In Abraham's case, duty is found in the doing of God's will, which is itself higher than the universal. His duty transcends the ethical. . . . [F]aith's paradox is precisely this, that the single individual is higher than the universal, that the individual determines his relationship to the universal through his relation to the Absolute (i.e. God), not his relation to the Absolute through his relation to the universal. That is, to live by faith means that one has an absolute duty to God and to God alone. In this tie of obligation the individual relates himself absolutely, as the single individual, to the Absolute—the God who commands. This duty alone is absolute and for this reason the ethical, for the person of faith, is relegated to the relative. In fear and trembling, this is faith's paradox— the suspension of the ethical.

Sören Kierkegaard, *Fear and Trembling*, from *Provocations, the Spiritual Writings of Kierkegaard*, compiled by Charles E. Moore (Walden, NY: Plough Publishing, 2002), 83–98.

this story risks glorifying violence, and such interpreters criticize Abraham for his uncritical passive obedience to God for a tyrannical demand. James's interpretation of Abraham's action certainly raises serious questions from our contemporary perspective: he praises Abraham for offering his son Isaac as a sacrifice, saying that "faith was brought to completion" by this act. Teachers and preachers approaching this text today need to think carefully about how people might hear James's praise for Abraham's potentially violent act. The horrifying reality of child abuse should make all of us pause before doing anything to imply that a parent is to be praised for binding and raising a knife over a child, even to demonstrate wholehearted obedience to a divine command.

Particularly since the sixteenth century, with its sharp disagreements on the topic of justification, interpreters have wrestled with James's claim that Abraham was justified by his works (2:21, 24), whereas Paul says that he was justified by faith (Rom. 4). Luther argues repeatedly that works are not part of justification but are the fruits of justifying faith. He therefore argues vociferously against James's interpretation of Abraham, saying that Abraham was already justified before the "work" of offering Isaac. At a particularly polemical moment, he says, "I almost feel like throwing Jimmy into the stove, as the priest in Kalenberg did."[14]

Other interpreters have sought to harmonize Paul and James on the topic of justification. The fifth-century bishop Cyril of Alexandria, for instance, explains the apparent contradiction by saying that Abraham's sacrifice of Isaac was based on faith, believing that God could still raise Isaac from the dead.[15] It was not the "works" alone which justified Abraham, but the faith on which the action was based. John Calvin in the sixteenth century and John Wesley in the eighteenth follow this line of reasoning, interpreting James to mean that works are the fruit of justification, not its cause. Calvin, for instance, harmonizes the two New Testament writers by saying, "to Paul, the word [justification] denotes our free imputation of righteousness before the judgment seat of God, to James, the demonstration of righteousness from its effects, in the sight of men."[16] This reading eases the tension between Paul and James, understanding the claim that "a person is justified by works and not by faith alone" to mean "a person is shown to be righteous by works, and not by faith alone." This is also the tack that contemporary Roman Catholic interpreter Luke Timothy Johnson recommends; he translates "justified" as "shown to be righteous" (vv. 21, 24, 25), which suggests something revealed, not something made to be true.

James moves on to offer a second biblical example of "being justified by works": Rahab, whose story is told in Joshua 2. James's portrayal of Rahab, however, may have been influenced not only by the narrative in Joshua, but also by extra-biblical Jewish traditions about her. According to legend, Rahab was a beautiful prophet who eventually married Joshua, and she was an ancestor of Jeremiah and Ezekiel. She was also seen as the "archetypal convert" to the Israelite religion.[17] How can Abraham's action be compared to the subversive and life-giving intervention of Rahab, who "welcomed the

14. Martin Luther, "Examination of Heinrich Schmedenstede," in *Luther's Works*, American edition, vol. 34, ed. Lewis W. Spitz (Philadelphia: Muhlenberg Press, 1960), 317.
15. Cyril of Alexandria, *Catena in Epistolas Catholicas* 17 (Oxford: Clarendon, 1840).
16. Calvin, *A Harmony of the Gospels Matthew, Mark, and Luke, Vol. III and the Epistles of James and Jude*, 285.
17. Sharon Dowd, "James," in *The Women's Bible Commentary*, ed. Carol A. Newsom and Sharon H. Ringe (Louisville, KY: Westminster John Knox Press, 1992), 460–61.

messengers and sent them out by another road"? (2:25). Abraham was prepared to give up the life of his son; Rahab preserves the lives of the messengers. In his exploration of these two exemplary figures in James, Robert J. Foster concludes that Rahab does something that "Abraham was never called to do; she entrusted God with her own life. She decides to take responsibility for the safety of the spies, first by hiding them and then by helping them escape back to their camp via the safety of the mountain hideouts. . . . Rahab forsakes the doomed world around her and entrusts her uncertain future (humanly speaking) to God, her only friend (cf. 4:4)."[18]

These two biblical examples present sharp contrasts in other ways as well: Abraham the wealthy prominent male ancestor of the Jews, and Rahab the marginalized non-Jewish female, identified

---

William Hulme in *The Fire of Little Jim* attests to finding comfort in James's emphasis on active faith in the aftermath of his daughter's tragic death. The passivity and "moral impotence" of Paul did not help in a situation where helplessness seems so obvious. "In the shock of bereavement one is overwhelmed by one's helplessness and powerlessness, a passive though agonized victim of a capricious and cruel world. One needs to have one's balance restored, and James helped me to do this. His affirmation of the power of faith to effect change was the light I needed to penetrate an otherwise dark and painful existence."

William Hulme, *The Fire of Little Jim* (Nashville: Abingdon, 1976), 117.

---

here as a prostitute, and therefore a sinner. Gay Byron highlights this liberative dimension of Rahab's story, pointing out that her example "demonstrates that God is on the side of the oppressed and responds to those of different ethnic, economic, social, and cultural backgrounds. . . . for contemporary readers she provides an invitation to pursue acts of justice—with engaged faithfulness."[19] Despite their obvious differences, James employs both of these characters to make his basic point that true faith is active, not passive. He is keen

---

18. Robert J. Foster, *The Significance of Exemplars*, 127.
19. Gay Byron, "James," in *The Women's Bible Commentary*, 3rd ed., ed. Carol A. Newsom, Sharon H. Ringe, and Jacqueline Lapsley (Louisville, KY: Westminster John Knox Press, 2012), 614.

to emphasize that righteousness by faith, as Byron puts it, means "engaged faithfulness."

In the fourth century, John Chrysostom saw that this message from James could be especially important for people outside of the church, arguing that non-Christians are attracted to Christianity by a "mode of life" that exemplifies love.[20] Throughout history, there have been stories of people drawn to follow Jesus because of the way that Jesus' followers lived. The legend of the fourth-century saint Moses the Ethiopian, for instance, tells of a leader of a group of bandits who took shelter in the monastery of Skete and was converted because of the compassionate way of life of the community there.[21]

On the other hand, as the contemporary "nones" often suggest in their reflections, corrupt or unjust behavior can turn people away from organized religious institutions like the church. In the sixth century, Gregory the Great cites James 2:18 ("Show me your faith apart from your works, and I by my works will show you my faith") to make exactly this point. He argues that priests should not accept bribes or amass wealth as part of their office, since such works cause "the innocent and poor" to "recoil from sacred orders." Corruption of the clergy prevents church leaders from living good lives worthy of their calling, and it turns others away.[22]

In the end, the message of James in this passage is simple: faith and deeds are inextricable. Anyone who claims to have faith but does not live it out in action is misguided. Which one is primary, faith or "works"? Several interpreters through the ages have favored the primacy of faith, arguing that a fundamental trust in God is the basis for good deeds. Teachers such as John Calvin and John Wesley appeal to the analogy of a tree to explicate this relationship, perhaps inspired by Psalm 1:3: "They are like trees planted by streams of water, which yield their fruit in its season." Using this image to interpret James, the works are fruit and faith is the root of the tree. Calvin, for instance, interprets James's emphasis on the connection

---

20. Chrysostom, Homily LXXII.5, on John 13:20, in *Homilies on St. John and the Epistle to the Hebrews,* http://www.ccel.org/ccel/schaff/npnf114.iv.lxxiv.html.
21. "Venerable Moses the Ethiopian of Scete," Orthodox Church in America, https://oca.org /saints/lives/2014/08/28/102414-venerable-moses-the-ethiopian-of-scete.
22. Gregory the Great, Epistle CX, "To Theoderic and Theodebert. Kings of the Franks,"http:// www.ccel.org/ccel/schaff/npnf213.ii.v.xlix.html.

of faith and works to mean that "fruits always come from the living root of the good tree."[23]

The last verse of this passage, though, challenges any easy assumption that faith is simply the prior condition that gives birth to good deeds. James concludes his discussion with an unusual analogy: "For just as the body without the spirit is dead, so faith without works is also dead" (2:26). That is, body is to spirit as faith is to works. In both cases, the second gives life to the first. Just as the spirit gives life to the body (an assumption that James's audience would have immediately accepted), so, too, *works* give life to *faith*. The writer here seems to be deliberately reversing the image of the tree and its fruits, and in the process, he reverses the common assumption that faith is "spiritual"' and works are "bodily." Works (or "deeds," which Luke Timothy Johnson suggests as a better translation) do not follow from faith; they animate it. Until we practice what we proclaim, our supposed "faith" is no better than a corpse.

FURTHER REFLECTIONS
Faith and Works, Justification and Sanctification

As discussed in "Further Reflections: Faith" (see p. 36), Christian history of interpretation of "faith" is long and contentious. It helps to be mindful of this historical baggage when we come to read James— and never more than here in chapter 2, in his famous passage regarding faith and works. "Faith by itself, if it has no works, is dead" (2:17), as James puts it bluntly. He emphasizes the importance of faith expressing itself in action, much to the consternation of interpreters like Martin Luther, who heard this as a denial of the central Reformation teaching of "justification by faith alone."

Because of its central role in Protestant thought over the centuries, this claim regarding justification by "faith alone" deserves a brief discussion of its own. Luther, writing in his sixteenth-century context and particularly shaped by his reading of Romans, insisted that the heart of the gospel is the free gift of grace in Jesus Christ, which

---

23. Calvin, *A Harmony of the Gospels Matthew, Mark, and Luke, Vol. III, and the Epistles of James and Jude,* 284.

alone covers our sins. We have only to turn to Christ and grasp hold of him in faith; we need nothing else to be righteous before God. We are "justified" (made righteous) only in Christ, by grace, through faith. This consolation of grace is great good news, since on our own we can never earn our way into God's good graces. Following in this tradition, many Lutheran (and other Protestant) scholars have continued to focus on justification by faith alone, apart from works, as the singular summary of Christian teaching.

Other Protestants since the sixteenth century, particularly those who identify with Reformed Protestantism, have agreed with Luther's emphasis on justification by faith, while also affirming the importance of "sanctification" as a lifelong process of maturing in faithful discipleship. This branch of the Christian family tends to see "faith alone" as that which justifies but "works" as the clear evidence

> **We're all bastards but God loves us anyway.**
>
> Will Campbell, *Brother to a Dragonfly* (Jackson: University of Mississippi Press, 2018), 187.

that grace is transforming one's life. For instance, the Heidelberg Catechism (1563) asks a question that logically follows from a strong doctrine of justification: Since we are redeemed, why must we do good works? Answer:

> Because just as Christ has redeemed us with his blood, he also renews us through his Holy Spirit according to his own image, so that with our whole life we may show ourselves grateful to God for his goodness and that he may be glorified through us; and further, so that we ourselves may be assured of our faith by its fruits and by our reverent behavior win our neighbors to Christ.[24]

This is what Christian tradition has called sanctification, the ongoing process of the Spirit working in us, making us live more and more in Christ. While justification is more of an event establishing our salvation, sanctification is more of a process of living out this salvation. John Calvin describes these together as a "double grace":

24. Heidelberg Catechism, in *The Constitution of the Presbyterian Church (U.S.A.)*, Part I, *Book of Confessions* (Louisville, KY: Office of the General Assembly, Presbyterian Church (U.S.A.), 2014), 4.086.

Christ was given to us by God's generosity, to be grasped
and possessed by us in faith. By partaking of him, we principally receive a *double grace*: namely, that being reconciled to
God through Christ's blamelessness, we may have in heaven
instead of a Judge a gracious Father; and secondly, that sanctified by Christ's spirit we may cultivate blamelessness and
purity of life.

This "double grace" of justification and sanctification has characterized much Protestant discussion of what we receive by faith—the
objective gift of reconciliation with God and the inner transformation of our beings to live more in conformity with Christ.

Roman Catholics also teach about justification and sanctification,
but whereas classical Protestants distinguish these two aspects of
salvation, Catholic teaching portrays justification and sanctification
as an organic whole. The *Catechism of the Catholic Church* makes this
clear when it says, "justification is not only the remission of sins, but
also the sanctification and renewal of the interior man."[25] In other
words, when God makes us righteous in Christ by the power of the
Spirit, God really makes us new, enabling us by grace to cooperate
with God's grace. This sets us on the lifelong path of sanctification.

Can this process of sanctification bring us to perfection in
this life? This too has been a subject of debate among Christians
through the centuries. Those who, like Calvin and many Roman
Catholic theologians, resonate with a strong Augustinian teaching
on the pervasiveness and tenacity of human sin, shy away from any
suggestion that "perfection" is in the realm of human possibility.
James, however, speaks frequently of perfection. The word
teleios ("perfect," or "mature") appears twenty times in the New
Testament, and five of these appearances are in James. This writer
is clearly concerned about completeness, wholeness, maturity.
For this reason, Elsa Tamez sees significant agreement between
James and the eighteenth-century theologian John Wesley, who
likewise emphasizes "Christian perfection." According to Wesley
and the tradition that follows him, Christians should seek complete
conformity to Christ in all that we think, say, or do. Mature Christians

---

25. *Catechism of the Catholic Church,* par. 1989, quoting the Council of Trent, http://www
.vatican.va/archive/ENG0015/__P6Y.HTM.

are "fully sanctified" in that they freely love God and neighbor. This does not mean that they never make mistakes but that they have pure hearts devoted entirely to God. "These Christians are known by their fruits, and keep the entire law, not a part of it, or even most of it, but all of it. To do this is a pleasure, a 'crown of joy.'"[26] For the Wesleyan tradition, justification is an event that comes first, followed by the process of sanctification, which may culminate in an experience of complete sanctification, even in this life.

The topic of justification has attracted lively ecumenical discussion in recent years, much of which has moved away from older polemics and toward new conversation partners. Such recent work on justification includes the groundbreaking Lutheran-Catholic "Joint Declaration on the Doctrine of Justification" (1999) cited on page 104, a document which has now been affirmed also by the worldwide Methodist and Reformed bodies. This development has been driven both by new ecumenical openness in the Catholic church since Vatican II and by new interpretations of Luther and Calvin that illumine the centrality of union with Christ in the thought of these two reformers. According to these recent interpretations, the Protestant emphasis on justification by faith does not mean simply that God declares us to be righteous, but that we are actually made righteous because of our participation in Christ's righteousness.[27] This does not dissolve the distinction between justification and sanctification, but it has enabled many Protestants to appreciate more fully how much Christians can profess a common faith in God who unites with us in Christ, thereby transforming us both from the outside in and from the inside out.

Finally, there has been important recent theological reflection on the meaning of justification by faith from the point of view of people who are oppressed. Andrew Sung Park, in *The Wounded Heart of God*, criticizes Western theology for interpreting justification almost exclusively in terms of those who actively commit sin and need forgiveness. What about the victims? Does the doctrine of

---

26. Tamez, *The Scandalous Message of James*, 69.
27. See, e.g., Carl E. Braaten and Robert W. Jenson, eds., *Union with Christ: The New Finnish Interpretation of Luther* (Grand Rapids: Eerdmans, 1998), and J. Todd Billings, *Calvin, Participation, and the Gift: The Activity of Believers in Union with Christ* (New York: Oxford, 2008).

justification and the sin it is meant to forgive have something to say to those who are the recipients of oppressive and abusive behavior? In response, Park connects the doctrine of justification (and sin) with the Korean concept of *han*: "the critical wound of the heart generated by unjust psychosomatic oppression, as well as by social, political, economic, and cultural oppression."[28] *Han* is characterized by sadness, bitterness, hopelessness, and the will to revenge. To pay attention to *han*, to the pain of the victims of sin, leads to revision of the doctrine of justification: "the doctrine of justification for the oppressor will be underpinned by the doctrine of justice for the oppressed."[29] Park suggests that we need to understand justification not by faith, but by love, which means that being made righteous by God coincides with justice for victims and real transformation of the world by God's grace. James, with his emphasis on the need to care for those who are hungry and poor, would surely agree.

28. Andrew Sung Park, *The Wounded Heart of God: The Asian Concept of Han and the Christian Doctrine of Sin* (Nashville: Abingdon, 1992), 10.
29. Ibid., 13.

3:1–12

The Dangers of the Tongue

For any self-identified teacher to comment on this passage in James is a double exercise in irony. "Not many of you should become teachers," says James. For we all make a lot of mistakes. And "we who teach will be judged with greater strictness." (3:1) Teachers are held accountable by human courts and by God, because of their power to influence the behavior of others. James's grave warning regarding the role of teachers should make anyone pause before stepping up to that podium or into that pulpit.

The further irony is that I am about to *speak* about how dangerous it is . . . to speak.

Given this treacherous situation, we can take comfort in two things: first, James did declare a few verses earlier that "mercy triumphs over judgment" (2:13). Reading his strong words about the importance of following the law and showing one's faith through works, it becomes clear that for James the law is fundamentally about neighbor-love, and the works that justify are the works of mercy. God's ways are just and merciful, not harsh and arbitrary. With fear and trembling, then, profoundly aware of mistakes past, present, and future, we trust that our mercy-filled God forgives and loves us despite our shortcomings.

Second, James's words do not apply only to self-identified, paid "teachers." He was likely speaking to those in his community who were particularly responsible for teaching wisdom to others. Yet his words are relevant to anyone today who speaks with authority—all those who have something to say, and write books or articles or blogs, preach or teach or counsel, or in any way use words to communicate their message to the wider world. So professional teachers are not the only ones who benefit from hearing James's words here; I think he speaks to a much wider audience.

Here is what he says: "The tongue is a fire . . . [it] sets on fire the cycle of nature, and is itself set on fire by hell" (3:6). Sticks and stones shall break my bones, but words shall never hurt me? No, says James, I don't think so.

This warning about the power of words to hurt—and to inflame further hurt—is hardly news to us. Anyone who has ever lived with an adolescent, or been an adolescent, knows this well. Adolescents, with their endearing mixture of vulnerability, honesty, and need to test social boundaries, create a great opportunity to see James's observation in action. The 2004 movie *Mean Girls* offers just one comic exploration of the way teenage girls can use words to insult and humiliate each other. Cruel words are whispered behind the back, spread over the phone and down high school hallways, transforming new student Cady from a kindhearted ingenue to someone more concerned with appearances, a "plastic. " James had it right: the tongue is a restless evil, full of deadly poison.

But we all know that the dangerous power of speech does not end with adolescence. Nineteenth century pastor and teacher Charles Deems observed that in his day there was an epidemic of what he called "much-teachingness." Its symptoms include "a disposition to be always taking the chair, much given to finding fault, correcting, playing the censor, putting on professional airs, having an opinion on every subject, with great readiness to give it dogmatically, dictatorially, pontifically, as being paramount, final, infallible, from which there is no appeal."

> The most frequent argument for silence is simply that words lead to sin. Not speaking, therefore, is the most obvious way to stay away from sin. The connection is clearly expressed by the apostle James. . . . James leaves little doubt that speaking without sinning is difficult and that, if we want to remain untouched by the sins of the world on our journey to the eternal home, silence is the safest way. Thus, silence became one of the central disciplines of the spiritual life.
>
> Henri Nouwen, *The Way of the Heart* (New York: Seabury, 1981), 35–36.

This is common "in social and business circles, and in religious assemblies. . . . It is a dangerous and hurtful habit, to be corrected by those who have formed it and to be avoided by those who have not."[1] Deems welcomes the observations of James, because he too recognizes the dangerous power of word-mongers to hurt and destroy.

Words paint pictures, they weave stories, they build worlds and then draw us in to play our parts. James himself does this, of course: skillfully, using the best rhetorical flourish of the Greek-speaking world, he compares the tongue to a bridle of a horse, the rudder of a ship, a fire, a spring of water, a fig tree, a grapevine. Many ancient writers use the metaphors of the bridle's control of a horse and a rudder's control of a ship to talk about small things having great effect. Philo, for instance, offers a very similar series of metaphors when he comments not on the power of the human tongue but on the power of the mind to direct the whole human being:

> when the charioteer is in command and guides the horses with the reins, the chariot goes the way he wishes, but if the horses have become unruly and got the upper hand, it has often happened that the charioteer has been dragged down. . . . A ship, again, keeps to her straight course when the helmsman grasping the tiller steers accordingly, but capsizes when a contrary wind has sprung up over the sea, and the surge has settled in it. Just so, when Mind, the charioteer or helmsman of the soul, rules the whole living being . . . the life holds a straight course, but when irrational sense gains the chief place, a terrible confusion overtakes it . . . for then, in very deed, the mind is set on fire and is all ablaze.[2]

Drawing on common images of his day, James recognizes both the power and the peril of speech, and muses on the contrast between the smallness of the instrument (bit, rudder, tongue) and the greatness of the effect (steering the horses or the ship, and controlling human society).

The book of Proverbs in the Israelite wisdom tradition also has much to say about the dangerous potential of human speech that is

1. Charles Deems, *Gospel of Common Sense* (New York: Wilbur Ketcham, 1888), 156–57.
2. Philo, *Legum Allegoriae* III, 223–224, in *Philo*, vol. 1, trans. F. H. Colson and G. H. Whitaker, Loeb Classical Library (Cambridge: Harvard University Press, 1929).

"crooked," "lying," "false," or simply "babbling." This kind of speech sows discord in families and in society, and the LORD hates it (Prov. 6:12–19; cf. 14:5, 25; 19:5, 9). Proverbs, like James, cautions against speaking too much: "When words are many, transgression is not lacking, but the prudent are restrained in speech" (Prov. 10:19). In his discussion of the power of words, James reveals his own deep formation in that wisdom tradition, as well as his awareness of the Greek philosophical world.

While James shares with other ancient writers both impressive rhetorical skill and awareness of the power of human speech, he differs from classical writers in his pessimism about human ability to control speech. By verse 8 he exclaims, "no one can tame the tongue—a restless evil, full of deadly poison." Is this an echo of the psalmist's description of evildoers: "They make their tongue sharp as a snake's, and under their lips is the venom of vipers" (Ps. 140:3)? Whether or not James has the psalmist in mind, he seems to have abandoned all hope that human beings themselves can steer the ship or keep the horses under control. Our tongues are hopelessly harmful, and we need to confess this.

Does this mean that we should stop speaking altogether? Is James calling us all to take vows of silence? It can be difficult to apply James's wisdom in a society built on the affirmation of the value of free speech, in which our children are taught from an early age to value words as they learn to read, write, and make persuasive arguments. But of course, James too is using words to move his audience. He is not remaining silent, nor does he call on others to stop speaking entirely. He wants his audience to recognize the dangerous potential in what he is doing. In essence, he is saying: look at how my words can move you. And now—you, watch out how you use words to move others.

"How great a forest is set ablaze by a small fire!" (3:5) says James. In this time of climate change, when forest fires rage regularly during the summer season in the American West, destroying forests and homes and threatening people's very lives, this image is especially poignant. Once a fire is started, especially in drought conditions, it spreads quickly, and the one who started it cannot keep it under control. Once a story is told, once a rumor is begun, once an insinuation is made about someone else's character, the fire spreads. And how much more in these days of tweets and re-tweets, Facebook postings and re-postings. How great a forest is set ablaze.

Professor Susan Benesch of Harvard University and American University's School of International Service founded an organization in 2010 called the Dangerous Speech Project. She and her staff document the links between rise in hate speech and outbreaks of violence around the world. They have identified five factors to discern the dangerousness of a particular speech act: the power of the speaker, the grievance of the audience, the explicitness of the call to violence, the particular social context, and the means of distributing the words.[3] The project is not trying to impede free speech, but it is pointing out that there are times when unmonitored free speech can incite genuine violence. How great a forest can be set ablaze by a small fire!

The fire started by human speech "sets on fire the cycle of nature," according to James—a phrase that literally means "cycle (or wheel) of birth." This term was used by Greek writers including Plato and Herodotus to describe the cycle of rebirth, the idea that human souls are immortal and migrate from body to body over the course of lifetimes until they return to their original unity. Given the open trade routes that linked the Greek-speaking world with India and other parts of Asia, it is entirely possible that the idea of transmigration of souls had itself migrated from India, where it is common to Hindu and Buddhist thought. The notion is attested in Greek philosophy from at least the sixth century BCE, and it is not surprising that the writer of James was familiar with it.[4] Some Christians at the time may well have assumed the existence of a "cycle of birth" and sought to integrate it with hope in future resurrection. There certainly seem to be Christians in the sixth century CE who still affirmed transmigration, given the fact that the Second Council of Constantinople officially condemned this view in 553.

Scholars disagree, however, on whether James has the original meaning of the term in mind here. Dale Allison, for instance, argues

---

3. Https://dangerousspeech.org/.
4. For history and interpretation of the cycle of birth, see John P. Keenan, *The Wisdom of James: Parallels with Mahāyāna Buddhism* (New York: The Newman Press, 2005), 102–7.

that by James's day "cycle of birth" had become a popular metaphor distant from its literal meaning, simply conveying "something like 'the ups and downs of life,' that is, life in its entirety, past, present, and future."[5] John Keenan, on the other hand, points out that the specific idea of transmigration was common in Greek-speaking society in the first century, and James was likely aware of its more developed meaning. Whether he himself means it literally, Keenan argues that James uses the metaphor for "the constant round of sufferings and vicious circles that our actions engender."[6] Our words perpetuate systems of injustice that seem to go around and around, never allowing us to break free from their pernicious influence.

Our words enflame the cycles of suffering and injustice, but James does not place all the responsibility for suffering on human agency alone. The tongue, he says, "is itself set on fire by hell" (literally, "gehenna," 3:6) The Greek term "gehenna," naming the place of final punishment after death or at the end of time, appears in the New Testament only here and in the Synoptic Gospels (e.g., Matt. 5:22, Mark 9:47), and it is often associated with fire. This claim that the tongue is "inflamed by gehenna" intensifies the evil associations of the tongue by suggesting that the final cause of the destructive power of human speech is hell itself. This points to a fundamental dualism in James's worldview: friendship with God is opposed to friendship with the "world," associated here with hell. Human speech should be rooted in relationship with God, whose word of truth gives life (1:18), not death and destruction.[7]

In 2015, the hit musical *Hamilton* ignited the imaginations of the American public when it opened on Broadway. Lin-Manuel Miranda's remarkable hip-hop retelling of the beginnings of the American experiment eventually won eleven Tony awards, a Grammy, and a Pulitzer Prize for Drama. Repeatedly, the character Aaron Burr in this musical reminds his fiery young friend: "Talk less. Smile more. Don't let them know what you're against or what you're for." Given what we know about the destructive power of words, we might all be

---

5. Dale C. Allison Jr., *A Critical and Exegetical Commentary on the Epistle of James*, International Critical Commentary (New York: Bloomsbury, 2013), 539.

6. Keenan, *The Wisdom of James*, 107.

7. See Luke Timothy Johnson, *Brother of Jesus, Friend of God: Studies in the Book of James* (Grand Rapids: Eerdmans, 2004), 165.

tempted to sing along with him. Talk less. Smile more. "The tongue is a fire," after all. Surely it would be better if we used it less.

But didn't the church begin with tongues of fire? Isn't that what Pentecost was about? "They were all together in one place. And suddenly from heaven there came a sound like the rush of a violent wind. . . . Divided tongues, as of fire, appeared among them, and a tongue rested on each of them. All of them were filled with the Holy Spirit and began to speak in other languages . . ." (Acts 2:1–4). Fiery tongues are the beginning of the church, empowering people to speak to one another in different languages, by the power of the Spirit. Bede the Venerable celebrates these the fiery tongues of Acts 2, saying that "Holy teachers are set on fire by [saving fire] both that they themselves may burn with loving and that by preaching they may set others on fire with fiery tongues, as it were."[8]

The difference is this: at Pentecost, the tongues of fire were sent by God, empowering people to speak by the power of the Spirit. The question is: Whose fiery tongues are inspiring us? *Whose* words are we speaking? In this passage, James reminds us to pay attention, so that our words spring not from our own self-aggrandizement, but from the Word of God.

Earlier I suggested that James's words offer important caution not only to self-identified teachers, but to a much wider audience. His opening address, "not many of you should become teachers, my brothers and sisters," (3:1) leads into a portrait of the dangerous power of words that is relevant to all who use language to move an audience. Yet James's words also offer a specific challenge to those of us who are church leaders or theological educators today. Gay Byron points this out, arguing that James reminds church leaders to "exercise their responsibilities in light of the presence and power of God," practicing more "self-control and contemplation" in light of the multiple challenges that face every community. Teachers, who are trained to use words in every situation, might be in particular need of James's wisdom here, which urges bridling the tongue and attending to the word of God first, before any words of our own making. Citing Michael Battle in a reflection on his own profession,

8. Bede the Venerable, *Commentary on the Seven Catholic Epistles,* trans. David Hurst (Kalamazoo, MI: Cistercian, 1985), 39.

Byron goes on: "The vocation of a divinity school professor is not only to articulate how to know God in our midst, it is also to know when to 'shut up' in the midst of God's presence. The teacher's vocation is to know how *and how not* to know God through text and experience."[9]

Centuries earlier, Martin Luther also cited James in his argument to listen for the word of God before all human words, to be taught before trying to teach others. He appeals to James 3:1 in arguing against papal authority, because humans need to listen to God alone, and not to any human-made commandments.[10] Elsewhere, he calls on this verse to caution church leaders who are quick to speak, even in situations where the Word is already being rightly taught. "Permit yourself to be taught," he counsels eager preachers. Perhaps he might have said: Talk less. Listen more.

> **Do not be your own teacher or anyone else's, and do not listen to yourself or to anyone else but only to the Word of God.**
>
> Martin Luther, "Commentary on Ecclesiastes," in *Luther's Works*, ed. Jaroslav Pelikan and H. T. Lehmann (Philadelphia: Muhlenberg, 1955–76), 15:77.

Ironically, a sixteenth century Catholic translation of the New Testament appealed to exactly the same verse against Protestant leaders, translating James 3:1 as "Be yee not many maisters my brethren. . . ." In the commentary on this text, the writer expands on the point: "He meaneth principally Sect-maisters that make them selves several Ringleaders in sundry sortes of new devised doctrines: every one arrogating to himself to be maister, and none so humble as to be a scholer, either to God's church and true Pastors, or to other guides and authors of the said sectes. So did Zuinglius disdaine to be Luthers scholer, and Calvin to be the follower of Zuinglius."[11]

---

9. Gay Byron, "James," in *True to Our Native Land: An African American New Testament Commentary*, ed. Brian K. Blount (Minneapolis: Fortress, 2007), 467. Citation from Michael Battle, "Teaching and Learning as Ceaseless Prayer," in *The Scope of Our Art: The Vocation of the Theological Teacher*, ed. L. Gregory Jones and Stephanie Paulsell (Grand Rapids: Eerdmans, 2002), 158.

10. Martin Luther, "Defense and Explanation of All the Articles," in *Luther's Works*, ed. Jaroslav Pelikan and H. T. Lehmann (Philadelphia: Muhlenberg, 1955–76), 15:77.

11. Annotation on 3:1, in *The New Testament of Iesus Christ, translated faithfully into English out of the authentical Latin . . . in the English College of Rhemes*, 1582.

Clearly, Christians have interpreted James's warning against teachers against a variety of their own theological opponents.

James seeks to cultivate awareness of the dangerous power of words, calling all his readers to listen well to the word of God before spinning out words of our own. "For all of us make many mistakes" (3:2), he cautions. This verse became a favorite of Augustine's, who used it to support his interpretation of the pervasiveness of human sin—the doctrine that became known as "original sin." All people make mistakes, Augustine affirms with James, and therefore no one can claim to be without sin by her own effort. "Human beings cannot tame themselves; God must tame them and their tongues."[12] This humbling reminder of our human tendency to err stands as a critical check on any illusions of our own personal or societal greatness.

Yet James follows this statement with another, apparently contradictory claim: "Anyone who makes no mistakes in speaking is perfect, able to keep the whole body in check with a bridle." Wait— is James saying now that perfection is possible, right after saying that all people make many mistakes? Interpreters disagree about whether perfection is truly possible, but many see this as an important check on the observation about universal mistake-making. To be sure, as the common proverb puts it, "to err is human," but this should not make us complacent about our errors. James is not offering a view of the world that says, "everything is going to hell in a handbasket, so we should just give up trying." Instead, he offers a realistic observation about human mistakes in order to chasten our view of ourselves—and to inspire us to seek a better way. John Wycliffe in the fourteenth century cites this verse in support of his argument that "every Christian ought to be serving God more completely and more perfectly than in fact he does, since no one serves God in every last detail, as he ought."[13] A few centuries later, John Wesley also cites James in support of his call for all people to seek to serve God more fully, even while recognizing that we make mistakes. In calling for Christians to be "perfect," Wesley "is not referring to

---

12. David B. Gowler, *James through the Centuries* (Malden, MA: Wiley Blackwell, 2014), 207; paraphrasing Augustine, "Sermon V.2 on the Sermon on the Mount."

13. Oliver O'Donovan and Joan Lockwood O'Donovan, eds., *From Irenaeus to Grotius: A Sourcebook in Christian Political Thought, 100–1625* (Grand Rapids: Eerdmans, 1999), 500.

Yes we was!

perfection in any absolute sense," clarifies Elsa Tamez. Rather, like James, the eighteenth-century reformer urges followers of Christ to have "a uniform following of Christ, a complete inward and outward conformity to our Master."[14] This does not mean that we never make any mistakes, but that we allow Christ to purify our hearts so that we can focus our desires on what God wills, not on ourselves.

> For people today, perfection is linked to success, competition, excelling at the expense of others. For James it is the opposite: for him it is to attend to the needy in order to be consistent with what we believe and what we read in the Bible.
>
> Elsa Tamez, *The Scandalous Message of James: Faith without Works Is Dead*, rev. ed. (Crossroad, 2002), 71.

Aaron Burr's counsel to "talk less" can be wise, if it allows us to think more, to pray more, to listen more closely for the voice of God through the clamor of the twenty-four-hour news cycle. Sometimes we all need to talk less. Burr's mistake is in the next line: "don't let them know what you're against or what you're for." Because that's the very point that James is trying to counter: we need to be clear about what we are for, about *whom* we are for, and our words and actions must match those commitments. We praise God and curse our neighbors with the same tongue—but James calls that "double-mindedness," and it is a betrayal of God's word. God's word cannot lead us to curse our neighbors, who are made in the image of God.

With this affirmation, James shifts his line of argument again. He began this passage with the observation of the power of the tongue (3:1–5) and then moved to a pessimistic vision of the tongue as a fire enflamed by hell, unable to be tamed (3:6–8). Beginning at verse 9, he points out the contradiction inherent in our inflammatory words: How can it be that human beings, who are good and made in the likeness of God, can curse other humans who are also made in the likeness of God? "My brothers and sisters," he laments, "this ought not to be so." (3:10)

This is the only New Testament affirmation that people (by implication, *all* people) are made in the image or likeness of God. (The

---

14. Tamez, *The Scandalous Message of James*, 68–69.

difference between *homoiosis*/likeness and *eikon*/image, which has been important in some Christian interpretations of Gen. 1:26, does not seem to be important to James, whose usage implies both.) All other uses of the phrase "image of God" in the New Testament refer to *Christ* as God's image (e.g., Col.1:15). Instead of a christological interpretation, James offers the common Jewish interpretation of "image of God" as a simple anthropological claim, carrying the moral imperative to treat all people with respect, not cursing them. What exactly he meant by "image of God" is not clear, but the conceptual content does not matter here; it is the ethical that prevails. All people are created "in the likeness of God," and this ought to shape the way we treat all our neighbors.

James begins and ends this passage by appealing to his audience as family: "brothers and sisters." This is a community with common ancestors, common stories, a shared commitment to the God who has spoken creation into being and who calls the people to listen and follow. The words here are those of an older brother, reminding his own beloved siblings what they should already know. And here is what he says: speak we must; but God's word—which is love and righteousness, mercy and redemption—that Word always comes first.

3:13–18

True and False Wisdom

James is fond of contrasts: between rich and poor, between blessing and cursing, between fresh and brackish water. Throughout the book, James repeatedly depicts a basic contrast between the word/law/wisdom of God, which is enduring and patient and life-giving, and the ways of "the world," which are fleeting and chaotic and death-dealing. This contrast, deeply rooted in Israelite wisdom literature, is on full display in this passage, as James returns to the theme of "wisdom" which he introduced in 1:5. In the earlier passage, the writer compared wisdom, which comes from God, with "double-mindedness," a condition in which one is tossed about "like a wave of the sea." Here, James describes wisdom as "first pure, then peaceable, gentle, willing to yield, full of mercy and good fruits" (3:17). The opposite of such wisdom, "envy and selfish ambition," (3:14, 16) is "earthly, unspiritual, devilish" (3:15). Clearly these two sorts of "wisdom" are at odds with each other, and the writer is doing his best to persuade the audience to choose the path that leads to righteousness.

True wisdom, among other things, is shown and not merely spoken, according to James. In this way, he weaves together themes from the previous two passages: 2:14–26, in which he emphasizes the importance of acting rather than just speaking, and 3:1–12, in which he issues serious warnings about dangerous speech. He may still have his sights set on those who would be teachers (as in 3:1), when he asks, "Who is wise and understanding among you?" (3:13) Those who claim to be wise, like those who claim to have faith (in 2:14–26) need not announce it, because their life will make it clear.

Again, as in chapter 2, we might hear Eliza Doolittle singing in the background, "Don't talk of stars burning above, if you're in love, show me!"[1] Or as James puts it, "Show by your good life that your works are done with gentleness born of wisdom" (3:13). Bede the Venerable appreciates this point in the early middle ages. He elaborates by saying this about those who would be teachers: "if anyone among them may be, or may appear to himself to be, wise or learned, let him show his learning more by living wisely and according to learning than by teaching others. For he who brings about the good which he can with a meek heart and a well-controlled mouth certainly gives plain evidence of a wise mind."[2] Wisdom, we might say, is a matter of showing, not just telling.

The phrase "envy and selfish ambition" appears twice in this brief passage, and the theme of envy continues in 4:1–10. Craving something that belongs to another is the source of violence and disorder, in contrast with the peace that characterizes "wisdom from above." (3:17) The connection of envy and discord is not unique to James; many Greek moral philosophers, including Plutarch, Plato, and Aristotle, share this observation that envy leads to social division and even violence. So too does the Israelite wisdom tradition; the book of Proverbs portrays envy as so strong and murderous that no one can stand before it (Prov. 27:4). Several other New Testament and other early Christian writers also underscore the violence associated with envy. Paul, in his first letter to the Corinthians, for instance, asks, "For as long as there is jealousy and quarreling among you, are you not of the flesh, and behaving according to human inclinations?" (1 Cor. 3:3).[3]

Even if it is not unique to James, this linkage of envy and violence is worth our attention today. What constitutes envy? It is the desire for something that belongs to another. It is a fixation on one's own lack, the hunger to have more or be more. Awareness of what one does not have leads all too easily to the urge to destroy the one who has in abundance. Several early Christian writers noted the connection of

1. "Show Me," from Frederick Loewe, *My Fair Lady* (New York: Columbia, 1964).
2. Bede the Venerable, *Commentary on the Seven Catholic Epistles,* trans. David Hurst (Kalamazoo, MI: Cistercian, 1985), 43.
3. For more, see Luke Timothy Johnson's essay "James 3:13–4:10 and the *Topos peri phthonou,*" in *Brother of Jesus, Friend of God: Studies in the Book of James* (Grand Rapids: Eerdmans, 2004), 191.

envy and violence in the story of Joseph's brothers, who envied the coat that Joseph wore as a sign of his father's special love, and who contemplated murder before selling him into slavery (see an allusion to this in Acts 7:9). James too warns, "where there is envy and selfish ambition, there will also be disorder and wickedness of every kind" (3:16). More directly, in the next chapter, he asserts, "you want something and you do not have it; so you commit murder" (4:2).

This dynamic is clearly at work in the character Gollum in Tolkien's epic *Lord of the Rings*. Originally a hobbit named Sméagol, long before the main action of the story, he and his relative Déagol go fishing one day. Déagol is pulled into the water by a fish, and at the bottom of the river he puts his hand on a ring—the long-lost Ring of Power that exercises control over anyone who holds it. When Déagol comes up and shows the treasure to his cousin, Sméagol demands the ring as a birthday present. Déagol refuses, and Sméagol strangles him. Envy in this case leads directly to murder. For the rest of his life, Sméagol (soon Gollum, because of the sound he makes in his throat) is driven by love of the ring, envying anyone else (first Bilbo, then Frodo) who takes possession of it. More than once, Gollum threatens to kill the Ring-bearer. Surely envy and selfish ambition lead Gollum—among others—to disorder and wickedness of many and various kinds.

Wisdom that is driven by envy and selfishness is not of God, says James. Its origins are elsewhere; he calls it "earthly, unspiritual, devilish." Just as the tongue in 3:6 is "set on fire by hell," so here false wisdom is "devilish," having its source in that power which is opposed to God, variously identified as the demons (2:19), "gehenna" (3:6), and the devil (4:7). James sees the cosmos in dualistic terms, with the wisdom and generosity of God coming down "from above," and the selfishness and destruction of the evil powers pervading the earth. Human beings are caught in a sharp tension between the two, and James pleads with his audience to choose the wisdom that comes from God. This is the distinctive move of James, not found in other Hellenistic literature on envy: he urges listeners to turn away from the ways of the world, characterized by envy and violence, and to turn to God. This call to conversion becomes even more clear in the following section, at the beginning of chapter 4.

Since James was written, it has been easy for Christian readers to use these verses to condemn the "false wisdom" of all kinds of opponents: "the Jews, the Greeks, Valentinians, Origenists, deniers of the Trinity, anti-Hesychasts, Jesuits, Roman Catholics, and even Nietzsche."[4] It is remarkably easy to recognize how envy and selfish ambition drive others, how others' wisdom is "earthly, unspiritual, and devilish." The question is: Can we see the ways that we too are infected by jealousy and resentment? It would surely be ironic for those who read and teach James to point out the strife caused by others, without at the same time confessing the ways that we ourselves are driven by the selfishness that leads to conflict.

In 1549, the first Book of Common Prayer of the Church of England adapted James's phrase "earthly, unspiritual, devilish" in its litany: "From fornicacion, and all other deadlye sin, and from al the deceytes of the worlde, the fleshe, and the devil: Good lorde, deliver us."[5] This phrase, "the world, the flesh, and the devil" has gone on to have its own life in English usage. For contemporary readers, the blanket condemnation of "world" and "flesh" needs interpretation, since it could lead (and has led) to destructive attitudes toward human bodies and the material creation. Deliverance from "the world" can sound like rescue of some pure disembodied spiritual self from the blood, sweat, and tears of earthly existence. Salvation from "flesh" can imply that everything to do with human bodies is dirty, so that our best hope is to shed this mortal shell and fly away. But such attitudes would be unfaithful to the Jewish and Christian affirmation that the world, including human bodies, is the good creation of a good God; after all, God pronounced every aspect of creation "good" at the very beginning of Genesis. This positive value of creation is affirmed in the opening line of the Nicene Creed: "We believe in one God, the Father almighty, maker of heaven and earth, and of all things visible and invisible." To say that the one God created *all things*, including heaven and earth, caterpillars and stars, microbes and mammoths, and all manner of messy human bodies, is to dismiss any dualism that places our ultimate hope in

4. Dale C. Allison Jr., *A Critical and Exegetical Commentary on the Epistle of James*, International Critical Commentary (New York: Bloomsbury, 2013), 562.
5. Ibid., 563.

the evacuation of our flesh. And James himself assumes that human bodies—especially vulnerable human bodies—matter, as he calls for his readers to "care for orphans and widows in their distress" (1:27). If we continue to use this litany, or some version of it, we need to be careful not to perpetuate the kind of dualism that condemns the entire created order as opposed to God.

"World, flesh, and devil," to use the prayer book language, are not synonyms for the material creation. They name the destructive patterns of behavior in human society, and the quasi-personal forces that drive them. To condemn envy and boasting as "earthly, unspiritual, devilish" is to point out how grasping, self-centered ambition flatly contradicts the peaceable ways of God. We do indeed need deliverance from these things. What the litany gets right is the posture of supplication: rather than reading James and immediately using it as a blueprint to diagnose the ills of others, the prayer book takes James as a tool for self-examination. Where have we ourselves followed the ways of the "world," meaning the distorted and unjust aspects of human society? When have we been drawn into the selfish schemes of "the world, the flesh, and devil"? Whenever and wherever we have been lured into these ways, we pray, good Lord, deliver us.

In contrast with the wisdom of "world, flesh, and devil," James exhorts his audience to take the other path, to embrace the wisdom "from above" that brings not violence but peace (3:17). His description of wisdom here would apparently have been beautiful if read aloud in the original language: "Nine of the words of the list start with either the Greek letter *alpha* or the Greek letter epsilon, two vowels that are fairly close in sound; some of these words also rhyme, three or more in a row."[6] We can tell from verses like this that the writer of James knew how to use words to move a crowd, and he was seeking to move them in the right direction. The right direction in this case is peace: those who are truly wise will show it by becoming peacemakers.

---

6. Margaret Aymer, *James: Diaspora Rhetoric of a Friend of God*, Phoenix Guides to the New Testament (Sheffield: Sheffield Phoenix, 2015), 28; citing Ben Witherington III, *Letters and Homilies for Jewish Christians: A Socio-Rhetorical Commentary on Hebrews, James, and Jude* (Downers Grove, IL: IVP Academic, 2007), 503. Reference to "eta" in the original amended here to "epsilon," as in the Greek.

In the preceding chapter, James chastises those who say, "Go in peace; keep warm and eat your fill" to anyone who does not have enough food or clothing (2:16). If "peace" remains merely a pleasant word of exchange, without active work toward the goal, it is meaningless. In the concluding verse of chapter 3, it is significant that he praises not just *saying* "peace" but *making* peace.

This emphasis on peacemaking comports well with the image of James, the brother of the Lord, in the book of Acts. Named there as the leader of the church in Jerusalem, James offers a compromise on an important controversy about how to respond to the "Gentiles who are turning to God" (Acts 15:19). In Acts 21, he also works to diminish conflict between Paul and certain Christian Jews in Jerusalem who are spreading rumors that Paul is teaching Jews living among the Gentiles to "forsake Moses" (Acts 21:21). James, in that case, offers Paul a way to publicly demonstrate his loyalty to the law, even as he also celebrates the ministry among the Gentiles. While we cannot determine the relationship between the author of this book and the James in the book of Acts (see introduction), such similarity in character suggests that there are common traditions about James as a peacemaker informing both writings.

The pure and peaceable wisdom that James advocates is "from above," that is, not solely from human effort, but flowing from God. As James says earlier, in 1:17, "[e]very generous act of giving, with every perfect gift, is *from above*, coming down from the Father of lights. . . ." Wisdom, then, is one of those "perfect gifts" for which we need to ask (1:5) and which God generously bestows. To those who ask, God gives the capacity to recognize and the strength to follow the ways of life—which are the ways of peace.

> True religion, then, demands the heart and the soul, not the deed and other externals, although these follow if you have the right heart. For where your heart is, everything else is. . . . And this is the reason why true religion is "without insincerity" (James 3:17) or hypocrisy, unlike that pharisaical religion which is only outward and does not change the heart.
>
> Martin Luther, Commentary on Psalm 2:12, in *Luther's Works*, ed. Jaroslav Pelikan and H. T. Lehmann (Philadelphia: Muhlenberg, 1955–76), 12:87.

There is a danger, of course, that reading this passage, with its emphasis on being peaceable and "willing to yield," could suppress the active pursuit of justice among people who are deprived of the basic necessities of life. Is James saying that those who do not have enough to eat should just accept their lot in life, and be "willing to yield" to the powerful? Does being peaceable mean being passive in the face of injustice? By no means. James's explicit concern for "widows and orphans" should check any effort to use this call for peace against those who rally for fair wages and just employment practices. Frederick Douglass, who quotes this verse from James ten times in his extant antislavery speeches, emphasizes that James says, "*first* pure, *then* peaceable."[7] This word order challenges any call to "peace" that does not first call for justice. "There could be no peace where there was oppression, injustice, or outrage upon the right,— none but the most hollow and deceitful peace could ever exist between the man who was on his back on the ground, and the man that stood on his neck with his heel. [. . .] The Divine arrangement was this, be first 'pure and then peaceable.'"[8] To be "pure" is to fight for the just treatment of those whom the world has mistreated, not to stand piously aside from that struggle.

Many African American leaders have taken James's emphasis on "pure, peaceable religion" as a challenge to white systems of oppression, which appeal to false wisdom. For Frederick Douglass, James 3:17 offers a definition of true religion that grounds his argument against any Christian support of slavery. In his 1847 speech "Love of God, Love of Man, Love of Country," he says:

> I love the religion of Christianity—which cometh from above—which is pure, peaceable, gentle, easy to be entreated, full of good fruits, and without hypocrisy. I love that religion which sends its votaries to bind up the wounds of those who have fallen among thieves. By all the love I bear to such a Christianity as this, I hate that of the Priest and Levite, that with long-faced Phariseeism goes up to Jerusalem and

---

7. See Margaret P. Aymer, *First Pure, Then Peaceable: Frederick Douglass Reads James,* Library of New Testament Studies (London: T&T Clark, 2007), 27. This verse is the focus of the entire volume.

8. Ibid., 50, quoting the Scottish reporter who wrote on one of Douglass's speeches.

worships, and leaves the bruised and wounded to die. I despise the religion that can carry Bibles to the heathen on the other side of the globe and withhold them from heathen on this side—which can talk about human rights yonder and traffic in human flesh here.[9]

Similarly, nineteenth-century African American political writer Maria W. Stewart emphasizes that pure religion actively cares for the most vulnerable, "the widow, the fatherless, the poor and the helpless." She follows James in connecting wisdom and pure religion: "Have you one desire to become truly great? O then become truly pious and God will endow you with wisdom and knowledge from on high. . . . Religion is pure; it is ever new; it is beautiful; it is all that is worth living for; it is worth dying for."[10] Pure, peaceable religion calls us not away from the struggle for justice, but into it.

The "just peacemaking" movement of the past few decades has tapped into the same wisdom of Douglass and Stewart, recognizing that making peace is an active enterprise, interwoven with the effort to establish justice. Like James, this movement emphasizes that peace has to be *made*, not just mentioned in holy, high-minded words. One model describes seven steps of just peacemaking, each beginning with a strong active verb: affirm, take, talk, seek, acknowledge, end, work.[11] Each of these is shaped in part by biblical teachings, particularly prophetic literature and the Sermon on the Mount—and therefore, unsurprisingly, several of the points resonate with the wisdom of James. For instance, the third principle, "talk with your enemy" counters the kind of self-centered ambition that James condemns in this passage; nations and people will only ever resolve conflict if they talk to each other. Listening to James in the context of just peacemaking discourse sharpens our ears to hear his counsel in practical political terms. When he advocates wisdom that is "pure, peaceable, willing to yield, full of mercy and good fruits, without

9. Ibid., 44.

10. Gay Byron, *True to Our Native Land: An African American New Testament Commentary*, ed. Cain Hope Felder, Clarice J. Martin, and Emerson B. Powery (Minneapolis: Fortress, 2007), 468, citing Marilyn Richardson, ed., *Maria W. Stewart: America's First Black Woman Political Writer: Essays and Speeches* (Bloomington: Indiana University Press, 1987), 32–33.

11. Glen Stassen, *Just Peacemaking: Transforming Initiatives for Justice and Peace* (Louisville, KY: Westminster John Knox Press, 1992), 89–113.

a trace of partiality or hypocrisy," he might be saying to us, "stop trying to make yourself great by tearing down everyone else. Come to the table, and be willing to listen to others." Agreeing to talk with those we call enemies is one concrete step toward making peace—for individuals, social groups, and nations.

James's call to be peaceable here addresses those in the community who are stirring up conflict. Although he identifies the problem of economic oppression at other moments, that is not his target here, which suggests that he is not primarily speaking to people who are impoverished. The problem in this passage is that some people wish to be wise, but they can see their lot in life only as a competition with others who have more. Jostling for more power and wealth, those who are driven by "envy and selfish ambition" sow conflict rather than a "harvest of righteousness." To this audience, James says, "this is not the true life of wisdom."

> Today we all are called to be disciples of the Lord,
>
> ....
>
> to serve the poor and homeless first, our ease and comfort last.
>
> H. Kenn Carmichael, "Today We All Are Called to Be Disciples," *Glory to God* (Louisville, KY: Westminster John Knox Press, 2013), 757.

The life rooted in wisdom bears "mercy and good fruits," "works done with gentleness." Here again, as in previous chapters, we glimpse James's emphasis on the productiveness of the faithful life. By repeating the word *karpōn* (fruit/harvest) twice in these two verses, James evokes a common biblical image: those who are rooted in wisdom, those who truly have faith, simply will bear fruit, just as the "trees planted by streams of water, which yield their fruit in its season" (Ps. 1:3). There is no choice, no independent "free will" in the matter; one who is wise and understanding will show this in her actions of mercy and peace.

4:1–10

Conflict between God and "the World"

In this passage, James's passionate argument with his audience escalates, as he cultivates one kind of conflict in order to condemn another. The true conflict, he insists, is the conflict between God and "the world." He points this out plainly in verse 4: "Adulterers! Do you not know that friendship with the world is enmity with God? Therefore whoever wishes to be a friend of the world becomes an enemy of God." This verse states a strong recurring theme, perhaps even the organizing center, of the whole book. You cannot be a "friend of God" and a "friend of the world." To be a friend means to share the same outlook, the same values, to be deeply united to the other.[1] The "world" represents the dynamic of competition and scarce resources, and friendship with this world produces conflict and destruction. God, on the other hand, is the ultimate giver of good gifts, and those who are friends with God are shaped by generosity and grace, as well as gratitude and humility.[2] These are fundamentally different worldviews, incompatible with one another. Here, James sounds similar to 1 John: "Do not love the world or the things in the world. . . . for all that is in the world—the desire of the flesh, the desire of the eyes, the pride in riches—comes not from the Father but from the world" (1 John 2:15–17). James, like the writer of 1 John, insists that we must choose: either God or the world. You cannot befriend both; they stand in absolute conflict.

1. Luke Timothy Johnson, *The Letter of James*, Anchor Yale Bible (New Haven: Yale University Press, 1995), 288.
2. Cf. Luke Timothy Johnson, "Friendship with the World and Friendship with God," in *Brother of Jesus, Friend of God: Studies in the Book of James* (Grand Rapids: Eerdmans, 2004).

On the other hand, James condemns the conflict that arises when one does not choose rightly. That is, if we choose to be "friends with the world," we have opted to live in a (false) reality in which life is a zero-sum game. We compete for resources and for attention, and we regard those who have more than we do as threats to our own well-being. This worldview creates conflict within ourselves ("your cravings that are at war within you") as well as conflict with those around

us. All we see is that we "want something and do not have it" (v. 2), and therefore we want to kill the person who has what we lack. This is petty conflict, conflict that fails to recognize what we really need to be resisting, which is "the devil," or "the ways of the world." James here sounds deeply frustrated with his audience for their failure to recognize the seriousness of the conflict that we really do face. Instead of "rebuking the devil," we are rebuking and harming our neighbors—the very ones whom God has called us to love. If his tone in these verses is harsh, this is simply an indication of how seriously James regards the choice that lies before us.

> [T]hose who allow their own desire to become their god, must inevitably hate other human beings who stand in their way and impede their designs.
>
> Dietrich Bonhoeffer, *Discipleship*, trans. Barbara Green and Reinhard Krauss (Minneapolis: Fortress Press, 2015), 248.

In some early church baptismal liturgies, candidates for baptism were asked to face the west, stretch out their hands and say "I renounce you, Satan . . . and all your works . . . and all your pomp . . . and all your worship."[3] They then turned to the east (the direction of the rising sun, and thus the symbol of resurrection) and affirm faith in the triune God. This embodied turning is exactly what James is calling for here: "resist the devil . . . draw near to God . . . cleanse your hands, and purify your hearts. . . ." Recognize the startling truth that God continues to give "all the more grace" to those who ask, and turn toward that life-giving power.

---

3. See, e.g., Cyril of Jerusalem, *Mystagogical Catechesis* 1.2, in Maxwell Johnson, *The Rites of Christian Initiation: Their Evolution and Interpretation*, rev. ed. (Collegeville, MN: Pueblo Books, 2007), 122–24.

The real world, James contends, is the world of God's grace and mercy. This is the world of wisdom into which the writer calls us.

The 1999 movie *The Matrix* offers a dualistic vision of the world every bit as stark as James's view, but in reverse. In the future society of the film, humans operate in a computer-generated simulated reality, while the truth is that their bodies are being used as sources of electrical energy for intelligent machines. The main character, Neo, with the help of the prophetic figure Morpheus, wakes up to this reality, and goes to war against the machines that enslave the human population. In a dramatic scene saturated with early Christian baptismal imagery of enlightenment, immersion, and rebirth, Neo is flushed from the system that had been feeding on his energy, detaching himself from illusory "reality" and turning toward the harsh truth of the "real world."

James, too, summons his audience to turn from the false illusory world toward the real world—but the real world, in this case, is the merciful and generous world of God, while the illusion is the competitive and violent world that we too often occupy. What James lacks in eye-popping visual effects, he makes up for with his fiery rhetoric. Like the long line of Israelite prophets before him, James condemns those who adopt the ways of the world by charging them with adultery: "Adulterers (literally, "adulterous women")! Do you not know that friendship with the world is enmity with God?" (4:4). With this, he recapitulates the fierce language of prophets like Hosea, Isaiah, and Jeremiah, who all describe the people of Israel and Judah as God's unfaithful spouse. Hosea offers a striking example, as God says to the symbolic children of Israel:

> Plead with your mother, plead—
> for she is not my wife,
> and I am not her husband—
>   that she put away her whoring from her face,
> and her adultery from between her breasts,
>   or I will strip her naked
> and expose her as in the day she was born,
>   and make her like a wilderness,
> and turn her into a parched land,

and kill her with thirst.
> Upon her children also I will have no pity,
> because they are children of whoredom.
> For their mother has played the whore;
> she who conceived them has acted shamefully.
> For she said, "I will go after my lovers;
> they give me my bread and my water,
> my wool and my flax, my oil and my drink."
>   (Hos. 2:2–5; cf. Isa. 1:21 and Jer. 13:27)

The gendered description of the wrongdoers here as "adulterous women," comparing unfaithfulness to God with a woman's unfaithfulness in marriage, begs for careful interpretation in our contemporary context, since it can reinforce negative stereotypes of women. This image implies a male-gendered God bound in marriage to a female-gendered people who wander away from their covenant commitments. By employing the ancient metaphor of the unfaithful people as female, the writer of James subtly associates infidelity with womanhood, playing into the cultural assumption that women are more fickle and unstable in their commitments than men. The need for cautious interpretation is heightened when we recognize that the language of "cravings" (4:1) and "covet" (4:2) parallel the language of "desire" in 1:14–15, which is similarly depicted as female. In chapter 1, desire lures, tempts and entices, giving birth to sin and ultimately death. When the same terminology shows up again in chapter 4, the words carry the same imaginative associations: cravings/desires are still gendered female, and they still give birth to destructive results—conflicts, disputes, murder. As with the passage in chapter 1, so too here: those who work with James today need to exercise caution about simply passing on such embedded stereotypes of women as dangerous temptresses or as paradigms of infidelity. This portrayal can damage women and undermine healthy relationships between women and men.

But again, given the rest of James's teaching, sexual activity and gender roles do not seem to be his concern here. The condemnation of craving and coveting has more to do with the destruction that follows when we seek immediate self-gratification rather than following the ways of God and loving the neighbor (see 2:8). In his own way, James is simply restating Jesus' teaching, "you cannot serve God and wealth" (Matt. 6:24). "Do you not remember this?" asks James. Do you not know that you cannot serve two different lords? In calling his audience "adulterers," he is trying to show them how their ways of selfishness are fundamentally unfaithful to God's ways of grace.

Early in the first chapter, James used the striking term "double-minded" (*dipsychos*) to describe one who is divided in loyalty, asking something of God but doubting that she will receive it (1:8). To be of two minds, unable to commit, is a major problem that James attacks from the beginning of the book. Here, he employs the term again as he targets those who attempt to befriend both the world and God, exhorting his audience, "purify your hearts, *you double-minded*" (4:8). For James, the choices are clear: "Either you believe that God generously answers prayers or God does not (1:8). Either you make friends with God or with the unjust world (4:4). Either you are in the community or you are out of it."[4] The decision is before you, and you must choose.

The contrast between the way of the world and the way of God is stark, but James's audience does not yet perceive it. He cajoles them for continuing to ask God for things to satisfy their selfish desires, rather than out of true desire for wisdom: "You ask and do not receive, because you ask wrongly, in order to spend what you get on your pleasures" (4:3). This verse may jar readers accustomed to hearing Jesus' words "ask and you will receive" (Matt. 7:7 // Luke 11:9), since these seem to be contradictory statements. Yet James is addressing a different issue from Jesus here. Jesus is seeking to teach his disciples a basic trust in God's benevolent generosity, embodied in the act of prayer. James concurs that God is gracious and benevolent and that we should turn to God as the giver of all good gifts; after all, he commands those lacking in wisdom to "ask in faith, never doubting" (1:6). At this point, however, he is criticizing prayer that emerges from selfish motives rather than sincere trust. This leads to the writer's outburst in the next verse: those who ask

---

4. Elsa Tamez, *The Scandalous Message of James: Faith without Works Is Dead*, rev. ed. (New York: Crossroad, 2002), 49.

✓ wrongly are being unfaithful and idolatrous, because they appeal to God only as the fulfiller of our own selfish desires.[5] Therefore, they may ask but will not receive.

We cannot know whether the writer of James knew John the Baptizer, but his teaching here certainly improvises on the same urgent refrain: "Repent, for the kingdom of heaven has come near!" (Matt. 3:2). Repent. Turn away from the world and to God. This ancient summons yet calls us today, as it called James's original audience. Pondering such a call to conversion, we might reflect with James on four basic questions:

1. *From* what do we need to turn?
2. *To* what do we need to turn?
3. *How* do we turn?
4. What will happen if we turn?

The first question inquires about what we need to turn away from. James calls this "the world." What is the "world," the *kosmos*, that needs to be resisted? We have already begun to describe this realm: the world, according to James, is the false reality in which we perceive ourselves in competition with others, fighting for attention and resources. It is the world that abides by "the myth of scarcity."

Walter Brueggemann narrates the whole saga of the Bible as the conflict between the "liturgy of abundance" and the "myth of scarcity," and these two terms line up well with the two ways, the two forms of wisdom, that James places before his readers. The "world" from which we need to turn is that world in which there is not enough to go around, and so we need to fight for it all. This mindset of scarcity drives us to fight for scraps, cursing those around us when they get in the way, even as we covet their stuff.

One story from Israel's history illustrates the conflict and jealousy that arise when people perceive the world in terms of scarcity, and God's response to such conflict. Some scholars think that this story informed James's own description of the conflict between friendship with the world and friendship with God. It is the story of Eldad and Medad from Numbers 11. Moses has just told God that he needs help

5. Johnson, *Brother of Jesus, Friend of God,* 208.

> We who are now the richest nation are today's main coveters. We never feel that we have enough; we have to have more and more, and this insatiable desire destroys us. Whether we are liberal or conservative Christians, we must confess that the central problem of our lives is that we are torn apart by the conflict between our attraction to the good news of God's abundance and the power of our belief in scarcity — a belief that makes us greedy, mean and unneighborly. We spend our lives trying to sort out that ambiguity.
>
> Walter Brueggemann, "The Liturgy of Abundance, the Myth of Scarcity," *Christian Century*, March 24–31, 1999, https://www.christiancentury.org/article/2012-01/liturgy-abundance-myth-scarcity.

carrying the burden of the people and their complaining, and God has responded by asking Moses to gather seventy elders to help him.

> So Moses went out and told the people the words of the LORD; and he gathered seventy elders of the people, and placed them all around the tent. Then the LORD came down in the cloud and spoke to him, and took some of the spirit that was on him and put it on the seventy elders; and when the spirit rested upon them, they prophesied. But they did not do so again.
>
> Two men remained in the camp, one named Eldad, and the other named Medad, and the spirit rested on them; they were among those registered, but they had not gone out to the tent, and so they prophesied in the camp. And a young man ran and told Moses, "Eldad and Medad are prophesying in the camp." And Joshua son of Nun, the assistant of Moses, one of his chosen men, said, "My lord Moses, stop them!" But Moses said to him, "Are you jealous for my sake? Would that all the LORD's people were prophets, and that the LORD would put his spirit on them!" (Num. 11:24–29)

The themes of jealousy and conflict are clear: Joshua wants to stop Eldad and Medad from prophesying, with the implication that their powerful words are detracting from Joshua's own authority. Moses, the paradigmatic "friend of God," chastises his assistant, celebrating the abundance of God's spirit that has come even upon these otherwise unknown Israelite leaders.

James 4:5 alludes to an unknown "scripture" that has puzzled interpreters for centuries and whose Greek grammar is far from clear. The NRSV renders the verse this way: "Or do you suppose that it is for nothing that the scripture says, 'God yearns jealously for the spirit that he has made to dwell in us'?" Given the context of James's discussion, it may be that this "Scripture" was a lost writing about Eldad and Medad. Early Christians knew and discussed this story, and there are references to such a now-lost writing in the *Shepherd of Hermas* and other ancient Christian book lists. The themes of this Israelite narrative are remarkably resonant with James's concerns: "desire, jealousy, 'the spirit,' speaking against others, the humble being exalted, the giving of grace, and God drawing near to the saints."[6] If James did in fact have this lost writing in mind, then "the quoted bit must have belonged to Moses' response to Joshua, after the latter raised his objection about Eldad and Modad [*sic*] prophesying; and *to pneuma* must have been the spirit that God told Moses he would give to the elders."[7] Dale Allison (who translates Medad as Modad) offers this interpretation of James's curious verse: "Just as Moses rebuked the jealous Joshua, who protested the grace unexpectedly given to Eldad and Modad, so James rebukes those in the synagogue who, out of envy and selfish desire, are cursing, disputing, slandering, and judging others."[8] The main point, for our purposes, is that the world from which we need to turn is the world of slander and jealousy, the world which inspired Joshua in this story to protest the good gifts given to Eldad and Medad, thinking that more for them meant less for him.

The world from which James calls us to turn is also identified with "the devil" (4:7), whom we are to "resist." The devil and "Satan" had become interchangeable terms by the first century, naming the wholly evil figure opposed to God and working for destruction of all good. For James, the devil stands as a contrast to God and God's merciful ways. The writer does not explore the history or metaphysical reality of the devil or the details of his relationship to the "demons" mentioned in 2:19. Allied with the "world," the devil is simply that power who is to be resisted. The devil's role as "accuser" is particularly appropriate in this context, since James is

---

6. Dale C. Allison Jr., *A Critical and Exegetical Commentary on the Epistle of James*, International Critical Commentary (New York: Bloomsbury, 2013), 621.
7. Ibid.
8. Ibid., 622.

rebuking people who stir up controversy and accuse each other. The traditional association of the devil with pride also resonates with James's overarching concerns to critique prideful self-assertion and instill humility.[9]

"Humility" begins to answer our second question in relation to James's call to conversion: *To* what do we need to turn? What must we do to live more holy and perfect lives? James says: become humble. "God opposes the proud, but gives grace to the humble" (4:6). This verse quotes the Septuagint version of Proverbs 3:34: "The LORD resists the arrogant, but he gives grace to the humble,"[10] quoted also by 1 Peter 5:5. This statement of divine preference for the humble echoes a theme we have seen many times already in James: attention to the "lowly" (1:9), "orphans and widows" (1:27), and "the poor" (2:5). It should come as no surprise that the writer here seeks to drive home the point that if we wish to align ourselves with God, we should seek the way of humility.

Nor is this theme unique to James. As we noted in discussion of those earlier passages, the writer here is echoing a classic biblical motif of reversal that we hear in prophets like Isaiah ("Every valley shall be exalted . . ." Isa. 40:4 KJV) and Jesus ("Blessed are the meek, for they will inherit the earth" Matt. 5:5). The blessing of the humble here also recalls Mary's Magnificat (Luke 1:46–55), in which the young woman sings of God scattering the proud "in the imaginations of their hearts" (Luke 1:51 KJV) and lifting up the lowly. Perhaps Jesus learned this song from his mother. Perhaps the writer of James did too (see commentary on 1:9–10).

Many early Christian writers quote James 4:6 for its clear opposition to pride and praise of humility. It was one of Augustine's favorite verses; as he says, "[t]here is hardly a page in the Bible which does not proclaim the message: 'God resists the proud, but gives grace to the humble.'"[11] Gregory the Great cites this verse against the Bishop of Constantinople when he wants to be called "universal

9. Ibid., 626.

10. Johann Cook, trans., "Proverbs," in *A New English Translation of the Septuagint: And the Other Greek Translations Traditionally Included under That Title*, ed. Albert Pietersma and Benjamin G. Wright (New York and Oxford: Oxford University Press, 2007), 626.

11. Augustine, *De Doctrina Christiana* 3.75, ed. and trans, R. P. H. Green (Oxford: Clarendon Press, 1995), 165.

bishop," saying that God will become his adversary if such arrogance persists, because "God resists the proud (James 4:6)."[12]

There is a danger that we might hear James's praise of humility as a call to grovel, or a call to crow over how unworthy we are. Neither of these is especially helpful. James is not saying that those who are poor and oppressed should celebrate their deprivation (go back and read 2:15–16). God cares for the lowly and summons the word-doers to do the same. Nor is James inviting us to call attention to ourselves by proclaiming that we are not good at something. This kind of self-deprecation turns one's focus inward, to one's own (supposed) shortcomings, rather than seeking to love the neighbor.[13] The pithy statement that "God opposes the proud, but gives grace to the humble" invites serious self-reflection for each person and each community. *From* what kind of selfish arrogance do we need to turn? *To* what kind of humility do we need to turn?

Humility is not a false rejection of God's gifts. To exaggerate the gifts we have by denying them may be as close to narcissism as we get in this life. No, humility is the acknowledgment of God's gifts to me and the acknowledgment that I have been given them for others. Humility is the total continuing surrender to God's power in my life and in the lives of those around me.

Joan Chittister, *Wisdom Distilled from the Daily* (New York: HarperCollins 1990), 65.

At verse 7, James launches into a series of strong imperative verbs: "submit," "resist", "draw near," "cleanse," "purify," "lament and mourn and weep." The writer is eager to direct his audience on *how* they are to repent, *how* they are to turn—the third question for us to ponder about conversion. The short sentences, with their firm, commanding tone, exude confidence that the devil will flee, and that God will draw near, if people submit and draw near to God.

---

12. Gregory the Great, "Epistle XX to Mauricius Augustus," in *Nicene and Post-Nicene Fathers*, Series 2, vol. 12: *Leo the Great, Gregory the Great* (Grand Rapids: Eerdmans), cited on Christian Classics Ethereal Library (CCEL): http://www.ccel.org/ccel/schaff/npnf212 .iii.v.v.x.html.
13. See Frederick Buechner, *Wishful Thinking: A Theological ABC* (New York: Harper & Row, 1973), 40.

But is it so simple? Do we act first, and then God responds? One of my students commented that one of the first Scriptures he memorized was James 4:8: "Draw near to God and he will draw near to you." But, he reflected, "That scripture has become much more problematic to me since coming to seminary. . . . Are we really afforded such agency in the proximity of God to us?!"[14] That is, do we just act independently, and then God reacts to what we have done? To say that our relationship to God follows such a simple if/then logic (if I do this, then God will do that) implies that we have the power and will to approach God ourselves. Many Christian interpreters over the centuries have wrestled with this claim in conversation with the whole of Scripture and human experience and have concluded that we do need to resist the devil and turn to God—but we cannot do it on our own. God's grace enables us to resist evil and choose the good. John Calvin, for instance, comments, "Of course, should someone infer from this passage that the initiative lies with us, and God's grace follows after, this is miles from the intention of the apostle. For though this is our duty, it does not directly follow that it is within our power. When the Spirit of God nerves us for our task, there is no derogation of His own person or prowess in fulfilling in us the very thing He commands."[15] In other words, the bare imperative for us to act does not keep the Spirit from acting in and through us. James's insistence that we need to "draw near to God" should be held together with his equally strong insistence that "every generous act of giving, with every perfect gift, is from above" (1:17)—so our act of turning to God is itself empowered by God's gift working within us.

Finally, what will happen if and when we turn? If we turn away from "the world" and turn to God, embracing the way of true humility by the power of God's wisdom at work in us, what will be the result? Simply this: God "will exalt you" (4:10). This is the divine action that so often follows human abasement throughout the Bible, as James already affirmed in his citation of Proverbs 3:34 a few verses earlier. Again, James is singing his own version of the song that Mary

---

14. C. J. Dates, private communication. Used by permission.
15. John Calvin, *A Harmony of the Gospels Matthew, Mark, and Luke, Vol. III, and the Epistles of James and Jude,* trans. A. W. Morrison, ed. David W. Torrance and Thomas F. Torrance (Grand Rapids: Eerdmans, 1972), 299.

lifts up in the Magnificat and Jesus reprises in his parable-telling: "For all who exalt themselves will be humbled, and those who humble themselves will be exalted." (Luke 14:11, cf. 18:14; Matt. 23:12). The God of Israel loves reversals of fortune, challenging human assumptions about what kind of power truly lasts.

The exaltation that James announces might sound simply like a future promise, a "pie in the sky by and by" kind of promise that eventually those who are humble now will get their reward. And there is a future dimension of James's teaching; as we will see in chapter 5, he does look ahead to the "coming of the Lord" (5:7), a day which will bring both judgment and mercy. This eschatological expectation does color his promise here, that those who humble themselves will (in some near future) be exalted. Christian interpreters have often connected this future expectation with the promise that "God will draw near to you" in 4:8, reading both of these as a promise that people will be drawn into the nearer presence of God after death. For instance, the popular hymn "Nearer, My God, to Thee," inspired by James, concludes with two verses that clearly celebrate being nearer to God after death:

> Or, if on joyful wing cleaving the sky,
> Sun, moon, and stars forgot, upward I'll fly.
> Still all my song shall be, nearer my God, to Thee.
>
> There in my Father's home, safe and at rest,
> There in my Savior's love, perfectly blest;
> Age after age to be, nearer my God to Thee.[16]

The future promise is real, but James's primary focus is not to turn attention to a distant future in which we might be nearer to God. He focuses on conversion now, on drawing nearer to God in the present by turning away from selfish desires and judging others, drawing nearer to the ways of God through humble repentance. Those who humble themselves now will be exalted—not just in the future, but

---

16. Stanzas 1–5, Sarah F. Adams, in *Hymns and Anthems*, by William Johnson Fox, 1841; stanza 6, Edward H. Bickersteth Jr., "Nearer, My God, to Thee," http://www.hymntime.com/tch/htm/n/m/g/nmgtthee.htm.

in the present moment, as the word of God bears fruit and God's beloved begin to see even now the harvest of righteousness.

FURTHER REFLECTIONS
World

James uses the term "world" (*kosmos*) three times in this letter. In one case, it seems to be a neutral term for the realm of human society ("the poor in the world," 2:5), but on the other two occasions, "world" clearly refers to a realm that is opposed to God. At the end of chapter one, he exhorts his audience, "Religion that is pure and undefiled before God, the Father, is this: to care for orphans and widows in their distress, and to keep oneself unstained by the world" (1:27). In chapter 4, he sets out a contrast that some scholars have taken to be the heart of the whole book: "Do you not know that friendship with the world is enmity with God? Therefore whoever wishes to be a friend of the world becomes an enemy of God" (4:4). As Luke Timothy Johnson has argued, *kosmos* for James is not simply the material world or social structures; it "points to a kind of measure or system of meaning." The "world" is that which does not take God's existence and claims into account.[17] In particular, the "world" that James indicts here is the Roman empire, driven by elite power and indulgence of selfish desires, not by mercy and justice.

The term "world" has had a varied history of interpretation in Christian thought, sometimes meaning the whole of creation, sometimes the whole inhabited earth, sometimes the realm of human activity corrupted by sin. It is always worth pausing to ask what a writer means when she refers to "the world" without further specification. From earliest centuries, Christian teachers have regularly insisted that the whole wide created order is good and not evil. This is why the Nicene Creed affirms that the one God in whom we believe is the "creator of all things visible and invisible," as well as being the "Father" of Jesus Christ. There is no separate malevolent creator of the material world; the same good God creates all that is,

17. Johnson, *Brother of Jesus, Friend of God*, 211–13.

pronounces it good, and redeems it when it goes astray. The opposition of God and world, therefore, does not mean that the created material world is inherently evil.

The "world" of human affairs, however, is corrupted by sin, which creates tension. John 1:10 plays with both senses of "world" when it says that the Word "was in the world, and the world came into being through him; yet the world did not know him." This tension is particularly evident in Johannine literature (see, e.g., John 17 and 1 John 2:15–17), setting up the common claim that Christians are to be "in, but not of, the world." How exactly are we to live this out? What aspects of the "world" are we to shun, and which ones acknowledge as good, or at least capable of transformation?

Christians have responded to this in vastly different ways. Though H. Richard Niebuhr's classic work *Christ and Culture* (1941) has received its share of critique in recent years, it continues to offer a helpful typology of ways that Christians have interpreted the relationship between Christ/the gospel and "culture," or the complex sphere of human affairs. These approaches closely parallel the ways that Christians have interpreted and relate to the "world." Some movements (e.g., Amish) present Christianity as sharply opposed to contemporary political, social, and economic life, so "friendship with God" means forming separate communities with distinctive dress, language, and communal life in order to resist the lures of the outside "world." Other Christians (e.g., the nineteenth century social gospel movement) affirm that the ways of God stand against the tendency of human politics to corrupt with power, but they work through existing systems to seek the transformation of "the world."

Recent awareness of environmental change has renewed Christian attention to the created world as good and vital to our call to stewardship. This has prompted new positive uses of the term "world" to refer to the good, and fragile, earth. Some theologians have even described the world as "God's body" (Sallie McFague, Grace Jantzen) to emphasize the intimate relationship of God to creation. "World" in this sense refers particularly to the created material earth, not the realm of human social affairs. At the same time, neo-apocalyptic forms of Christianity pray for the destruction of this world in order that God's new heaven and earth may come.

4:11–17

Warnings against Judging or Presuming to Know the Future

4:11–12

Do Not Judge

James returns here to one of his favorite themes: the destructive power of the tongue (cf. 1:19, 26; 3:1–12). "Do not speak evil against one another, brothers and sisters" (4:11), he urges. In so naming his audience in familial terms, he also shifts away from the harsher tone of the preceding passage, in which he condemned his hearers as "adulterers." There, his rhetoric reached a fever pitch as he exhorted his audience to choose between the ways of the world and the ways of God. Here, he speaks in more intimate terms to members of his own community, his "brothers and sisters," pleading with them to live out what they already know.

What should they already know? They should definitely know the ✓ content of Leviticus 19. James has already reminded his audience of this key portion of the Torah in chapter 2, when he condemned their acts of favoritism toward the rich (2:1; cf. Lev. 19:15), and when in verse 8 he explicitly quotes the "royal law" to "love your neighbor as yourself" (2:8; cf. Lev. 19:18b). He will return to this major portion of the Torah in 5:4 when he condemns the oppression of the laborers as a transgression of Lev. 19:13: "You must not exploit or rob your neighbor. You must not keep back the laborer's wage until next morning." The book of Leviticus, and particularly chapter 19, is a gold mine of God's word for James, and he wants his audience to dig into it.

The point in this passage is that speaking evil against someone else violates God's word, which says, "You shall not go around as a slanderer among your people, and you shall not profit by the blood of your neighbor: I am the LORD" (Lev. 19:16). Judging and slandering a neighbor violates this portion of the law; by extension, James says that speaking evil against someone else is the same as speaking against the whole law (similar to the logic employed in 2:10). To slander and judge is to place oneself above the law, to assume that it does not apply to you. But the only one who is truly above the law is God. Those who slander others assume the role of judge and thus take the place of God. Therefore, transgressing the law is the equivalent of idolatry.

"If you judge the law you are not a doer of the law but a judge." This phrase "doer of the law" so clearly echoes the phrase "doer of the word" (1:22) that it seems likely that the author means these as synonyms. To be a doer of the word is to be a doer of the law. The word that gave us birth (1:18), and which was implanted in us with the power to save our souls (1:21), is the same word that we are called to "do." And what is this word? None other than the law, the life-giving guidance in the ways of justice and mercy that God offered the people of Israel at Sinai, and in Jesus Christ.

Living out that same life-giving law, Jesus too speaks memorably against judging the neighbor: "Do not judge, so that you may not be judged. For with the judgment you make you will be judged, and the measure you give will be the measure you get" (Matt. 7:1–2; cf. Luke 6:37). Both teachers, James and Jesus, interpret the Torah guidance against judging the neighbor, but they draw out different conclusions. Jesus says: do not judge, because your judgment of others (without honest self-examination) will ricochet. James says: do not judge, because to judge another person is to usurp the place of God, who alone is "lawgiver and judge." Jesus is pragmatic about human relations in this passage; James is theological. No one but God has the right to act as supreme judge of another.

This is good advice to any of us who tend to take upon ourselves the authority to pronounce judgment on others' behavior, since careless judgment can too easily slide into slander. In the eighteenth century, Jonathan Edwards quoted James as he reflected on the enthusiastic outbursts of the Great Awakening. In "Some Thoughts concerning the Revival," he argues that forbidding the practice "of judging our brethren in the visible church" would help the revival.[1] Clearly, he was overhearing disapproving comments from some people regarding the emotional responses of revival worshipers, and he sought to remind his readers that their job was not to judge their neighbors with harsh words but to recognize that the behavior they witnessed might just be the work of the Spirit.

We might wish that such a tendency to judge others had faded in the eighteenth century. I suspect, however, that every reader of James today can think of occasions when we have either said or heard harsh words about someone else based on snap judgments rather than patient understanding of another child of God. Perhaps the offense was inappropriate clothing or whispering too loudly during the sermon or accidentally dropping papers from the church balcony. And the "judgment" was an unduly sharp word after the worship service. Or perhaps the offense was walking in the wrong neighborhood or playing your music too loudly or failing to speak in the right way at the right time. And the judgment was harsher by far. Be careful, says James. "There is one lawgiver and judge . . . so who, then, are you to judge your neighbor?"

Of course, every functioning human society needs to acknowledge and respond to harmful behavior when it occurs. Every human society, therefore, needs some people who judge when genuine wrongdoing occurs and how justice is to be restored. How are civil judges to interpret James's challenge? "There is one lawgiver and judge who is able to save and to destroy. So who, then, are you to judge your neighbor?" (4:12). For that matter, how are parents and guardians to exercise judgment about children's behavior, to encourage works of mercy, and to steer young people away from acts that harm others and themselves? Isn't some kind of "judgment" necessary precisely to nurture the love of neighbor that the law commends?

In James's terms, the law itself provides the tool by which we are to discern how to act, and it can be used as a tool to evaluate the behavior of others (as the writer himself does in indicting his audience on several counts of failing to keep the law!). The law provides

1. Jonathan Edwards, *The Great Awakening: A Faithful Narrative*, The Works of Jonathan Edwards Series (New Haven, CT: Yale University Press, 1972), 4:479.

a means for identifying and addressing truly harmful behavior: envy, murder, slander, treating the rich with favoritism and failing to care for those in need. But calling the community to keep the law is not the same thing as being a "judge." To be a "judge" here is to place oneself above the law, beyond the reach of others to hold you accountable for your behavior. This is what James condemns.

So yes, every society needs civil authorities to keep citizens safe and whole. Every family needs mature adults to guide children as they grow up, so that they might evolve into compassionate and just human beings. James is not against these things. He is urging people instead to remember that God alone is the final judge and lawgiver; all of us, then, should judge with responsibility, conscious of the possibility of mistake, "for the improvement, not the humiliation, of the person blamed . . . otherwise we set up ourselves above the law and the lawgiver."[2]

Although James may not have been addressing civil government or the judicial system, these words provide a good opportunity to reflect on the relevance of his critique to criminal justice systems today. The reminder that God alone is the lawgiver and judge stands as an important call to humility to any who sit on the bench holding lives and fortunes in their hands. Especially in light of the hundreds of exonerations of people wrongly convicted in the United States since the early 1990s,[3] it seems more vital than ever to exercise justice with humility, heeding James's challenge, "who are you to judge your neighbor?" And when someone is convicted fairly, James's warning about judgment invites us to consider what true human justice looks like. Does it look like speaking evil and destroying the full humanity of those convicted? Or is there another way? Might human justice systems seek the restoration of humanity to those who have harmed their neighbors? Might those in prison, even for the most violent of crimes, be themselves invited to reflect on James's words "who are you to judge your neighbor?"—so that they might have the opportunity to learn, repent, and work to repair the harm done to victims and their families? This is the aim of "restorative justice,"

2. Joseph B. Mayor, *The Epistle of St. James*, 3rd ed. (Grand Rapids: Kregel, 1990), 538.
3. See https://www.innocenceproject.org/ and https://www.innocenceproject.org/all-cases/#exonerated-by-dna.

which brings victims, offenders, and community members together to seek repair of the damage done by crime. No one in this system is "above the law," since all engage together in the hard work of enacting what James calls "the royal law according to the scripture, 'You shall love your neighbor as yourself'" (2:8).[4]

4:13–17

Do Not Boast about Tomorrow

James shifts his attention again at this point, from the "brothers and sisters" of the community who are speaking evil about one another, to "you who say." The phrase "you who say" echoes multiple prophetic passages in which wrongdoers utter smooth words to avoid following God's ways, immediately followed by the prophet's ferocious condemnation of their unjust behavior (see, e.g., Isa. 5:19; Jer. 14:15; Amos 8:5–6). We can imagine that the original audience would have heard this formula and thought immediately, "Uh-oh. Here it comes." In these verses, James targets wealthy merchants who travel and make money for their own benefit, without a thought for others or about their own mortality. They may be members of the Jewish-Christian community itself, or James may be critiquing the wealthy classes for the benefit of his own community, who were attracted to their way of living. This passage is the first half of a final two-part condemnation of the wealthy, addressed to traveling merchants (4:13–17) and landowners (5:1–6).

Commercial travel in Palestine became easier under Roman rule because of the unification of the empire, protection of trade routes, and more paved roads—all of which enhanced the trading routes already established during the Hellenistic era. It was therefore easy for a merchant to travel to various cities and ports for economic gain, as described in this passage. How much easier in our own time, when so much global trade does not depend on physical travel across roads and airways, but on the trade routes of high-speed Internet! What might James have to say to us about commercial ventures today?

---

4. See the work of Restorative Justice at http://restorativejustice.org/#sthash.PTJbbDbU.dpbs.

The question James poses, for the first century as well as the twenty-first, is this: Whose business are we "doing"? Are we doing God's business or our own? In the passage immediately before, James underscores the importance of "*doing* the law" (4:11), just as in the first chapter he exhorts his audience to "be *doers* of the word" (1:22). Here, he mocks those who blithely say, "I think I will go to such and such a town for a year or so and *do business* there—making money for myself." It is not the practice of trading as such that James objects to; he objects to the focus on human effort rather than the sovereign wisdom of God, and the focus on personal gain rather than heeding God's law, which requires mercy toward others.

The irony that James highlights is that personal gain is only ever fleeting. It is no secure basis on which to build a lasting future. We can hear the disbelief in James's voice when he reminds his audience, so busy with their business plans, "you do not even know what tomorrow will bring. What is your life? For you are a mist that appears for a little while and then vanishes" (4:14). In other words, if you plan for the future without recognizing that you do not control the future, you are living an illusion. With this word of caution against presumptuous future planning, coupled with the comparison of human life to mist, smoke, or shadow, James is drawing on a long tradition with roots in both wisdom and prophetic literature, including Proverbs 27:1 ("Do not boast about tomorrow, for you do not know what a day may bring") and Psalm 144:4, which compares human life to a "passing shadow." Other biblical passages that compare human life to mist or smoke include Hosea 13:3, Psalm 68:2, and Wisdom of Solomon 2:2–4 and 5:14. In all these passages, this image implies that those who disappear like mist or smoke have ignored or rejected God.[5] Implicitly, James is contrasting the passing nature of shadows and mist with the enduring character of the law/wisdom/word of God.

James, however, is not only looking back to the prophets and the wisdom writings as he develops his theme. He is also looking sideways, at the rabbi Jesus, who likewise warns against putting one's trust in riches that perish, rather than in the lasting wisdom

5. Pheme Perkins, *First and Second Peter, James, and Jude,* Interpretation: A Bible Commentary for Teaching and Preaching (Louisville, KY: John Knox Press, 1995), 130.

of God. The "parable of the rich fool" in Luke 12:15–20 poignantly depicts a man so impressed with his own grain production that he tears down his barns and builds bigger ones to store all his goods. Confident of his own future well-being, he relaxes to "eat, drink, and be merry"—and immediately God demands his life, so that he is not able to enjoy his own wealth. Jesus, like James in this passage, is warning his listeners not to trust in the goods of material wealth rather than the goodness of God. As Margaret Aymer points out, the underlying theme of this passage is the impending judgment on the rich. "James's point is clear: such transience is the best that the 'world' (*kosmos*) has to offer, so the choice to befriend the 'world' rather than to do good is a choice for the impermanence of sin rather than for the power of faith or wisdom in the eternal God."[6]

Of course, even as we heed James's reminder of the fleeting nature of private gain, we also need to recognize that material wealth passed down through generations has a lasting effect on power and privilege in society. In latching onto James's caution about the ephemeral character of wealth, especially for those in positions of privilege, it is vital not to be naive or self-deceived about the benefits that really do accrue from inherited goods. In the United States this is clearly connected to the privilege of white people, whose wealth as a group far outstrips the wealth of people of color.[7] What does James have to say to those of us who are able to live comfortably, not only because of what we have earned, but because of who our parents and grandparents were, and how they were able to accrue resources and pass them on? At least two implications seem to follow from James's cautionary words, for those in positions of racial-economic privilege:

1. Even inherited wealth and power can vanish, due to economic shifts, political change, or natural disaster. For instance, in mid-twentieth-century Britain and France, a combination of high taxes, inflation, and nationalization sharply curtailed the value of inherited wealth for the aristocracy, which

---

6. Margaret Aymer, *James: Diaspora Rhetoric of a Friend of God* (Sheffield: Sheffield Phoenix, 2015), 31.
7. For 2016 statistics, see the sobering report on the racial wealth divide by Dedrick Asante-Muhammed, Chuck Collins, Josh Hoxie, and Emanuel Nieves, for the Institute for Policy Studies, "The Ever Growing Gap," http://www.ips-dc.org/wp-content/uploads/2016/08/The-Ever-Growing-Gap-CFED_IPS-Final-2.pdf.

significantly shifted political and economic power.[8] More dramatically, following the Russian revolution of 1917, aristocratic families were officially reclassified as "former people," deprived of their wealth and property, and forced into exile or hard labor. Inheritance may not literally vanish overnight, but it is not eternal.

2. Those who benefit from inherited wealth and privilege ought not to boast (4:16) or focus solely on making money for personal gain (4:13) but use their goods to do "the right thing" (4:17), which is to live out the merciful law of God. Those who have resources need not be paralyzed by guilt but do need to consider how to use these resources in service of God's law.

What about James's caution "you do not even know what tomorrow will bring"? Does this mean we should never engage in future planning, in building institutions or investing our time and money in long-term visions? Not necessarily. After all, caring for marginalized communities is a long-term project that requires sustained effort. Seeking to love the neighbor is a lifelong practice. James calls his audience repeatedly to endurance, which is nothing if not a long-term investment of time and effort. It is not a repudiation of the future that James recommends here, but a humility about our ability to control it. "If the Lord wishes" ought to begin all our future planning, he reminds us (4:15). In the sixteenth century, John Calvin particularly commended the expression "God willing" as an abbreviated form of James's appeal: "Let us, however, say it is right and useful, when we make any promise for future time, to make a habit of these expressions: 'God willing,' or 'God permitting.' Naturally I do not want to make a fetish of this, as though the omission should be an offense. . . . James means to arouse those who take no respect for the providence of God from their unconcern."[9] Followers of Islam, as well as Arab Christians, often use a similar

---

8. See Thomas Piketty, *Capital in the Twenty-First Century* (Cambridge, MA: Harvard University Press, 2014).

9. John Calvin, *A Harmony of the Gospels Matthew, Mark, and Luke, Vol. III, and the Epistles of James and Jude*, trans. A. W. Morrison, ed. David W. Torrance and Thomas F. Torrance (Grand Rapids: Eerdmans, 1972), 303.

phrase *inshallah* or *in sha'allah*, meaning "if God wills," before stating future plans.[10] This, like James's use of the term, affirms that despite our best efforts, we do not control the future; our plans are always situated within the larger mysterious context of God's plan.

The theological theme that surfaces in these discussions of "God's will," as Calvin notes, is divine providence. James reminds his audience, then and now, that even wealthy and powerful human beings do not determine the course of history; we need to exercise humility in our assumptions about what will and will not happen, because we cannot just make it so. We need to recognize what "the Lord wishes" in the midst of it all. Yet, particularly since the horrors of the twentieth-century world wars and genocides, many Christians have been challenging any simple notion of divine providence that would say *whatever* happens is directly caused by God's will. Did God intend and will the Holocaust? The Armenian genocide? What about hurricanes like Katrina, Andrew, Maria? Can we really say that the massive scale of human and environmental destruction in each of these events is God's will? Is God the only actor on the stage of history, and human beings just passive instruments of divine manipulation?

Surely not, and surely this is not what James is saying. After all, he chastises his audience, not God, for their unjust ways in slandering their neighbors and failing to "do the word." He does not treat his audience like automatons but like free persons who know what they are supposed to do but do not always do it. So, when he instructs them to say, "if the Lord wishes," he is not eliminating the role of human agency in historical events. He is calling them to acknowledge that humans alone do not control future events. And he is calling them (and us) to consider what it is that "the Lord wishes," and to shape our own plans accordingly.

For Christians, the phrase "if the Lord wishes," or "God willing," reminds us of the petition "your will be done" in the Lord's Prayer. In both cases, we might be tempted to think that attention to God's will detracts from our own choice, so that when we pray for God's will to be done, we are abandoning our own responsibility to decide and act. But divine will and human activity do not relate to each

10. John L. Esposito, ed., "Insha Allah," in *The Oxford Dictionary of Islam* (Oxford: Oxford University Press, 2014), 138.

other simply as "either/or." At times, to be sure, humans struggle with God's will (as Jesus himself struggled in Gethsemane, saying "not my will, but yours be done," Luke 22:42). Yet repeatedly in Scripture, God works in and through human decisions—not apart from them—to accomplish good things: in the Joseph story, in Hannah's prayer, in Cyrus the anointed deliverer, in Mary's "yes" to the angel. Jesus in his teaching on prayer, and James here in this passage, direct our attention to "the Lord's wishes" not to render us passive, but so that we may align our actions with God's saving intentions for the world.

"Anyone, then, who knows the right thing to do and fails to do it, commits sin" (4:17). In this final indictment of the passage, James implies that everyone who is listening to him should know "the right thing to do." Be a friend of God, not the world. Cultivate the word that has been implanted in you. Pay attention to God's law, and just do it. For those engaged in business transactions, like the traveling merchants in James 4, this means: stop boasting, and show humility in your dealings with others. Stop pretending that you rule the universe. Pay attention to where your profits go, and remember that your chief religious duty is to care for widows and orphans, the most vulnerable members of society (1:27). Do not show favoritism to the rich (2:1–7) but show mercy to your neighbors as yourself (2:8–9). Pay fair wages to your workers and pay them on time (5:1–4).[11] At this point, James implies that his listeners still have the possibility to repent and turn to the just and merciful ways of God. In the next passage, it is no longer clear that such repentance is possible.

FURTHER REFLECTIONS
Providence

As noted in the commentary, James 4:13–17, with its injunction to precede all planning with the words "if the Lord wishes," surfaces the tricky theological topic of divine providence. Traditionally, "providence" refers to the ways that God acts in human history,

---

11. See Edgar McKnight and Christopher Church, *Hebrews–James* (Macon, GA: Smyth & Helwys, 2004), 395–97.

by preserving, accompanying, and guiding all things toward their appointed end. By framing all of our activity within the broader, more startling scope of God's reconciling activity, affirmation of divine providence chastens any presumption that humans alone control the course of events.

Classical discussions of providence often turn to Old Testament narratives like the Joseph cycle (Gen. 37–50) for inspiration. This long narrative offers a rich source of reflection on divine providence, which works in a hidden way through the very human deeds of Joseph and his brothers. The brothers sell Joseph into slavery, and as a result he ends up in Egypt, eventually in a position of power so that he can provide for his brothers when there is a famine in Canaan. When Joseph eventually reveals himself to his brothers, he says, "do not be distressed, or angry with yourselves because you sold me here; for God sent me before you to preserve life" (Gen. 45:5). The story concludes, "even though you intended to do harm to me, God intended it for good, in order to preserve a numerous people" (Gen. 50:20).

Perhaps shaped by his knowledge of the Joseph story, the apostle Paul likewise affirms the mysterious goodness of divine providence when he says, "We know that all things work together for good for those who love God, who are called according to his purpose" (Rom. 8:28). Though this might sound unrealistically optimistic, it is again a deep affirmation that, despite all appearances to the contrary, nothing at all is able to separate us from the "love of God in Christ Jesus our Lord." God works in and through "hardship, distress, persecution, famine, nakedness, peril, and sword" to accomplish God's own purpose, which is the redemption of the world in Jesus Christ.

John Calvin, who knew a good deal about hardship and persecution in his lifetime, still wholeheartedly affirms that God is at work in every detail of human history. So-called "general providence" is not enough, according to Calvin. God does provide for the world and its creatures through general laws of nature, but this is not a full account of God's providential care. Rather, God operates by "special providence," that is, God not only watches over creation but directs and guides all things to the divine end:

> For [God] is deemed omnipotent, not because he can indeed
> act, yet sometimes ceases and sits in idleness, or continues by
> a general impulse that order of nature which he previously
> appointed; but because, governing heaven and earth by his
> providence, he so regulates all things that nothing takes place
> without his deliberation.[12]

Why is an understanding of general providence insufficient,
according to Calvin? Because it does not leave enough room to
see events in the created world as the direct result of God's favor
or God's judgment. Calvin draws from Scripture to claim that God
directly wills events in history. The events of life are not simply neutral; they tell us something about God's favor or God's judgment,
and we need to respond appropriately by repenting or by giving
thanks. Thus, Calvin even argues that God directly wills "natural"
occurrences (which, for Calvin, means that what insurance companies call "acts of God" really are acts of God).

Traditional understandings of divine providence like Calvin's
have emphasized that God is the omnipotent force directing and
guiding all things. While there is something right about this, it has
also tended to obscure the real creaturely agency through which
God works. This position seems to suggest that God is the only real
agent, so every single thing that happens is God's will.

Such a view of providence has become increasingly difficult in
light of the horrors of the twentieth century, which ought to stop
the mouths of any who would claim that God meant the Holocaust,
or Hiroshima, or My Lai, for the good of humanity. As theologians
have been rethinking the doctrine of God in general, so they have
been reformulating understandings of divine providence in particular. Is it still possible to affirm that God is at work in the world, in
spite of all evidence to the contrary? And if so, how?

Daniel Migliore, inspired by other theologians such as Karl Barth
and Jürgen Moltmann, proposes a fresh Trinitarian rethinking of
providence for these times. Migliore begins with Barth's claim that
God is not "sheer almightiness" but is the God we come to know
most clearly in the life, cross, and resurrection of Jesus Christ. This

---

12. John Calvin, *Institutes of the Christian Religion,* ed. John T. McNeill, trans. Ford Lewis Battles
(Philadelphia: Westminster, 1960), 1:200.

means that the God of providence is not only free and powerful but also loving. Furthermore, the God of providence is triune, as "creator, redeemer, and consummator," who confronts and overcomes evil in, through—and sometimes in spite of—us. This leads Migliore to offer three basic claims about God's providence:

1. "The love of God the creator and provider is at work not only where life is sustained and enhanced, but also where all that jeopardizes life and its fulfillment is resisted and set under judgment."[13] This means that God not only sustains life but also resists evil—and calls Christian disciples to do the same. This reinterpretation of God's preservation leads not only to patience but also to our resistance to evil.

2. "The love of God the redeemer is at work in both the heights and the depths of creaturely experience, both when the creature is strong and active and when the creature is weak and passive."[14] Here, Migliore acknowledges God's solidarity with the suffering of the world. This point echoes the work of Jürgen Moltmann, who in *The Crucified God* (1974) makes the claim that on the cross, God really experienced death. This means that evil and death are taken into God's own being. Ultimately, these are conquered, as we see in the resurrection, but at this point, on the cross, what we see is God's radical identification with creaturely experience even to the point of death.

3. "The love of God the sanctifier is at work everywhere, preparing for the coming reign of God, planting seeds of hope, renewing and transforming all things."[15] This reinterprets God's "rule" not as domination but as the work of life in the midst of death. This is God's rule interpreted through the cross, the work of the Spirit, and the groaning of creation.

This way of interpreting providence might help us hear James's words "if the Lord wishes" not as a call to complacency but as a reminder that we ought always to evaluate our own plans in terms of the more mysterious and merciful plans of the triune God.

---

13. Daniel L. Migliore, *Faith Seeking Understanding: An Introduction to Christian Theology*, 3rd ed. (Grand Rapids: Eerdmans, 2014), 137.

14. Ibid., 138.

15. Ibid., 139.

5:1–6

Critique of Rich Oppressors

In this passage, James intensifies the sharp critique of "rich people" that he began in 4:13–17. Walter Rauschenbusch spoke admiringly of this passage in 1907, saying that James "pronounces an invective against the rich which would seem intolerably denunciatory in the mouth of a modern socialist preacher."[1] With stark apocalyptic language, James continues his reminder that riches do not last, so no one should place ultimate hope in accumulated treasure. But whereas the prior passage addressed traveling merchants, this section speaks to wealthy landowners who live in luxury and mistreat their workers. Perhaps because of their greater degree of wealth, the "rich people" here receive even more scathing judgment than the merchants of preceding verses; James describes their wealth as already rotting away, while eschatological judgment looms because of the landowners' unjust treatment of their workers, and their murder of "the righteous one" (5:6). By the end of these six verses, there is little hope of redemption for the rich, clad like medieval skeletons in their rotten and rusted attire.

In the preceding section, James derides the arrogance of those who plan for the future without recognizing that they do not control the future. Here, the author condemns those who live in luxury, regardless of the cost to other people, assuming that extravagant wealth will protect them from death and judgment. In both cases, the root problem is arrogance, forgetting the limits of human power and human achievement, and mistaking ourselves for God.

1. Walter Rauschenbusch, *Christianity and the Social Crisis* (1907; repr., Louisville, KY: Westminster/John Knox Press, 1991), 99.

"Come now, you rich people, weep and wail for the miseries that are coming to you," (5:1) begins James ominously. This is the only appearance of the command to wail, or "howl" (*ololuzontes*), in the entire New Testament; but the verb appears eighteen times in the Septuagint (the Greek version of the Old Testament), eleven of which are in Isaiah and nine of those eleven in the first part of Isaiah alone. Isaiah 13–15 has a particularly high concentration of this verb, as the prophet calls the people of Israel to wail for the destruction of the empires of Babylon, Moab, and Philistia.[2] So, for instance, "Wail, for the day of the LORD is near; it will come like destruction from the Almighty!" (Isa. 13:6). By employing the same term here, James kindles his audience's memory of apocalyptic judgments against ancient empires, who were judged for their own arrogance and trust in worldly power.

Does this threat of impending destruction offer any hope to the listener? There is no explicit hope for the rich here, though these words could be taken as a last-ditch invitation to the wealthy to repent before imminent destruction.[3] Perhaps by commanding the rich to weep and wail, they might be induced to change their ways. But are the "rich people" in the passage really James's main concern? Those of us who worry about this question might be revealing more about our own power and privilege than about the justice that James demands. The apocalyptic judgment may not be comforting at all to the wealthy, but it offers real consolation to those who are oppressed.[4]

Though ancient and medieval writers almost never cite this passage, biblical interpreters since the nineteenth century have turned to it with renewed vigor, because its sharp critique of the "rich" resounds with startling relevance in societies with wide economic disparity between rich and poor. Pedrito Maynard-Reid, writing in late twentieth-century Jamaica, provides one good example:

> [James's] words speak not only of the other world, but address

2. Specifically, Isa. 13:6, 13:8; 14:31; 15:3. See Pedrito Maynard-Reid, *Poverty and Wealth in James* (Maryknoll, NY: Orbis, 1987), 82.
3. See Joseph B. Mayor, *The Epistle of St. James,* 3rd ed., repr. (Minneapolis: Klock & Klock Christian Publishers, 1977), 230.
4. Maynard-Reid, *Poverty and Wealth in James,* 97.

this world. His intense language demonstrates that he opposes the structures that enable the rich to increase their wealth at the expense of the poor—structures that fatten some and allow them to live in luxury while others are exploited and live in misery and filth, eking out a mere existence. James' indignation is an unqualified condemnation of the intolerable nature of such existence. His epistle condemns unjust situations in his and our historical contexts.[5]

For those readers who confront unjust and unequal economic conditions in the world every day, James's observation, "You [rich people] have lived on the earth in luxury and in pleasure; you have fattened your hearts in a day of slaughter" does not sound like it belongs to a distant time and place, but to our very own.

As with 1:9–11, interpreters debate about who exactly James means by "the rich" here. Unlike the earlier passage, however, in 5:1–6, James explicitly criticizes the accumulation of wealth in a series of vivid images, so there is no doubt that he has actual economic disparity in his sights. Accumulated wealth of a small privileged class, for James as for the biblical prophets and Jesus, is not innocent. Economic disparity is always bound up with larger systems of social and political oppression. So, for instance, in first-century Palestine as well as in the contemporary world, when wealth is concentrated in the hands of a few, the drive to increase profits leads all too easily to unjust labor practices. In our own time, companies seek to lower the cost of labor to maximize profit. Massive economies depend on low-paid workers to produce enough goods for the wealthy to consume,

> [James offers] a fierce declaration of God's judgment on the wealthy as *sinners*, whose wealth is accumulated and held in defiance of God's law requiring justice and compassion, and is used to pervert the structures of society to their own ends with impunity. The indictment, based on a tradition already ancient when James wrote, sounds remarkably "modern" even now.
>
> Sondra Ely Wheeler, *Wealth as Peril and Obligation: The New Testament on Possessions* (Grand Rapids: Eerdmans, 1995), 103.

5. Ibid.

to drive the economic engines forward and the stock market higher. Concentrated wealth, then, tends to lead to greater oppression of the poor. It is not wealth in the abstract that James condemns but the actions that seem to emerge inevitably when there is grave disparity in wealth and power.

Economic injustice is also intertwined with other forms of oppression. In her reading of this passage, Gay Byron reminds us that "rich people" are not just individuals, but systems and institutions that perpetuate oppression of the non-elite (which often include gender and racial oppression).[6] In the United States, for instance, it is difficult to read this passage and not think of the lives of migrant farm workers, both documented and undocumented. The agriculture industry currently depends on immigrant labor, primarily from Mexico and Central America, to harvest produce, because repeated studies have demonstrated that even unemployed American workers will not do this work. These migrant laborers are subject to brutal hours, low pay, and sometimes slavery conditions, because of the demand for affordable produce in the American grocery store. How do these workers hear James when he calls out, "Listen! The wages of the laborers who mowed your fields, which you kept back by fraud, cry out, and the cries of the harvesters have reached the ears of the Lord of hosts" (5:4)? "You" in this context does not only name isolated managers and farm owners, but the systems that support low wages and unjust working conditions.

Whoever is included in the "rich," James lashes them with pro-phetic/apocalyptic judgment of biblical proportions: "Your gold and silver have rusted, and their rust will be evidence against you, and it will eat your flesh like fire . . ." (5:3). Taking up the rhetoric of his brother-prophets Isaiah, Jeremiah, Ezekiel, and Amos, James threatens the fire of judgment on those who have not followed the just and merciful ways of God (see e.g. Isa. 10:16–17; Jer. 5:14; Amos 1:12–14). He refers to a coming "day of slaughter," like the "day of Lord" that Isaiah foretells: "Wail, for the day of the Lord is near; it will come like destruction from the Almighty! . . . See, the

6. Gay L. Byron, "James," in *True to our Native Land: An African American New Testament Commentary*, ed. Cain Hope Felder, Clarice J. Martin, and Emerson B. Powery (Minneapolis: Fortress, 2007), 469.

day of the LORD comes, cruel, with wrath and fierce anger, to make the earth a desolation, and to destroy its sinners from it" (Isa. 13:6, 9). Done with his call to conversion, James is declaring that God's concern for the poor is real, and that neglect of God's command to care for the neighbor carries dire consequences.

Nor is such prophetic judgment limited to "the God of the Old Testament," as if the God of the prophets was some other God than the one who sent Jesus. James's anger here recalls not only Amos and Isaiah but also Jesus' teaching regarding wealth, particularly in the Gospels of Matthew and Luke. When James says, "You have laid up treasure for the last days," he may have been pondering the "parable of the rich fool" told by Jesus (Luke 12:13–21), in which a man seeks to store up wealth for the sake of his own later comfort, rather than using his treasure to care for others. Jesus there and James here seem to be saying that the treasures of the wealthy should be given out as wages, rather than hoarded, only to rot and rust. Or perhaps James was recalling Matthew 6:19–20: "store up for yourselves treasure in heaven, where neither moth nor rust consumes." Perhaps he had just been telling his own children the parable of rich man and Lazarus (Luke 16:19–31). That tale too portrays a man of wealth condemned to eternal torment because he "feasted sumptuously every day" while Lazarus, the beggar outside the rich man's gates, longs to eat even the morsels that fall from his table. There will be a day of reckoning, say Isaiah, Jesus, and James. God does see and hear, and God will respond to "the cries of the harvesters."

All readers who dismiss such fiery speech as quaint "fire and brimstone" preaching of another age do well to pause and notice what whips up James and his prophetic band to such fury: injustice and oppression.

> God did not appoint gold to go to waste, or clothes to be eaten by moths, but intended them to sustain human life.
>
> John Calvin, Commentary on James 5:3, in *A Harmony of the Gospels Matthew, Mark, and Luke, Vol. III, and the Epistles of James and Jude*, trans. A. W. Morrison, ed. David W. Torrance and Thomas F. Torrance (Grand Rapids: Eerdmans, 1972), 306.

God does not condemn the rich for a failure to keep odd and outdated practices, but for failing to care for the poor. Wealth is to be used for the good of the wider community, not just private consumption. The "rich people" whom James addresses have such excess that they clearly could use some portion of it to help others, since it is going to waste—but they choose not to. This is the heart of the problem. As on so many previous occasions, James here is reminding his readers of the law that they should already know. In this case, the "rich people" are explicitly ignoring the teaching of Leviticus 19:13: "You shall not defraud your neighbor; you shall not steal; and you shall not keep for yourself the wages of a laborer until morning." This teaching is expanded in Deuteronomy, which says, "You shall not withhold the wages of poor and needy laborers, whether other Israelites or aliens who reside in your land in one of your towns. You shall pay them their wages daily before sunset, because they are poor and their livelihood depends on them; otherwise they might cry to the LORD against you, and you would incur guilt" (Deut. 24:14–15). What might sound like an idiosyncratic commandment is eminently practical: in the first century when James was writing, laborers were usually day laborers, not slaves, and thus particularly dependent on daily wages for their very survival.[7] To withhold wages at the end of a day was (and is) to prevent the hungry from having sufficient food.

James's judgment concludes with a cryptic last verse, which refers to the murder of "the righteous one, who does not resist you." This is the final charge in James's list of accusations against the rich. But who is this "righteous one"? Because the object of oppression shifts here from the plural ("laborers" and "harvesters") to the singular ("the righteous one"), and because Jesus is seen as the righteous innocent victim of unjust murder, many early Christian interpreters read this as a reference to Jesus. Bede the Venerable, for instance, interprets the "righteous one" as Jesus, crucified at the hands of the rich. He also interprets the destruction of Jerusalem in 70 CE as God's righteous punishment for these sins.[8] Several ancient as well as a few modern interpreters follow this same christological reading. Unfortunately, such interpreters sometimes use this interpretation also to condemn Jews for the murder of Jesus, suggesting that James

---

7. Elsa Tamez, *The Scandalous Message of James: Faith without Works Is Dead,* rev. ed. (New York: Crossroad, 2002),16.

8. Bede the Venerable, *Commentary on the Seven Catholic Epistles,* trans. David Hurst (Kalamazoo, MI: Cistercian, 1985), 56.

was writing here to wealthy members of the Jewish community who were particularly guilty for Jesus' conviction and crucifixion. Though the term "the righteous one" may spark fruitful christological reflections for a contemporary reader, two cautions are in order: (1) there is no suggestion in the text that the writer of James is referring to Jesus, and (2) if an interpreter does take a christological turn, she should beware of the anti-Jewish sentiments that have sometimes accompanied such a reading. The "you" whom James targets for the murder of the righteous one does not and should not be read as a veiled reference to Jews who are somehow more responsible for Jesus' death.

Instead of this interpretation, it is much more straightforward to read "the righteous one" as a singular representation of the innocent poor people, oppressed by the actions of the wealthy. James may well have in mind the "righteous poor man" who is oppressed by the "ungodly" in the Wisdom of Solomon; in that text, the wicked ones conspire together: "Let us oppress the righteous poor man; let us not spare the widow or regard the grey hairs of the aged. But let our might be our law of right, for what is weak proves itself to be useless" (Wisdom of Solomon 2:10–11; see 2:12–20 for the rest of the passage). Such a reading is much more in keeping with the rest of James's concern in this passage. Though he does not refer to the possible connection with the Wisdom of Solomon, John Calvin also interprets the "righteous one" in James as the oppressed poor, who simply have no power to resist. Calvin writes,

> When [James] adds that *the righteous one . . . doth not resist*, he means that the audacity of the rich increases, since those they crush are without any means of resistance. Yet at the same time he gives warning that the vengeance of God will be all the more ready and swift, as on man's side the poor are unprotected. I grant that the reason for the just making no resistance is that he ought to bear injuries with patience: at the same time, I think the reference is to his essential weakness, which is, that he does not resist because he has no force, and has no human assistance.[9]

9. Calvin, *A Harmony of the Gospels Matthew, Mark, and Luke, Vol. III, and the Epistles of James and Jude*, 308.

Calvin demonstrates sensitivity to the poor here, going beyond telling them to endure their lot with patience and instead recognizing that those who are poor have little recourse to end their oppression at the hands of the rich. In the contemporary global economy, those who are poor are often likewise crushed by political and economic systems governed by the wealthy, unable to resist effectively because of the layers of oppression that leave them little time or energy to do more than survive.

In light of the numerous Two-Thirds World countries today, not least in Latin America, in which vast tracts of land are owned by a handful of wealthy people or, in many instances, large multi-national corporations that fail to pay decent wages to their labourers, would-be Christians need to reflect long and hard on this passage. . . . To what extent do we tacitly endorse such injustice by our purchases from such companies, often without even being aware of their practices, or by supporting politicians who promise tax cuts for the upper and middle classes, when programmes helping the needy at home and abroad are slashed in the process and not likely to be replaced by private-sector equivalents? To what extent do the well-to-do Christians in the West and North live lives little different from those described in 5:1–6, . . . even if we plead innocent of the more blatant forms of oppression described in this text?

Craig L. Blomberg, *Neither Poverty nor Riches: A Biblical Theology of Material Possessions* (Grand Rapids: Eerdmans, 1999), 158.

Amid such prophetic denunciation, the good news is this: God hears the cry of the poor now, as God always has. The cries of the defrauded laborers have already "reached the ears of the Lord of hosts," according to James—a deliberate allusion to the exodus story, in which the cries of the people reach God and prompt God's intervention (Exod. 2:23). This image also recalls the "woe-oracle" of Isaiah 5:7–9, in which the landowners accumulate more and more property but fail to do justice. The "LORD of hosts" sees bloodshed and hears a cry, and therefore the many "large and beautiful houses" are made desolate. Such destruction sounds like bad news to those who have large and beautiful houses, but it is profoundly good news for those who have suffered because of the privilege of those house-dwellers. Above all, it is an affirmation that God listens and responds to oppression. As Pedrito Maynard-Reid puts it, "James states that God hears the cry of the poor. God responds to the cry and struggle of the poor. Thus the oppressed have the right to cry out to God to demand their just due."[10] On the day of judgment, God will listen, and the suffering of the poor will end.

Who is this Lord who will deliver the poor from their oppression? James uses a distinctive term for God here: "Lord of hosts" (*kuriou sabaōth*), literally "lord of armies." This is a common name for the God of Israel in Hebrew Scripture, particularly in Isaiah, emphasizing God's power and God's concern for the poor. Maynard-Reid illumines the meaning of this title, saying, "As in Ps. 147:3–4, the One who heals the broken-hearted is the same mighty God who 'determined the number of the stars,' so here (and also at Isa. 5:9). He who is Lord of Hosts is the protector of the oppressed and ill-treated."[11] However, "Lord of hosts" only occurs twice in the New Testament: here and in Romans 9:29. The image of God as a commander of vast heavenly armies would have carried double resonance for James's original audience: looking back, recollecting Isaiah's prophetic promise of deliverance, and looking around, as a

> The bread of the needy is the life of the poor;
>
> whoever deprives them of it is a murderer.
>
> To take away a neighbor's living is to commit murder;
>
> to deprive an employee of wages is to shed blood.
>
> Ben Sira 34:25–26

subversive challenge to the imperial power of Rome. Many readers of Scripture in recent decades have raised concerns about how images of God reinforce oppressive human power; so, for instance, images of God as male warrior or supreme Father can bolster the power of males in our societies and endorse military power as a clear expression of divine justice. These critiques are vital, challenging the subtle ways that our language for God can undergird and uncritically

10. Maynard-Reid, *Poverty and Wealth in James,* 98.
11. Ibid.

support human power schemes. In referring to God as "Lord of hosts" here, however, James slyly employs a military metaphor not to support human imperial power, but to subvert it. "You rich people … who have benefited from the power of Rome," he might be saying, "your armies do not have the last word. The Lord of hosts has heard our cries, and all the powers of heaven will deliver us."

5:7–20

Final Exhortations
to the Community Being Tested

5:7–11

Patience in Suffering

From condemnation of the rich, James now turns to comfort of the "beloved" (literally, the "brothers," members of James's own community). From scathing judgment of wealth gained through unjust labor practices, the writer turns to pastoral exhortation to patience and endurance. In other words, James shifts here from addressing the oppressors to addressing his primary audience: those who have endured suffering and oppression. This begins the final section of the book, summing up themes that James has visited already: endurance in the face of troubles, guarding one's tongue, and the mercy of the Lord.

"Be patient, therefore, beloved, until the coming of the Lord," says the author. This reference to the "coming of the Lord" is surely the reason that these verses (5:7–10) are appointed as the epistle reading in the Revised Common Lectionary for the third Sunday in Advent, Year A. James's call to attentive patience in light of the approaching day of the Lord suits well the season of Advent, when Christians turn their eyes to the approach of the Messiah. More on that later. But first, why does James say, "be patient"? What kind of patience is called for in the face of the injustices that James has so sharply condemned in the preceding passage? Are we just to sit back and wait for the Lord to appear and fix everything that needs fixing?

The word translated "patient" here does not mean passivity. Instead, it suggests an attitude of waiting on alert for something that is expected but cannot be controlled.[1] This is a tricky balance, since the call to be patient amid suffering has sometimes led to tolerance of evil injustice and oppression, particularly in African American and other minority communities. It can sound like a call simply to accept whatever suffering comes, without protest or resistance. But such an interpretation would misunderstand what James is calling for. Gay Byron suggests that those who suffer should not simply remain in silence but "acknowledge their trials and tribulations by exercising *hypomonén* [the word translated as "endurance" in v. 11] and responding to suffering and injustice with acts of compassion and kindness."[2] This is active, not merely passive patience.

Together with the call to patience, James calls his audience to endurance, a term which also denotes strong and active perseverance in the face of troubles. Those who "endure," like Job, root themselves firmly in God and trust that they will receive divine blessing despite the immediate evidence to the contrary.

Although patience and endurance are not passive qualities, James does remind his audience of their limits—as he has from the beginning of the book. God alone is the giver of all good gifts. (1:17) God alone is the source of wisdom (1:5). God alone is the judge and lawgiver (4:12). So here, the call to "be patient . . . until the coming of the Lord" reiterates a familiar theme: the importance of recognizing the limits of human wisdom and human action. We do not control the future (unlike the false perception of the wealthy merchants in 4:13–17). But we can expect it, with faith and confidence that the righteous one is on the way and will bring the mercy that is promised. And meanwhile, we can live out that mercy in our own lives.

During this time of waiting, there is real suffering in the world, and James knows it well—especially the suffering caused by unjust labor practices and backbiting in the community itself. How are we to respond to such suffering in the meantime, as we wait for the day of the Lord? Is there any way in which suffering itself can be redemptive? Gay Byron helpfully quotes Martin Luther King Jr. on

1. Elsa Tamez, *The Scandalous Message of James: Faith without Works Is Dead*, rev. ed. (New York: Crossroad, 2002), 45.
2. Gay Byron, *True to Our Native Land: An African American New Testament Commentary*, ed. Cain Hope Felder, Clarice J. Martin, and Emerson B. Powery (Minneapolis: Fortress, 2007), 469–70.

this theme, reflecting how one's own suffering can indeed be a source of healing. King says, ". . . recognizing the necessity for suffering I have tried to make of it a virtue. If only to save myself from bitterness, I have attempted to see my personal ordeals as an opportunity to transform myself and heal the people involved in the tragic situation which now obtains. I have lived the last few years with the conviction that unearned suffering is redemptive."[3] This comes from the mouth of someone who has known suffering but who refuses to give up hope. So, too, James counsels his audience not to despair in the face of real suffering, but to trust firmly in God's providential work in and through suffering to bring about redemption.

Back in 1:19–21, James employed a gardening metaphor, alluding to the "implanted word" that God has given, which we need to tend by clearing away the weeds of wickedness, so that it may bear fruit. Here, he returns to another agricultural image: the farmer waiting patiently for the crop, through both early and late rains. Earlier, the call was to activity: tend, nurture, weed. At this point, the call is to steadfast patience, watching for what God will do with the crop that has been sown. These are equally important aspects of James's message throughout the book, and the farming/gardening metaphor holds them together well: be active in doing the word—and recognize the limits of your activity. Fulfill the law—and know that God is able to do far more than you can ask or imagine. So, wait— not with bored distraction, but with bold and attentive confidence that the Lord is on the way.

Whether we encounter this passage in Advent or at another time of year, anyone reading verse 5:7 may wonder what James means by the "coming (Parousia) of the Lord." First, do the "Lord" in verses 7–8 and the "Judge" in verse 9 refer specifically to Jesus, or does this passage refer to the "day of the Lord" described in prophetic texts like Amos 5:18–20 or Zephaniah 1:14–16, without christological intent? Reading this passage in the Advent season certainly suggests a christological reading. Scholars disagree about the original intent, however, and it is difficult to tell from the text. Robert Foster argues that this is likely to mean Jesus, since Parousia is used so frequently

3. Byron, "James," in *True to Our Native Land,* 474–75, n. 38, quoting King's reflections on "Suffering and Faith" in 1960.

in the New Testament for this expected second coming.[4] But Pheme Perkins (among others) argues there is no indication that the return of Jesus is meant and interprets "the coming of the Lord" in line with the prophetic texts of the Old Testament.[5] Whether or not Jesus is implied, James is clear that the coming of the Lord is sure and should be a source of strength for those in distress.

Another question about the Parousia is just how "near" it is, and what that means for our own response. Is it imminent, which would suggest refraining from calling for immediate social justice because the Lord is about to return? Or is this closer to the "Day of Judgment" adapted from Jewish apocalypticism, which functions not to undermine human action but to judge and transform unjust social structures? Pedrito Maynard-Reid argues that James here is closer to the prophetic apocalyptic speech of Judaism, such as the *Dies Irae* of Zephaniah 1:11–15. James's words point to God's final judgment, but they also empower life in this present world.[6]

James goes on to direct his audience to "the prophets who spoke in the name of the Lord" as examples of patience, suffering, and endurance. He lifts up Job in particular as an example of endurance. This is the only reference to the figure of Job in the entire New Testament. Job joins the quartet of biblical exemplars whom James cites in the course of his address: Abraham (2:23), Rahab (2:25), here Job, and later Elijah (5:17). All he says about this particular prophet is "you have heard of the endurance of Job," without further detail. The King James Version translates this as "the patience of Job," a

> We are waiting, blessed Savior,
> We are watching for the hour
> When in majesty descending,
> Thou shalt come in mighty
> power;
> Then the shadows will be
> lifted,
> And the darkness rolled away,
> And our eyes behold the
> splendor
> Of the glorious crowning day.
>
> Fanny J. Crosby, "Waiting for Thy Coming," *Sacred Songs No. 2*, ed. I. D. Sankey, J. McGranahan, G. Stebbins (New York: Biglow & Main Co., 1899), 29.

---

4. Robert J. Foster, *The Significance of Exemplars for the Interpretation of the Letter of James* (Tübingen: Mohr Siebeck, 2014), 148–49.
5. Pheme Perkins, *First and Second Peter, James, and Jude,* Interpretation: A Bible Commentary for Teaching and Preaching (Louisville, KY: John Knox Press, 1995), 89.
6. Pedrito Maynard-Reid, *Poverty and Wealth in James* (Maryknoll, NY: Orbis, 1987), 95–98.

phrase which has become proverbial in the English language.[7] We can
assume, since this is no more than a passing allusion, that the audience
had the full story of Job in their imaginations and that listeners would
immediately call to mind the details to fill out the example that James
evokes.

However, it is not so clear to the contemporary reader. To be
sure, the biblical Job does exhibit impressive endurance in the face
of terrible loss and suffering, refusing to "curse God and die," as his
wife counsels. "And throughout the book he remains stubbornly
persistent both in his refusal to give in to his accusers (Job 27:2–6)
and in his desire for an audience with God (Job 23:3–4)."[8] But even
so, is "endurance" the clearest virtue that we see in the portrait of Job
in the Old Testament book?

Recent scholars have explored this question, and some have
concluded that James's reference to Job is likely informed not just
by the familiar book of the Hebrew Bible, but by the *Testament of
Job*, a Second Temple text in which the dying Job tells the story of
his life and offers counsel to his children. This text develops Job's
story more fully, focusing on his qualities of patience and endurance.
According to the *Testament of Job*, the patriarch plans to destroy
symbols of idolatry in a nearby temple; an angel warns him that if he
does this, the Accuser (*Satan*) will bring him great suffering, yet if
he endures that suffering, he will gain a reward. In sharing this story
with his children, Job focuses on the importance of endurance and
counsels them to embrace that quality in their own lives. In addition,
the *Testament* portrays Job as a wealthy man who is kind and just to
those who are poor, so that widows and orphans lament his death.[9] If
James's original audience knew this text (which is quite likely), then
the author's reference to the example of Job not only suggests the
value of endurance, but also offers a counter example to the wealthy
landowners whom James has just condemned in 5:1–6. "Job was a
righteous wealthy person *who having been brought low* endures non-
judgmental suffering, and in his humiliation, as a beggar on a dung

7. See Tod Linafelt, "The Patience of Job," on Bible Odyssey, https://www.bibleodyssey.org/en
    /people/related-articles/patience-of-job.
8. Ibid.
9. For a complete discussion, see Foster, *The Significance of Exemplars for the Interpretation of the
    Letter of James*, ch. 6 (128–64).

hill . . . he is (or perhaps becomes) well aware that 'the rich [would] disappear like the flower of the field' (1:10). As such, he is a shining example to a messianic community that may have judged others by their outward appearance and ostentatious wealth (2:1–5)."[10] The reference to Job in this single verse in James, then, originally evoked a depth of associations that are invisible to contemporary readers who do not know the *Testament of Job*, but only the biblical book. The full narrative clarifies why James appeals to Job as a paradigm of endurance, and it also evokes a number of other virtuous qualities of Job that are quite pertinent to James's own concerns: wise and compassionate use of wealth, care for the poor, guarding the tongue, showing wisdom, doing the royal law, and resisting Satan.

In response to Job's patient endurance, James says, "the Lord is compassionate and merciful." According to the end of the biblical book, "the Lord gave Job twice as much as he had before" (Job 42:10): more sheep, camels, oxen, donkeys, and children. He lived to see four generations and died "old and full of days" (Job 42:17). Many commentators have struggled with the implications of such an ending to the story; are readers supposed to understand that children are simply replaceable and that material abundance is a fitting reward for years of unjust suffering? Augustine explicitly cautions against using the example of Job to foster "avarice," because Job received double what he had lost. Readers should not come away thinking that if we just endure long enough, God will repay us twofold. According to Augustine, Christians should wish for the eternal rewards that are ours in Christ, not material recompense.[11]

Yet for those who suffer poverty and oppression now, it is important to emphasize that God has compassion on those who suffer—and Job sees this compassion in his own life, not after death. James exalts God as the giver of joy to those who endure suffering: "we call blessed those who showed endurance" (5:11). Blessing may not be limited to this life, but surely God does bestow blessings even in this life. The Lord lifts up the lowly (1:9), "gives grace to the humble"

10. Ibid., 162–63. Italics in the original.
11. Augustine, "On the Creed: A Sermon to the Catechumens," section 10, http://www.ccel.org/ccel/schaff/npnf103.iv.vii.x.html.

(4:6), blesses those who endure. This is the word of hope for victims of unjust suffering, both in the first century and today.

5:12

On Swearing

This verse deserves its own separate treatment, because it sits as a hinge between two larger sections, turning both forward and back, with its own particular concern. The discussion of oaths is not directly connected to what precedes and follows it, and yet rhetorically it does link these two sections. In continuity with the preceding verses, James speaks to "my beloved" (literally "brothers") again— the fourth time in seven verses that he uses this term of endearment (vv. 7, 9, 10, and 12). Verses 7–12 together thus have a particularly pastoral tone, addressed to James's beloved community. "Above all" looks both forward and back, continuing and intensifying the mode of exhortation, as if to say, "if you remember nothing else that I have said to you, remember this." Several scholars interpret this verse as a transition to the conclusion of the letter, as it sets up a contrast between wrongful use of words that tear down community (swearing oaths) and upbuilding use of words that strengthen community (prayer, as discussed in 5:13–18), in order that the community may not fall under the judgment that is coming.[12]

James has already expressed sharp concern about the destructive power of speech in 3:1–12. Here he returns to the danger of the tongue, saying, "Do not swear." Such a command today sounds initially like a prohibition of profane language. When I was growing up, it was simply a given in my house that we did not use profanity—ever. And we certainly never used anything approaching the Lord's name in vain. I still recall when I was about six years old and in a moment of frustration whined, "Oh, Gohhhh. . . ." Even without the final d, it was enough to merit a gentle reprimand from my father. Words mattered in our family, and use of any profane language was considered cheap, ugly, and low.

---

12. Foster, *The Significance of Exemplars for the Interpretation of the Letter of James,* 177.

My children find this very quaint, as do most of my colleagues. And it seems to be a liability in some parts of contemporary culture in which regular use of profanity demonstrates not bad taste but authenticity and approachability. My own discomfort with profanity also carries dangerous overtones of class privilege, since profanity was associated in my mind with people who were not well-educated enough to know better.

What then do we make of James's counsel to his beloved ones: "do not swear"? Despite initial impressions, James is not primarily talking here about the use of profane speech, although some later interpreters have read him this way. He is talking about legal oaths. And like rabbi Jesus, James clearly prohibits any such swearing: "do not swear, either by heaven or by earth or by any other oath, but let your 'Yes' be yes and your 'No' be no, so that you may not fall under condemnation." Indeed, James's language here is unusually close to that of Jesus, who says in Matthew 5:33–37:

> Again, you have heard that it was said to those of ancient times, "You shall not swear falsely, but carry out the vows you have made to the Lord." But I say to you, <u>Do not swear at all, either by heaven</u>, for it is the throne of God, <u>or by the earth</u>, for it is his footstool, or by Jerusalem, for it is the city of the great King. And do not swear by your head, for you cannot make one hair white or black. <u>Let your word be "Yes, Yes" or "No, No"</u>; anything more than this comes from the evil one. (parallel text underlined)

Some scholars see this as the closest parallel to a saying of Jesus in the entire letter of James.[13]

Such complete prohibition of oaths was unusual in first century Judaism.[14] Both James and Jesus are reinterpreting and intensifying the Torah prohibitions against swearing falsely, as commanded in Exodus 20:7 ("You shall not make wrongful use of the name of the LORD your God, for the LORD will not acquit anyone who misuses his name"), and Leviticus 19:12 ("And you shall not

---

13. William Brosend, *James and Jude* (Cambridge: Cambridge University Press, 2004), 150; cf. Dale C. Allison Jr., *A Critical and Exegetical Commentary on the Epistle of James*, International Critical Commentary (New York: Bloomsbury, 2013), 728.
14. William Brosend, *James and Jude* (Cambridge: Cambridge University Press, 2004), 151–52.

swear falsely by my name, profaning the name of your God: I am the LORD"). While the Torah cautions against false oaths, Jesus and James challenge the use of any oaths at all. There should be no need for oaths to testify to the truth of one's speech, implies James. Just say yes or no, and mean it.

Interpreters over the years have disagreed on how literally to take James's prohibition, particularly because it seems to contradict other portions of Scripture like Exodus and Leviticus, which permit swearing lawful oaths. John Chrysostom takes James's counsel against oaths very seriously, even though he knows it will bring ridicule.[15] Cyril of Alexandria argues that Christian lives should be more convincing than any oath, and that Christians should refuse to swear oaths at all, because to swear by anything in creation gives that thing "more value than it has by deifying it."[16]

In the sixteenth century, Anabaptist leader Menno Simons also took this verse very seriously, arguing that Christians should never swear oaths, even if it leads to condemnation and death by human authorities.[17] The current Mennonite Confession of Faith continues Simons's teaching on this matter:

> We commit ourselves to tell the truth, to give a simple yes or no, and to avoid swearing of oaths.
>
> Jesus told his disciples not to swear oaths at all, but to let their yes be yes, and their no be no [Matt. 5:33–37; James 5:12]. We believe that this teaching applies to truth telling as well as to avoiding profane language [Eph. 4:15, 29]. An oath is often sworn as a guarantee that one is telling the truth. This implies that when one has not taken an oath, one may be less careful about telling the truth. Jesus' followers are always to speak the truth and, in legal matters, simply to affirm that their statements are true.
>
> Jesus also warned against using oaths to try to compel God to guarantee the future. In faith, we commit our futures to God [Matt. 5:34–36].
>
> Throughout history, human governments have asked

---

15. Chrysostom, Homily VIII on Acts 3:1, http://www.ccel.org/ccel/schaff/npnf111.vi.viii.html.
16. Gerald Bray, *James, 1–2 Peter, 1–3 John, Jude.* Ancient Christian Commentary on Scripture, New Testament, vol. 11 (Downers Grove, IL: InterVarsity Press, 2000), 59.
17. David B. Gowler, *James through the Centuries* (Chichester: Wiley Blackwell, 2014), 291–92.

citizens to swear oaths of allegiance. As Christians, our first
allegiance is to God [Acts 5:29]. In baptism we pledged our
loyalty to Christ's community, a commitment that takes
precedence over obedience to any other social and political
communities.[18]

This confession offers three reasons why Christians should not
swear oaths: (1) we should tell the truth *at all times*, not just under
oath; (2) God, not humans, governs the future, so we should not
use oaths to try and force God to act; and (3) we owe ultimate allegiance to God alone, and then to the Christian community, not
ultimately to any other social or political community. This refusal
to swear oaths has traditionally applied not only to courts and other
legal circumstances but also to membership in any societies that
require oaths for membership. According to Menno Simons and his
heirs, Jesus' (and James's) prohibition of oaths simply calls us to true
and honest communication: in church, court, business, family—in
short, in all aspects of life.

John Calvin, among others, thinks that Simons goes too far and
claims that James does not forbid all oaths, but any dishonor to the
name of God. "James is not discussing the taking of oaths in the
widest sense, any more than is Christ," says Calvin. "To grasp James's
message, we must give first place to what the Law lays down: 'Thou
shalt not take the Name of thy God in vain.' This makes certain that
there is some legitimate use of God's Name."[19] Debate continues
today over whether James is offering absolute prohibition of all
oaths (as Simons contends) or more limited targeting of casual or
voluntary oaths (as Calvin argues).

What James and Jesus share with the older Torah tradition is a
concern to treat the name of the Lord with reverence. Swearing,
even by heaven or earth, is an indirect appeal to God's name, and
is therefore inappropriate. Calvin says, "it is no more permissible
to swear by heaven and earth, than by the Name of God outright.
Christ gives the reason: God's glory is set on all things, and His

18. Mennonite Confession of Faith, article 20, http://mennoniteusa.org/confession-of-faith
/truth/.
19. John Calvin, *A Harmony of the Gospels Matthew, Mark, and Luke, Vol. III, and the Epistles
of James and Jude*, trans. A. W. Morrison, ed. David W. Torrance and Thomas F. Torrance
(Grand Rapids: Eerdmans, 1972), 312–13.

light is everywhere. So there is no other sense or purpose in men taking the words *heaven* or *earth* for their oaths, than if they named God Himself: to speak like this, effectively names the Creator in His created things."[20] In other words, Calvin sees "heaven and earth" as an indirect appeal to the name of God, and thus not only blasphemous but dishonest. Though we may think Calvin overly scrupulous in his reading of "heaven and earth" as substitutes for the name of God, such substitutes were in fact common in first century Jewish practice.[21] Pronouncing the name of God was not permitted, so people used other phrases, including "heaven and earth." Calvin's point, following James, is that such substitutions borrow their power from the holy name of God and are therefore trying to cheat the law prohibiting taking the Lord's name in vain.

Above all, James calls his audience to truthful speech that honors God. Words matter in this family. After all, God is the one who "gave us birth by the word of truth" (1:18); how can we honor God unless our words reflect this truth that gave us birth?

5:13–18

Faithful Prayer

Do not swear, says James in the preceding verse. That is, do not use the name of the Lord as a shield to guarantee your own honesty. Just speak truthfully at all times, saying yes or no, without need to appeal to heaven or earth or anything else. Behind this prohibition of swearing stands concern about misuse of the name of God. In this passage, James encourages a better use of the name of God: not for swearing, but for healing.

How do you pray when you are suffering? How do you pray when you are sick? What do you think happens when you pray? These are key questions that James takes up in this passage on prayer. It might seem like a sudden shift of subject, but on closer inspection, we can see that this call to prayer is intimately related to themes that James has already explored: the need to rely on God for all good gifts (1:5,

---

20. Ibid., 312.
21. Allison, *A Critical and Exegetical Commentary on the Epistle of James*, 735.

1:17), the power of speech (3:1–12), and concern to heal the community's internal divisions (4:1–2, 11–12; 5:9). And though prayer is not only about words, James's introduction to prayer at this point provides a strong contrast to earlier discussions of words that "set on fire the cycle of nature" (3:6). Unlike the destructive power of speech to harm others and betray God, prayer offers an example of positive and powerfully upbuilding power of speech.

In 5:13, James calls his audience to turn to God in all situations of life, whether suffering or joy: "Are any among you suffering? They should pray. Are any cheerful? They should sing songs of praise." Sometimes when we are suffering, it is difficult to muster the energy to pray. It can be easier to sink into despair. But James advises otherwise: Are any of you suffering? Then pray! Likewise, in times of celebration, we may simply revel in the pleasure of the moment without giving thought to its source. James again calls for a wider vision: are you cheerful? Then sing and praise God! Recognize the source of all good things, and remember to ask for what you lack and give thanks for what you have.

> **James 5:13: Is any among you afflicted? Let him pray. Is any merry? Let him sing psalms. Note: That it is not only David's Psalms that they are urged to, but such as are by men fitted to their proper uses; which confuteth them that condemn all humane hymns of composed words in God's Service.**
>
> Richard Baxter, *A Paraphrase on the New Testament, with Notes Doctrinal and Practical* (1685)

James goes on to focus particularly on prayers for those who are sick (5:14–15). A 2016 study by Baylor University researchers concludes that 90 percent of Americans have at some point in their lives prayed for healing, more often for others than for themselves. These statistics suggest that many Americans, knowingly or not, have taken James's teaching to heart. In addition to verbal prayer, more than a quarter of those interviewed have practiced laying on of hands, and nearly 20 percent have done so multiple times. According to this study, and somewhat to the surprise of researchers, prayer for healing was not usually a substitute for medical care but a complement to it. The lead researcher, Jeff Levin, states, "Outside of belief in God, there may be no more ubiquitous religious expression in the U.S. than use of healing prayer."[22]

This provocative study opens the door to additional questions, which later research might address: What proportion of these prayers are individual and spontaneous, and what proportion are communal? How many of these are prayers in the context of public worship? Fifty-three percent of people report participating in a prayer group, but what is the relationship between this group and the 87.4 percent who report praying for healing for others? What do these practices

---

We cannot measure how you heal or answer every sufferer's prayer,
Yet we believe your grace responds where faith and doubt unite to care.
Your hands, though bloodied on the cross, survive to hold and heal and warn,
To carry all through death to life and cradle children yet unborn.

The pain that will not go away, the guilt that clings from things long past,
The fear of what the future holds, are present as if meant to last.
But present too is love which tends the hurt we never hoped to find,
The private agonies inside, the memories that haunt the mind.

So some have come who need your help and some have come to make amends,
As hands which shaped and saved the world are present in the touch of friends.
Lord, let your Spirit meet us here to mend the body, mind, and soul,
To disentangle peace from pain, and make your broken people whole.

John Bell, "We Cannot Measure How You Heal," Text © 1989 WGRG, Iona Community (admin. GIA Publications, Inc.). All rights reserved. Used by permission.

---

of prayer actually look like (e.g., momentary thought, prolonged prayer out loud in the presence of the afflicted person, or prayer in a group on behalf of others)? Furthermore, as the researchers frankly acknowledge, this study does not examine effects of prayer, only the practice. Additional research may explore these questions. What

---

22. Jeff Levin, "Prevalence and Religious Predictors of Healing Prayer Use in the USA: Findings from the Baylor Religion Survey," *Journal of Religion and Health* 55, no. 4 (August 2016): 1136–58.

this study does reveal, however, is that in some form, prayer for healing is a very familiar practice among American Christians.

Though this study of healing prayer does not address the question of what people mean by prayer, many Americans think of prayer primarily as individual and meditative, seeking God's presence or assistance in our own lives. This personal aspect of prayer is not wrong, but James would regard such an individual interpretation of prayer, apart from the praying community, as oddly distorted. This becomes especially clear beginning in verse 14, when the author continues his series of questions: "Are any among you sick? They should call for the elders of the church and have them pray over them, anointing them with oil in the name of the Lord." The sick one is to call the elders, and the elders are to respond. The sick one is not expected to pray alone. Sickness here is a threat to the whole community, and the question is how the community will respond. Will they be like the world, leaving the sick aside and focusing on the strong? Or will they be "friends of God," who reach out to God and to one another in mercy and compassion?[23]

James 5:14–15, with its discussion of prayer and anointing with oil by "the elders" for the purpose of healing, has generated much controversy in Christian interpretation. Originally this passage was understood as encouragement for members of the Christian community to pray for and anoint one another in times of need. In early Christian centuries, oil blessed by a bishop was often taken home and used in this way when people fell ill. By the ninth century, however, anointing with blessed oil could only be done by a priest, and it came to be associated with forgiveness of sins at the time of death rather than a prayer for healing during the ordinary course of life. Eventually in the Western church this practice of anointing people at the brink of death developed into the formal sacrament known as "extreme unction."[24] In the sixteenth century, the Council of Trent interprets James 5:14–15 as teaching the "matter, the form,

---

23. Luke Timothy Johnson, *The Letter of James,* Anchor Yale Bible (New Haven, CT: Yale University Press, 1995), 342–43.
24. Allison, *A Critical and Exegetical Commentary on the Epistle of James,* 741.

the proper minister, and the effect" of this "Sacrament of Extreme Unction."[25]

The official *Catechism of the Catholic Church* today emphasizes that the whole church has the responsibility to pray for healing, and that all the sacraments can contribute to healing of the sick, because of the presence of Christ:

> "Heal the sick!" The Church has received this charge from the Lord and strives to carry it out by taking care of the sick as well as by accompanying them with her prayer of intercession. She believes in the life-giving presence of Christ, the physician of souls and bodies. This presence is particularly active through the sacraments, and in an altogether special way through the Eucharist, the bread that gives eternal life and that St. Paul suggests is connected with bodily health.[26]

In addition to this general mandate to heal the sick, and following the teaching of Trent, the Catholic Church continues to cite these verses from James as the scriptural warrant for the particular sacrament of "Anointing of the Sick" (which has since Vatican II been the preferred name for this sacrament):

> However, the apostolic Church has its own rite for the sick, attested to by St. James: "Is any among you sick? Let him call for the elders [presbyters] of the Church and let them pray over him, anointing him with oil in the name of the Lord; and the prayer of faith will save the sick man, and the Lord will raise him up; and if he has committed sins, he will be forgiven." Tradition has recognized in this rite one of the seven sacraments.[27]

The Catechism here explicitly interprets "elders" as "presbyters," or priests, meaning those ordained by a bishop. Only priests and bishops are permitted to administer the sacrament. The gracious effects of such anointing are multiple: uniting the sick person to the passion of Christ; strength to face suffering; forgiveness of

25. James Waterworth, *The Canons and Decrees of the Sacred and Oecumenical Council of Trent* (London: Dolman, 1848), 104–5.
26. *Catechism of the Catholic Church*, par. 1509, http://www.vatican.va/archive/ENG0015 /__P4K.HTM.
27. Ibid., par. 1510.

sins; "restoration of health, if it is conducive to the salvation of his soul"; and preparation for passing over to eternal life.[28]

Reformers in the sixteenth century sharply criticized the Catholic interpretation of James's words, which undergirded the sacrament of extreme unction. Luther, for instance, argues against extreme unction (and against the accompanying interpretation of James) on three grounds: (1) only Christ can institute a sacrament, not James; (2) James's words here are general, not specific to the situation of one dying; and (3) these words are about healing of the sick, not anointing those about to die, and they call for anointing by elders, not priests.[29] Behind this rejection of priestly authority lies Luther's consistent concern about the medieval church and its leaders assuming more power than they ought. He reacts against extreme unction in part because it is yet another example of the church trying to control and limit access to God's free gift of grace. Calvin also rejects the sacrament of extreme unction, adding to Luther's criticisms his strong assertion that the miraculous gift of healing was only temporary, no longer operative after the first century.[30] As a result of this controversy in sacramental theology and biblical interpretation, most Protestants from the sixteenth century until the twentieth did not practice anointing of the sick for healing.

In recent years, however, as the sixteenth-century controversies have receded, Catholic teaching and practice have emphasized more fully the entire healing ministry of the church and connected the sacrament of anointing more explicitly with the central sacraments of baptism and Eucharist/Lord's Supper. At the same time, many Protestant denominations have reintroduced worship services for healing and wholeness, and even options for individual anointing of the sick. The most widely used Lutheran worship resource in the United States, *Evangelical Lutheran Worship* (2006) offers one example, providing a simple healing service that can be included in

28. Ibid., http://www.vatican.va/archive/ENG0015/__P4P.HTM , par. 1532.
29. "The Babylonian Captivity of the Church," in *Luther's Works*, ed. and trans. Theodore G. Tappert (Philadelphia: Fortress Press, 1967), 36:118–22.
30. John Calvin, *A Harmony of the Gospels Matthew, Mark, and Luke, Vol. III, and the Epistles of James and Jude*, 314. See Calvin's *Institutes of the Christian Religion*, ed. John T. McNeill, trans. Ford Lewis Battles (Louisville, KY: Westminster John Knox Press, 2006), 4.19.18–21 for extended argument against extreme unction as continuing sacrament of the church.

a service of Holy Communion or a Service of the Word. It includes prayers of intercession, laying on of hands with optional anointing, and a final blessing. In keeping with Luther's concerns, the service does not purport to be a sacrament, and it does not primarily address those who are dying, but "all who are in need of healing."[31] The Presbyterian Church (U.S.A.)'s *Book of Common Worship* (2018) offers even more extensive resources for healing and wholeness, with materials for both corporate and individual prayer. The prayer to accompany the laying on of hands and anointing reads as follows:

> Gracious God, source of all healing,
> in Jesus Christ you heal the sick
> and mend the broken.
> We bless you for this oil
> pressed from the fruits of the earth,
> given to us as a sign
> of healing and forgiveness,
> and of the fullness of life you give.
> By your Spirit,
> come upon all who receive this ministry of compassion,
> that they may know your healing touch
> and be made whole,
> to the glory of Jesus Christ our Redeemer. Amen.[32]

Although James himself does not clarify whether the "name of the Lord" (v. 14) refers to Jesus Christ or to the Holy One of Israel, this prayer presumes a clearly developed Trinitarian logic: "God" is the source of healing, Jesus Christ the mediator of healing, and the Spirit the effective power that makes healing happen. More clearly than James, this prayer affirms that God alone is the source of healing power, eliminating any uncertainty that might arise from James's statement "The prayer of faith will save the sick" (5:15).

The healing that James envisions has multiple dimensions (all of which are suggested in the prayer above). It includes physical

---

31. Evangelical Lutheran Church in America, *Evangelical Lutheran Worship* (Augsburg Fortress, 2006), 276–78.
32. "Service for Wholeness for a Congregation," in *Book of Common Worship* (Louisville, KY: Westminster John Knox Press, 2018), 738.

sickness, to be sure, but also sin, which needs to be forgiven. Healing may also imply, or anticipate, participation in the final resurrection, as James says, "The prayer of faith will save the sick, and *the Lord will raise them up*; and anyone who has committed sins will be forgiven" (5:15). "Raise them up" is likely a double reference, both to healings (recalling Jesus' own healing stories) and to the resurrection of the dead, when the righteous will be raised.

Above all, James portrays healing prayer as the ordinary responsibility of the Christian community. Though parts of the Christian tradition now endow particular leaders (priests) with authority to administer sacramental healing, the entire community is called to pray for the healing of those who are sick. The broad communal responsibility for healing prayer becomes even more clear in verse 16, when James urges his audience to confess their sins to one another and pray for each other. At this point, "elders" are not the only ones with the right to pray, but all are summoned to pray for and with each other. Biblical commentators from the early church to the present have called attention to this profoundly democratic impulse in James. The irascible Martin Luther, for instance, who wishes to throw James into the fire because of the discussion of faith and works in chapter 2, calls 5:16 "one of the best verses in that epistle" because of its counsel for Christians to pray for one another. He points to Monica's unremitting prayers for her son Augustine as an example of the efficacy of ordinary prayer and then cites this verse from James, saying "prayer is a powerful thing, if only one believes in it, for God has attached and bound himself to it [by his promises]."[33] John Calvin also finds great practical wisdom in this verse; he uses it to argue against the practice of private confession to a priest, instead promoting mutual confession and mutual prayer, saying that prayer is more effective if we know the difficulties of another person and can struggle with them in their troubles.[34]

This counsel to pray for one another is all the more striking when we notice how often James has earlier rebuked his audience for their

33. *Table Talk*, ed. and trans. Theodore G. Tappert, in *Luther's Works*, vol. 54 (Philadelphia: Fortress Press, 1967), 454.

34. John Calvin, *A Harmony of the Gospels Matthew, Mark, and Luke, Vol. III, and the Epistles of James and Jude*, 316.

misuse of words: speaking without acting (2:16), cursing the neighbor (3:9), boasting and envious speech (3:14), disputes and conflicts (4:2), speaking evil about each other (4:11), and grumbling against each other (5:9). Here, human words are redeemed in prayer, as prayers of faith heal the sick and enable forgiveness. Knowing the destructive potential of words, we are not to remain silent, implies James. Instead, direct your words to the One who has implanted the word of life in you. In that way, the word may bear fruit, saving not only *"your* souls" (1:21), but also the sick (5:15), thus healing the whole wounded community.

It is grace that we can confess our sins to one another. Such grace spares us the terrors of the last judgment. The other Christian has been given to me so that I may be assured even here and now of the reality of God in judgment and grace. As the acknowledgment of my sins to another believer frees me from the grip of self-deception, so, too, the promise of forgiveness becomes fully certain to me only when it is spoken by another believer as God's command and in God's name.

Dietrich Bonhoeffer, *Life Together,* Dietrich Bonhoeffer Works, vol. 5, ed. Gerhard Ludwig Muller and Albrecht Schonherr, trans. Daniel W. Bloesch and James H. Burtness (Minneapolis: Fortress, 1996), 113.

Nor does James offer this advice in the abstract. For those who might ask, "what does the effective 'prayer of the righteous' look like?" he points to the prophet Elijah. "Elijah was a human being like us, and he prayed fervently that it might not rain, and for three years and six months it did not rain on the earth" (5:17). For a first century Jewish-Christian audience, Elijah was a very familiar character. James's hearers would have immediately recalled the prophet's power of prayer: praying for drought, providing food and then by prayer raising the son of the widow in Zarephath, confronting the prophets of Baal on Mt. Carmel with the power of prayer, and then fleeing to the desert to escape the wrath of Jezebel, before being sustained and recommissioned as God's prophet (1 Kgs. 17–19). Beyond these biblical stories, Elijah had major importance in Jewish tradition of the time as a signal of the coming messiah, as we can tell from the frequent references to Elijah in the Gospels.

Outside the Gospels, however, Elijah is only mentioned twice in the New Testament: in Romans 11:1–14, and here. Why is he mentioned so often in the Gospels, and so little elsewhere? This may be another clue to James's Jewish context: unlike Paul, who writes primarily to Gentiles, James can make a brief allusion to this figure, because he knows that Elijah already lives in the rich imaginative world of his hearers. And why does James choose him as an exemplar for prayer? Not only do the biblical stories of Elijah exemplify the power of prayer, but also Elijah's very name ("My God is YHWH") underscores the need for the messianic community to remain steadfast in commitment to God amid their current tribulation. In addition, Elijah's raising of the son of the widow may inspire James to allude to this prophet, since this verse falls in the context of prayer for healing and raising.[35]

We lose some benefit of the saints' examples when we imagine them to be demigods or heroes, who enjoyed a special relationship with God. We gain no increase in confidence from the fact that they win their petitions. James would have this gentile or pagan superstition knocked clean away, and tells us to consider the saints in the infirmity of their flesh, and learn to attribute all they have won from God not to their merits, but to the efficacy of their prayer.

John Calvin, *A Harmony of the Gospels Matthew, Mark, and Luke, Vol. III, and the Epistles of James and Jude*, 317–18.

Elijah is the perfect representative of YHWH in the narrative of 1 Kings, but James emphasizes that he was also a regular human being. This emphasis on ordinary humanity of the prophet seems to be James's own unique contribution to Elijah interpretation. Forerunner of the messiah, yes, remarkable servant of God, yes—but for James, most importantly, "a human being like us." If he can pray like that, then we can too. Not just the illustrious appointed leaders of the community can pray, insists James. All members of the community can and should pray for each other, and God will hear.

This passage on prayer concludes with the affirmation that Elijah prayed again, "and the heaven gave rain and the earth yielded

---

35. For full discussion of Elijah as exemplar in James, see Foster, *The Significance of Exemplars for the Interpretation of the Letter of James*, ch. 7 (165–91).

its harvest" (5:18). The language here echoes Genesis 1:11 (Septuagint), as though Elijah's prayers have brought rain that restored creation to its original pristine state, with plants and trees bursting forth from the steamy new soil, green leaves unfurling. It also echoes 2 Chronicles 7:14, in which God says to Solomon, "if my people who are called by my name humble themselves, pray, seek my face and turn from their wicked ways, then I will hear from heaven, and will forgive their sin and heal their land." In our situation of global climate change, this particular outcome of prayer catches our attention. More than ever, we are aware of the effect of changing patterns of heat and cold, rain and drought, on the future of life on earth. Should we then pray for rain, as Elijah did? On the one hand, such a prayer could be selfish, just one more effort to manipulate God to our purposes and one more attempt to intervene in global systems to benefit ourselves. Yet prayer in the context of global climate change might be something else again. Perhaps, in this day, we might hear more clearly this prayer for rain in the wider context of James's call to pray for the sick and to confess our sins to one another for the sake of forgiveness and healing. Perhaps we might recognize the sick today not just as our neighbor-humans but also as the whole earth. Perhaps the call to confess our sins to one another might be an invitation to acknowledge honestly the ways that we have wounded not only ourselves and other people but also the very planet entrusted to our care. Taken together, this passage might invite a holistic self-offering in prayer that pleads for God's mercy and forgiveness. In prayer, we might join ourselves to God's work of righteousness, so that not just we ourselves, but the entire earth "may be healed" (5:16).

FURTHER REFLECTIONS
Prayer

James speaks about prayer at the beginning and the end of the letter, framing his address to the "twelve tribes" with attention to the generosity of God and the power of prayer. In 1:5–8, he urges his listeners, if they lack wisdom, simply to ask God in faith, and God will grant their request. At the end of the book, in 5:13–18, James returns to the topic of prayer explicitly, reiterating that "the prayer of faith" is powerful. Prayer with anointing can "save the sick," and bring forgiveness of sins and healing, just as Elijah's prayer kept it from raining for three and a half years and then brought the rains again.

These discussions raise a couple of basic questions about prayer. First, what do we believe about "healing" and other miracles in a post-Enlightenment world? Can prayer really cause such things to happen? James suggests that the prayer of faith brings healing to those who are sick. Does this mean a miraculous, instantaneous restoration to perfect physical health? On this question, we cannot ignore the historical distance between James's original audience and our own; neither can we ignore the differences of interpretation on this question among Christians in the world today. James's first century audience did indeed witness dramatic physical healings, associated with the personal power of certain religious leaders. The Gospels describe Jesus himself performing many healing miracles, and the apostles in Acts do the same, in the name of Jesus. Many Christians in the world today describe similarly dramatic instances of physical healing prompted by prayer. Those who have not experienced such healing themselves should refrain from judging too quickly that such incidents do not or cannot happen today.

Yet healing, and "salvation," come in a variety of forms, not just instantaneous dramatic restoration of physical health. Healing may involve the calming of an unquiet mind or the realization of joyful purpose by someone in despair. Frequently, healing involves the mending of broken relationships, allowing freer communication where there has been misunderstanding and hurt. In each of these cases, healing may be closely linked to forgiveness of sin, as we recognize the ways in which we have harmed ourselves, other people, and the world around us and breathe in God's grace that loves us into a new way of being.

At the same time, to say with James that "the prayer of the righteous is powerful and effective" (5:16) can lead to a dangerous arrogance that presents prayer as human effort, purified by our own righteousness. This prompts the second basic question: What really makes prayer "effective"—the power of our words, or our faith, or God's generosity?

The answer to this lies in reframing how we understand what prayer is: not our own independent effort, but our attentive communion with God, who already knows what we need before we ask. James has earlier reminded his hearers that God "gives to all generously and ungrudgingly" (1:5) and that God has already given us birth "by the word of truth" (1:18). Our prayers do not come from ourselves alone; they emerge from that word already implanted in us. When we pray, then, we do so out of God's generous grace already at work within us.

James did not have a Trinitarian theology of prayer, just as he did not have an explicit Christology. He does, however, root his understanding of prayer in the living word of truth that gives us life, is implanted in us, and which we are called to *do*. Thinking with James as well as with later Christian Trinitarian thought, we might describe prayer as our participation in God who is at once the source of our praying (as the word of life implanted), the one who prays with and through us, and the one to whom we address our prayers. Prayer is not just a conversation in which we are "over here" talking to God "over there." It is conscious articulation of our relationship with God who is at once behind, beneath, beside, and before us, beckoning us to abundant life.

If prayer is about our communion with God, and if God knows what we need before we ask, then what is the point of our asking? Why pray for healing, or relief from suffering, at all? Karl Barth, in

---

God is holy communion within God's own self. In Christ, we glimpse this communion in the heart of God, and we also realize that this holy One-in-Three seeks communion with us. In prayer, we enter into this communion, as we acknowledge that God is at once the source of our prayer, the one to whom we pray, and our companion in prayer. When we turn to prayer, before we even open our lips, we are surrounded and suffused by the mystery of the Holy Trinity.

Who is the God we encounter in prayer? God is source, goal, and companion in prayer, the Holy Trinity that envelops us as we pray, drawing us (if we open ourselves to it) into ever deeper communion with God. True prayer is thus participation in God.

Martha L. Moore-Keish, *Christian Prayer for Today* (Louisville, KY: Westminster John Knox Press, 2009), 11.

his book on prayer, says that all prayer is basically petition, or supplication. This seems to suggest that we simply "ask, and the door shall be opened to you," no matter what the request. But Barth did not mean that prayer is asking God to do stuff for us. Rather, asking is invocation, calling out to God to remind him that "he is [our] Father and [we] are his children."[36] Petition, according to Barth, points to a deeper relationship, even participation in God.

5:19–20
Bringing Home the Wanderers

To our modern ears, these last two verses of James sound oddly disconnected from the preceding section, and hardly like a conclusion at all. What does prayer for healing (in vv. 13–18) have to do with rescuing wanderers from the truth? And how does this appeal to bring back sinners from wandering offer a satisfying ending to this book?

Here at the end as at the beginning, it is helpful to remember that we are not James's original audience, so the author is not addressing our modern questions and expectations. We should not fault him for that, as if a distance of nearly two millennia constitutes literary or moral failure. Instead, we might notice the ways that James ends by subtly reiterating themes that have been consistent throughout his address and closes with a vision of reconciliation meant to sustain his beloved community in its time of trial.

To begin these final verses, James addresses his own community in intimate terms, calling them one last time "my brothers and sisters" (*adelphoi mou*)—as he did at the very beginning of the book in 1:2 (and throughout; see 1:16, 19; 2:1, 5, 14; 3:1, 10, 12; 5:12). Clearly, James is concerned above all to offer a word of hope and healing to his particular community, which is being tested from the outside and divided on the inside. In this he ends as he began: by reaching out to his brothers and sisters. He is speaking to those whom he knows and loves, who share with him a commitment to

36. Karl Barth, *Prayer*, 50th anniversary edition, ed. Don E. Saliers, trans. Sara F. Terrien (Louisville, KY: Westminster John Knox Press, 2002), 78–79.

the way of truth (however imperfectly they may follow it). He seeks
to knit this community into a more coherent whole, as he did in
cautioning against partiality (2:1–13), warning against the power of
harsh speech (3:6–12) and judging each other (4:11–2), and calling for members of the community to pray for each other in times of
sickness and suffering (5:13–18).

In such a context of a community in need of greater wholeness,
"wandering" suggests a real threat. This is not innocent meandering.
To "wander" is to leave the path of life. "Not all those who wander
are lost," wrote J. R. R. Tolkien famously in *The Fellowship of the
Ring,* alluding to the apparent wanderings of Strider/Aragorn.[37] But
for James, as for the tradition that formed him, those who wander
are indeed lost. James has used this same verb before, though one
cannot tell this from the NRSV translation. In 1:16, the author
cautioned "do not be deceived," but this common idiomatic phrase
literally means "do not wander."[38] A wanderer is not a hidden
king, nor a heroic explorer who boldly seeks new worlds and new
civilizations. One who wanders, like the sheep who "go astray"
(same verb) in Matthew 18:12–13, risks death—both immediate
and eternal. Naturally, the author calls on his community to bring
back such wanderers, promising life and forgiveness in return.

Though it may seem odd to us, the connection between prayers
for healing and bringing back the wanderers was not so odd in the
first century Jewish-Christian world. Several Old Testament texts,
from a variety of genres, speak of people "turning back and being
healed."[39] For instance, Proverbs 3:7–8 reads, "Do not be wise in
your own eyes; fear the LORD, and *turn away* from evil. *It will be a
healing* for your flesh and a refreshment for your body." The call of
Isaiah presents this connection in the negative: "Make the mind
of the people dull, and stop their ears, and shut their eyes, so that
they may not look with their eyes, and listen with their ears, and
comprehend with their minds, *and turn and be healed*" (Isa. 6:10).
As both these examples suggest, "turning back" is the opposite of

37. From "All That Is Gold Does Not Glitter," in ch. 10 of J. R. R. Tolkien, *The Fellowship of the Ring* (New York: Ballantine Books, 1954, renewed 1982), 193.
38. See 1 Cor. 6:9, 15:33. For other uses of this phrase in the New Testament and early Christian literature, see Allison, *A Critical and Exegetical Commentary on the Epistle of James,* 263 n. 49.
39. See Allison, *A Critical and Exegetical Commentary on the Epistle of James,* 780.

wandering. To turn, or to turn back, is to return to the way of God, which is the way of life. In the background of the entire book of James lies the "two ways" theme of wisdom: the earthly, unspiritual, devilish wisdom of the world (3:15) which we are to reject, and the peaceable, gentle, patient wisdom of God, which James summons his audience to choose. This same "two ways" theme may be reiterated here. Turning back to this way brings life in all its fullness: body, mind, and spirit, for the individual and for the community. This connection of turning back and being healed may well lie in the background of James's concluding verses.

Some scholars think James was working specifically with Ezekiel 34 in his closing. In Ezekiel 34:4, God indicts the false "shepherds of Israel," saying, "You have not strengthened the weak, you have not healed the sick, you have not bound up the injured, you have not brought back the strayed, you have not sought the lost." By contrast, in Ezekiel 34:16, God declares, "I will seek the lost, and I will bring back the strayed, and I will bind up the injured, and I will strengthen the weak."[40] Some ancient Christian liturgical traditions offer similar exhortations. For instance, 1 Clement 59.4 reads "save those among us who are in distress . . . raise up the fallen . . . heal the weak. Turn back those of your people who wander . . . raise up the weak." This could reflect a primitive church order, even earlier than the *Didache*.[41] James represents this same tradition here, inviting the community to participate in God's work of healing the sick (through their prayers) and bringing back the wanderers.

> Whether it is through critical readings of the Bible or through innovative social and spiritual initiatives to reach the disenfranchised, African American churches—given their diaspora realities of suffering, pain, triumph, and hope—are best positioned to reclaim the "wanderers" and to provide a witness of God's love in the world.
>
> Gay Byron, "James," in *True to Our Native Land*, 472.

James's final transition from prayers of healing to bringing back the wanderers may also have been inspired by the example of Elijah

---

40. Ibid.
41. Allison, *A Critical and Exegetical Commentary on the Epistle of James*, 747.

from the preceding verses. Elijah was instrumental in bringing back the wandering Israelites from their erroneous ways; so too James connects the prayers of the faithful with bringing back the wanderers from the wrong path.[42]

"Whoever brings back a sinner from wandering will save the sinner's soul from death . . ." This sounds like the one whose soul is saved is the "sinner," but the original text is more ambiguous. "The sinner's soul" (NRSV) is actually the nonspecific "his/her soul" in the Greek, and it could refer either to the wanderer or to the one who brings him back. The one who brings back the wanderer might save her own soul or that of the sinner, and she might "cover the sins" of herself or those of the sinner. The NRSV opts for the scholarly consensus: the one being saved is the sinner, while the sins that are covered might belong to the sinner or to the one who brings the wanderer back to the right path.[43] It is worth lingering over the ambiguity. Who really benefits from a strict calculation of whose sins belong to whom? In a beloved community, do not the wandering ways of one affect the whole? Could it be, in fact, that in rescuing a brother or sister from death, we save not only that one but also ourselves?

James says that such a rescue "will cover a multitude of sins." This is likely an allusion to Proverbs 10:12 (or to a popular line based on this proverb): "Hatred stirs up strife, but love covers all offenses."[44] To cover sin is to make it invisible, so that God does not see and judge. This does not imply deceit, like a "cover-up operation" that tries to hide the truth. Rather, to "cover sins," for James as for the Israelite tradition that shapes him, is the equivalent of forgiving. It is a gracious act that acknowledges past wrongdoing but heals the person and the community from the consequences of that wrongdoing.

Christians reading this passage today may think of the gracious intervention of Jesus Christ at this point, since we have centuries of interpreting Christ's life, death, and resurrection as the defining act of God in "covering the sins" of humanity, saving sinners from death.

---

42. See Foster, *The Significance of Exemplars for the Interpretation of the Letter of James*, 188–90.
43. Allison, *A Critical and Exegetical Commentary on the Epistle of James*, 783–87.
44. Ibid., 788.

Such a christological interpretation may lead to rich reflections—for instance, on the way Jesus leads wanderers back to the ways of God and on the ancient image of "covering" as a metaphor for how Jesus conveys God's forgiveness. There is no indication, however, that James has Jesus in mind here. Rather, James seeks to empower his brothers and sisters to seek out the wanderers and bring them home. They (and we) are the main actors. "God is not named, and there is not even a divine passive here. So James concludes characteristically by emphasizing the importance of human beings doing what is right."[45] God, the giver of all good gifts, has "given us birth by the word of truth" (1:18); now we are to bear fruit through rescuing, saving, forgiving.

This final word of empowerment is also a word of mercy. James has offered stern warnings along the way, rebuking his community for their partiality and backbiting, for their envy and greed. He has castigated those who speak pious words without living out their faith in action, and he leaves little hope for those who oppress the poor. Yet throughout, he has also offered a vision of God who is generous and merciful, who calls people to love their neighbors and walk in the ways of peace. In the midst of judgment, he has also proclaimed that "mercy triumphs over judgment" (2:13). And it is this vision of a merciful, healed, and healing community that closes the book. Bring back those who wander, he says. All those who have forgotten the way, who have gotten tangled in thickets of ambition and envy, lured by the shiny objects of fame and fortune, who have said hurtful things and ignored the poor—do not give up on them, says James. You, brothers and sisters, by walking in the paths of righteousness and peace, you may yet bring them home.

45. Ibid., 782.

Postscript: An Enduring
Word in an Age of Fear

As I have lived closely with James for the past few years, I have grown to admire many aspects of this writing, and two especially: how seamlessly this writer weaves together multiple elements from biblical tradition to speak to the issues of his day, and how timely his words are for us now. Neither of these was apparent to me at the outset, when just about all I knew of James was Luther's judgment on this writing as a "right strawy epistle." It did not take long, however, for James to wind his way into my heart. With time and attention, I grew to marvel at how deeply he is steeped in the breadth of the bible: the law (especially Leviticus 19), the prophets (such as Amos and Isaiah), and wisdom literature (especially Ben Sira). Attending to all these streams of Scripture, James speaks interchangeably of the law, the word, and the wisdom of God as the life-giving gift that we should embrace and nurture. With rhetorical skill and pastoral wisdom, he seeks to interpret for his own time the richness of the whole Bible, not just one piece. As a professor of theology in a seminary, I find in James a surprising model for my own work. How might I, like James, speak with coherence from the whole breadth of Scripture? How might these words empower me to speak as courageously as he of God's righteousness?

Not only did James speak truth to his original audience; he continues to speak with power to the contemporary world. For instance, each time I have preached or taught on James, people resonate strongly with his teaching on the dangers of speech. No one has needed to be convinced of the truth of his cry, "How great a forest is set ablaze by a small fire! And the tongue is a fire" (3:5b–6a). In these divided political times, in these days of tweets and re-tweets that spread like wildfire, there is no doubt about the truth of James's warning. His calls to "be quick to listen, slow to speak, slow to anger" (1:19), and not to speak evil against one another (4:11) have met many head nods in my audiences.

So, too, have people responded readily to James's condemnation of partiality and his call to works of mercy and justice. When groups encountered his portrait of a gathering in which well-dressed people are treated better than those who come in "dirty clothes" (2:2), they always had stories of their own to share, sometimes confessing their own implicit bias, and other times describing behavior they had witnessed in worshiping congregations. Everyone concurred with James's affirmations that religion means to care for widows and orphans (1:27), to love the neighbor without partiality (2:8–9), and to attend to the bodily needs of those who lack food or clothing (2:15–16).

Not everyone found James's words comfortable, of course, which is as it should be. I don't think James intended his audience to be comfortable. Even those who agreed with the need to care for "widows and orphans" sometimes felt directly challenged by his words about "rich" and "poor." More than one person in classes I taught raised a hand to insist that not all rich people are bad and that not all people who are poor are morally upright. True, I tried to say on those occasions. Yet James is not talking primarily about individual moral purity. He is condemning the suffering caused by unjust economic systems— and pointing out how readily we who have economic resources seek to protect them. He, like Jesus, is seeking to illumine our tendency to focus on our own economic stability above all else. I am grateful to James for holding up this mirror and making me squirm.

Above all, in this time of rapid change, I have valued James's emphasis on the enduring word of God and our corresponding call to endurance. We live in a world in which society, technology, churches, and academic institutions, all are changing in ways that can be disorienting and anxiety-making. In such situations, we can be tempted to act out of fear. As individuals, we fight or flee—curling up and defending ourselves or running as far away as possible from the apparent threat. As groups, we draw in, solidify existing relationships, clarify boundaries, declare who is in and who is out. Such responses are hard wired in human beings. We developed over eons of evolutionary history to be defensive, groupish creatures, convinced of our own rightness and suspicious of those whose views of the world are different from our own. These presuppositions only harden when we feel ourselves and our tribe to be under threat. It is as natural as breathing to be on the alert when we are in unfamiliar territory, to fight or flee in order to protect ourselves and our tribe. But James calls us to an alternative wisdom that can help counter such fear.

First, James reminds us that God is a generous and ungrudging gift-giver who has already "given us birth by the word of truth" (1:18). *Already* we have been given this word, which is life. Before we speak any words ourselves, God has already spoken. Grace precedes us. Such reminder comes as welcome reassurance amid times of turmoil.

This word that is life, and light, does not remain outside of us, but by God's grace it settles deep within us. As James says, "welcome with meekness the implanted word that has the power to save your souls" (1:21b). Nurture and tend that word, that wisdom, urges James—not the wisdom of "envy and selfish ambition," but the wisdom that is "pure, peaceable, gentle, willing to yield, full of mercy and good fruits" (3:17). Slow down, guard your tongue, listen.

Yet this life-giving word does not simply sit back and tolerate the world of injustice. God's word is also the law of righteousness. The "law" (which is also word, which is also wisdom) not only offers life and light to us, but it also declares that "you shall love your neighbor as yourself" (2:8). The word, in other words, bears fruit. Care for orphans and widows in their distress. Show mercy to those who are suffering. Do not envy others. Do not treat rich people better than those who have little to wear.

Finally, this word endures—and so should we. Over and again, James presents a contrast between things that wither and fade (flowers, riches, mist) and that which endures (true wisdom, the word and the doing of the word, the "Father of Lights"). Be patient. In these days when we are tempted to fear, God has already given us what we need: the Word, which is love for one another and for the whole wounded world. The word is this: in spite of appearances to the contrary, God is faithful in love, and so should we be. Do not lose heart. Do not fear. Tend the garden, especially the most vulnerable plants that need particular care. Stop, look, and listen for that word. And then: just do it.

For Further Reading

Allison, Dale C., Jr. *A Critical and Exegetical Commentary on the Epistle of James*. International Critical Commentary. New York: Bloomsbury, 2013. The most thorough, authoritative, critical commentary available today.

Aymer, Margaret. *James: Diaspora Rhetoric of a Friend of God*. Phoenix Guides to the New Testament. Sheffield: Sheffield Phoenix, 2015. Short introduction to James, framing the epistle as a "homiletic letter, intended to be heard by diaspora communities—that is, migrant people."

Gowler, David B. *James through the Centuries*. Wiley Blackwell Bible Commentaries. Chichester: Wiley Blackwell, 2014. Details the reception history of James, including attention to music, art, literature, and film.

Johnson, Luke Timothy. *The Letter of James*. Anchor Yale Bible. New Haven, CT: Yale University Press, 1995. Fresh reading of James from a literary-social perspective, arguing for the possibility that the letter might be written by James the brother of Jesus.

Maynard-Reid, Pedrito. *Poverty and Wealth in James*. Maryknoll, NY: Orbis, 1987. Written by a Jamaican scholar and Seventh-day Adventist pastor, this work was one of the first to pay close attention to the social context of James, arising first from the text itself rather than sociological theory.

Tamez, Elsa. *The Scandalous Message of James: Faith without Works Is Dead*. Rev. ed. New York: Crossroad, 2002. Originally based on a series of lectures given by Tamez in 1990, published in revised edition with study guide by Pamela Sparr and additional resource materials from the United Methodist Church. Tamez focuses her interpretation on three angles: oppression, hope, and praxis.

Index of Ancient Sources

Apocrypha

Pseudepigrapha

Apostolic Fathers

New Testament Apocrypha

Index of Subjects

CPSIA information can be obtained
at www.ICGtesting.com
Printed in the USA
BVHW030433240919
558962BV00040B/71/P